Trading Options on Futures: Markets, Methods, Strategies, and Tactics

John W. Labuszewski

John E. Nyhoff

WILEY

JOHN WILEY & SONS

New York • Chichester • Brisbane • Toronto • Singapore

Library of Congress Cataloging in Publication Data:

Labuszewski, John.
     Trading options on futures.

     Bibliography: p.
     Includes index.
     1. Financial futures.   2. Put and call transactions.
I. Nyhoff, John E.   II. Title.

HG6024.3.L33   1988   332.64′4   87-29656
ISBN 0-471-60676-6

Printed in the United States of America

10 9 8 7 6 5 4 3

Foreword

Fixed income, equity, and currency markets have experienced tremendous volatility in recent years. This volatility has arisen as the price inflation of the 1970s has been replaced by financial asset inflation in the 1980s.

The potentially deleterious effects of this volatility are magnified by the growth in the financial markets, raising the stakes in a macroeconomic sense. Further, it is clear that the capital markets now transcend political boundaries—the major economies are inextricably bound together.

For better or worse, risk management has become a 24 hour a day task, demanding quick responses to dynamic market conditions.

Financial futures and options were developed in response to these conditions. They provide perfectly suitable vehicles to transform the risk represented by marketplace volatility into a source of opportunity. Options can alter the risk/reward profile of a fixed income, equity, or currency portfolio to achieve the desired results—quickly, effectively, and efficiently.

TONE GRANT
President
Refco Group Ltd.

February 1988

iii

Acknowledgments

The authors would like to express their sincere appreciation to our colleagues who made immeasurably valuable contributions to this effort. In particular: Takashi Aragane, Mutsuo Asaba, Suzanne Bishopric, Kyo Cho, Dennis Collins, Robert J. Dantone, Maryrose Dombrowski, H. Patrick Faust, Yusuke Ikeda, Dennis L. Heskel, Michael P. Kamradt, Yasuyuki Kato, Heidi Labuszewski, James F. Meisner, Ikunori Morita, Marion Nyhoff, Horoiku Sago, Motoaki Sakaguchi, Yasuhiko Sawa, Diane E.G. Spikes, Yoshiki Suzuki, Keisuke Taguchi, Takeshi Sugihasi, Toshiki Tsunoda, Yasuto Tsuruta, and to the many others who supported this effort but whose contributions may have been inadvertently overlooked.

Special recognition must be extended to our employer, Refco Group Ltd.; its chairman, Thomas H. Dittmer; and its president, Tone Grant. Thank you for your generous support, infinite patience, and constant encouragement during the preparation of this publication.

JOHN W. LABUSZEWSKI

JOHN E. NYHOFF

February 1988

Contents

1

Introduction to Options

Options are an old business concept. However, this concept has enjoyed a renaissance of interest in recent years as evidenced by the trade of options on instruments as diverse as stock indexes, bonds, grain, and livestock. Many of these options are offered on an exchange-traded and over-the-counter (OTC) basis, domestically and in the international marketplace.

While options on many different instruments are actively traded, it was not too long ago that options enjoyed very limited interest. For many years, the trade of options for specified commodities was banned under the auspices of the Commodity Exchange Act (CEAct) enacted in 1936. This did not prevent the trade of options for individual equities in the over-the-counter market.

In 1973, the Chicago Board Options Exchange (CBOE) introduced exchange traded stock options. The success of this concept provided the impetus for the Commodity Futures Trading Commission (CFTC) to authorize the trade of commodity options on domestic commodity exchanges beginning in 1982. This development led to a new burst of interest in options both domestically and in international circles.

CONCEPTS AND TERMINOLOGY

This section is intended to introduce these markets, concepts and terminology associated with the markets, and a basic understanding about the mechanics of the markets.

Identifying Options

Options can be distinguished from one another on the basis of three criteria: *type*, *class*, and *series*.

The option type refers to whether an option is a *call* or a *put*.

A *call* option grants the buyer the right, but not the obligation, to *buy* from the seller or writer the underlying instrument at a predetermined strike or exercise price on or before a predetermined date. The buyer pays a negotiated price or premium to the seller in return for the rights conveyed.

If a call is an option to buy, a *put* may be thought of as an option to sell.

A *put* option grants the buyer the right, but not the obligation, to *sell* to the seller or writer the underlying instrument at a predetermined strike or exercise price on or before a predetermined date. The buyer pays a negotiated price or premium to the seller in return for the rights conveyed.

The second criteria which identifies an option is referred to as the option class. All options which are of the same type, that is, put or call, and share a common expiration date are of the same class.

For example, all call options exercisable for gold futures contracts which expire in the month of November 1987 are of the same class. When an option expires, all rights held by the buyer become null and void. Thus the expiration date defines the effective life of an option.

The expiration date must be distinguished from the exercise date. The exercise date is the day upon which the option holder actually exercises his right to buy (in the case of a call) or to sell (in the case of a put). The expiration date is the last day upon which such purchase or sale may take place.

An "American-style" option permits exercise at any time on or before the expiration date. A "European-style" option permits exercise only upon the specified expiration date. A "modified European-style" option may permit exercise during a limited "window" or range of dates.

The third and final criteria which completely identifies a given option is the option series. All options of the same class which share a common strike or exercise price are of the same series.

The following chart illustrates the three criteria:

Identifying an Option

	Type	*Class*	*Series*
Put or call:	Call		
Expiration:		Dec. '87 Call	
Strike price:			86 Dec. '87 Call

For example, all call options on T-bond futures which expire in the month of March 1988 with an exercise price of 84 percent of par constitute an option series. Normally, exchanges establish a number of strike prices at regular intervals surrounding or "bracketing" the current underlying market price. If bond futures were trading at 88, for example, there may be options available "struck" at 82, 84, 86, 88, 90, 92, and 94.

Options on Futures versus Physicals

Implicit in our discussion thus far is that an option may be exercised for a particular underlying commodity; for example, gold, T-bonds, deutsche marks (DM), and so forth. But these commodities may be available in different forms.

For instance, an option may be available calling for the delivery of a T-bond futures contract or for an actual T-bond. For the most part, this discussion will focus on options exercisable for futures contracts; however, there are advantages and disadvantages associated with either concept.

Options on futures tend to enjoy greater liquidity and interest than options which call for the actual delivery of a cash instrument. This is most clearly exemplified when you consider the bond option competition which had existed between the Chicago Board of Trade (CBOT) and the CBOE.

In 1982 and 1983, respectively, CBOT and CBOE introduced options exercisable for T-bond futures and for actual cash T-bonds. The CBOE market has never enjoyed much interest while the CBOT market has become the second most active exchange traded option worldwide (second only to the CBOE's OEX stock index option discussed next).

CBOT locals were able to make a tighter market than were CBOE traders because they could readily hedge the risk to which they were exposed by taking an offsetting position in the highly active T-bond futures market trading in the adjacent pit. CBOE traders, however, did not have ready access to the cash bond market. Even if they did, spreads in the cash bond markets are not as tight as spreads in the bond futures market and you cannot readily short cash bonds. Finally, the amount of capital required to use the cash market as an offset vehicle may be prohibitive to many locals.

Secondly, to restate the obvious, CBOT bond futures do not call for an actual delivery of bonds. This may be important, for example, to a financial institution attempting to "cross-hedge." CBOE options call for the delivery of a recently issued 30-year bond. This may be an advantage for an institution trying to hedge a 30-year bond. But if an institution is trying to cross-hedge a nondeliverable bond by, for example, selling calls, it may have to swap out of the original bond and into a deliverable bond in order to satisfy an exercise.

By contrast, it is much simpler to be exercised into a short position in the bond futures contract and simply offset that position with a long transaction. This same rationale may be used to explain in part the Chicago Mercantile Exchange's (CME) success with options on foreign currency futures relative to the Philadelphia Stock Exchange's (PSE) options on actual foreign currency.

Another instance to consider, however, is the relative success of the CBOE's option on the S&P 100—known by its ticker symbol of OEX. This option has attracted much more volume and activity than have competing products exercisable for futures, for example, the CME's option exercisable for S&P 500 futures.

Again, simplicity and ease of exit and entry appear to be factors. The OEX is a "cash-settlement" contract, that is, the contract is settled in cash upon exercise at the prevailing value of the index multiplied by $100. By contrast, a CME S&P 500 option is exercised into the S&P 500 futures contract. While S&P 500 futures are highly liquid and readily offsetable, it is still much easier to simply settle the contract in cash and not trade in futures.

Another factor is that the CBOE OEX contract is sized to be compatible to retail trading activity. The OEX is valued at $100 times the index—if the index is at 200.00, the contract represents a value of $20,000. The S&P 500 "futures-options" are valued at $500 times the index. Under similar circumstances, the CME's contract is valued at $100,000.

While bond options have attracted a largely institutional clientele, stock index options are largely retail. Of course, a number of over-the-counter products have appeared in recent years as well, exercisable for actual financial instruments. These products have enjoyed considerable market penetration although it is impossible to get a clear indication of their volume because trade of these products is fragmented over many different trading desks at different institutions worldwide.

Many of these products will continue to grow because the OTC market is capable of being more responsive to market demands than are the exchanges. As a result, OTC market participants are constantly developing new, innovative option products.

Profiting from Call Options

When a trader buys or sells futures, this implies a strongly bullish or bearish price expectation, respectively. Similarly, option strategies may be categorized as bullish or bearish, but options provide much more subtlety than do futures.

You can identify an option strategy which is strongly bullish or strongly bearish, mildly bullish or mildly bearish, or completely neutral, allowing you to capitalize on a flat market expectation. For example, you can buy (or hold or go long) a call option. This is a strongly bullish market position. Similarly, a long put may be described as a strongly bearish market position.

By contrast, if you sell (or write, grant, short—all of these terms being synonymous) a call, you have assumed a neutral to mildly bearish market position. A short put is a neutral to mildly bullish market position.

⚙ Once purchased, there are three ways in which an option may be disposed: (1) the option buyer may exercise the option; (2) the buyer may allow the option to expire unexercised or "abandon" the option; and (3) the option may be offset, that is, the buyer may subsequently sell the option, or the seller may subsequently buy the option back.

Let us illustrate a scenario where a call option is exercised or is permitted to expire unexercised.

Example: Assume that Eurodollar futures are trading at 92.50 and a trader expects a major bull move. He buys or goes long one call on Eurodollar futures struck at 92.50 for a 20 basis point premium (see Figure 1–1).

By expiration, our trader's expectations are realized: Eurodollars rally 50 basis points to 93.00. If our trader exercises this call option, he realizes a 50 basis

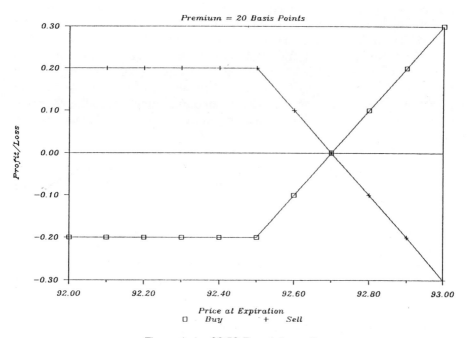

Figure 1–1   92.50 Eurodollar call.

point gain on expiration because he buys Eurodollar futures at the 92.50 strike when they are actually valued at 93.00. His net return equals the 50 basis points realized on exercise less the original 20 basis point premium for a net profit of 30 basis points or $750 ($25 per basis point).

Assume that Eurodollars fall to 92.00 instead of rising. It would be foolish to buy at 92.50 something valued at 92. Hence, the trader simply abandons the option by refusing to exercise it. Thus he limits his loss to the 20 basis point premium ($500).

What about the call writer's returns? The seller's returns are simply a mirror image of the returns which accrue to the option holder.

Example: In the foregoing example, the trader who had shorted the call would bring in 20 basis points to his account immediately upon sale. If the market rises to 93, the short is forced to sell at 92.50 something valued at 93.00. This implies a 50 basis point loss cushioned by the initial receipt of the 20 basis point premium for a net loss of 30 basis points ($750). If the market falls to 92.00, the option is abandoned, and the writer counts the entire 20 point premium ($500) as profit. Interestingly, if the market remains stable at the 92.50 strike price, the option is similarly abandoned, and the writer retains the full 20 basis point premium.

The Eurodollar futures price must appreciate noticeably before the option can be profitable for the holder. Specifically, Eurodollars must advance to a minimum price of 92.70 before the holder will realize any profit. Likewise, if Eurodollars stay under 92.70, the writer will realize a profit.

Why? Consider that if Eurodollars advance to 92.70, the holder can exercise by buying at 92.50 something valued at 92.70. This implies a 20 basis point profit. This profit is offset by the initial forfeiture of the 20 point premium for a net zero return. By the same reasoning, the call writer realizes a zero return at this level. This, therefore, is the call *breakeven point.*

The *breakeven point* at which both the buyer and the seller of a call realize zero profit and zero loss (without considering transaction costs) equals the call strike price *plus* the premium paid up-front from long to short to secure the option.

Note that it is in the call holder's interest to exercise the option if it is about to expire even when the market is between the strike price and breakeven point even though a net loss results! For example, if the market rises to 92.65 the buyer may exercise for a gain of 15 basis points on exercise, reduced by the initial 20 point premium for a 5 point loss. But had the buyer refused to exercise, he would have suffered a loss of 20 basis points, equal to the entire option premium. Thus by exercising even when a net loss results, the buyer can limit his loss.

This example illustrates that the premium, once paid, does not enter into a decision of whether or not to exercise the option. The premium represents a "sunk cost" and is forfeit at the moment the holder buys the option.

Profiting from Put Options

If calls represent options to buy, puts represent options to sell. Thus where a long call position is essentially bullish, a long put position is essentially bearish; where a short call is mildly bearish to neutral, a short put is mildly bullish to neutral.

It is sometimes difficult to think of buying an essentially bearish market position. Nonetheless, one must think of the rights and obligations conveyed through the purchase and sale of a put, that is, the right to sell, the obligation to buy, rather than the overt market action which creates those rights and obligations.

Let us illustrate a scenario where a put option is exercised or is permitted to expire unexercised.

Example: Assume that Swiss franc futures are trading at 55.00 cents per franc and a trader expects a major bear move. He buys or goes long one put on Swiss franc futures struck at 55.00 for a 1.50 premium (see Figure 1–2).

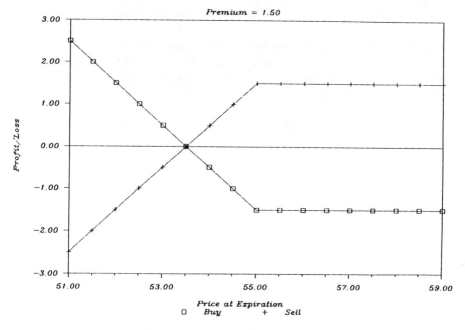

Figure 1-2   55.00 Swiss franc put.

By expiration, our trader's expectations are realized: francs fall to 52.20. If our trader exercises this put, he realizes a 2.80 gain on expiration because he sells "Swissie" futures at the 55.00 strike when they are actually valued at 52.20. His net return equals the 2.80 realized on exercise less the original 1.50 premium for a net profit of 1.30 or $1,625 ($12.50 per .01 cents).

Assume that francs rally to 57.80 instead of falling. It would be foolish to sell at 55.00 something valued at 57.80. Hence, the trader would simply abandon the option by refusing to exercise it, limiting his loss to the 1.50 premium ($1,875).

What about the put writer's returns? The seller's returns are simply a mirror image of the returns which accrue to the option holder.

Example: In the foregoing example, the trader who had shorted the put would bring in 1.50 cents per franc to his account immediately upon sale. If the market falls to 52.20, the short will be forced to buy at 55.00 something valued at 52.20. This implies a 2.80 loss cushioned by the initial receipt of the 1.50 premium for a net loss of 1.30 basis points ($1,625). If the market rises to 57.80, the put is abandoned, and the writer counts the entire 1.50 cent premium ($1,875) as profit. Note that if the market remains stable, the writer also counts the entire 1.50 cent premium as profit.

The Swiss franc futures contract must fall noticeably before the option can be profitable for the holder. Specifically, francs must fall to a maximum price of 53.50 before the holder will realize any profit. Likewise, if Swiss francs stay over 53.50, the writer will realize a profit.

The *breakeven point* at which both the buyer and the seller of a put realize zero profit and zero loss (without considering transaction costs) equals the put strike price *less* the premium paid up-front from long to short to secure the option.

	Call	*Put*
Long	Strongly Bullish	Strongly Bearish
Short	Mildly Bearish to Neutral	Mildly Bullish to Neutral

In-, At-, Out-of-the-Money

Because the question of whether or not an option may be expected to be exercised occurs frequently, the options trade has developed unique terminology to refer to options which are economical or uneconomical to exercise. When the market price exceeds the strike price for a call option, the holder may be expected to exercise. When the underlying market price is less than the call strike price, the option will be uneconomical to exercise.

The former option is *in-the-money* while the latter option is *out-of-the-money*. Finally, you have the unique case where both market and strike prices are equal. This option is *at-the-money*.

Consider the case of the Eurodollar call discussed in the example above. Should the market be less than the 92.50 strike price, the holder cannot be expected to exercise—thus, an out-of-the-money option. It is only when the market price exceeds the 92.50 strike that the option is in-the-money.

A call is an option to buy; a put is an option to sell. Thus the definitions of in- and out-of-the-money are reversed in the context of a put.

It is profitable to sell when the market price is less than the exercise price, that is, when the put is in-the-money. It is unprofitable to sell when the market price is greater than the exercise price. This is an out-of-the-money put option.

In our Swiss franc example, the put is in-the-money when the market is less than the 55.00 strike. The put is out-of-the-money when the market is greater than the 55.00 strike.

In- and Out-of-the-Money

	Call	*Put*
In-the-Money	Market > Strike	Market < Strike
At-the-Money	Market = Strike	Market = Strike
Out-of-the-Money	Market < Strike	Market > Strike

Risk and Return

An option contract grants the holder the right, but not the obligation, to buy in the case of a call and sell in the case of a put. The writer takes on the obligation to sell in the case of a call and buy in the case of a put, but only upon demand of the option buyer!

Because the holder owns a right and not an obligation, he can limit losses to the premium paid upon purchase. (Clearly, a holder could not be expected to exercise an out-of-the-money option.) But an option holder is permitted to participate in favorable market movements, limited only by the fixed premium paid upon purchase. If the market moves considerably in his favor, considerable profits may ensue. Thus the option holder's losses are limited to the premium while his returns are "open-ended" and limited only by the extent to which the market may fluctuate.

An option writer's risks and returns are a mirror image of that of the holder. This means the writer's returns are strictly limited to the premium received upon purchase while the losses are open-ended. A basic asymmetry exists, therefore, between risk and reward inherent in the option buyer's and seller's positions.

Despite the open-ended risk, writing options retains certain advantages. For example, the option writer receives the premium in cash up front and enjoys use of those funds over the life of the option. Additionally, the holder must hope that the market moves sufficiently to permit a profitable exercise or a sale at a profit while the writer may profit even when the market remains stable—or even if it moves slightly in-the-money!

This asymmetry of risk and return distinguishes options from futures. Both buyer and seller of a futures contract experience similar risks and profit potential. A futures contract may be thought of as a *double-edged blade*. The market may move favorably or unfavorably resulting in profits or losses of potentially similar magnitude.

Options, by contrast, represent *single-edged blades*. If the market moves favorably for the holder, large returns ensue. If not, losses are limited to the option premium. Of course, the reverse reasoning applies to option writers.

Finally, it must be noted that the option premium is negotiated competitively in the market to balance this basic asymmetry between risk and reward inherent in the option buyer's and seller's positions.

PRICING FUNDAMENTALS

Option pricing can be one of the most complex, but perhaps the most significant, topic a prospective option trader must address. The importance of being able to identify the "fair-value" of an option is evident when you consider the meaning of the term fair-value in the context of this subject.

A fair-market value for an option is such that the buyer and seller expect to break even in a statistical sense, over a large number of trials (without considering the effect of transaction costs, commissions, etc.).

This means if a trader consistently buys overpriced or sells underpriced options, he can expect, over the long term, to incur a loss. By the same token, an astute trader who consistently buys underpriced and sells overpriced options might expect to realize a profit.

But how can a trader recognize overpriced or underpriced options? What variables impact upon this assessment? A number of mathematical models may be used to calculate these figures, most notably, the models introduced by Black-Scholes and Cox-Ross-Rubinstein. The purpose of this section, however, is not to describe these models, but to introduce some of the fundamental variables which impact upon an option premium and their effect.

Intrinsic and Time Value

Fundamentally, an option premium reflects two components: *intrinsic value* and *time value*.

$$\text{Premium} = \text{Intrinsic value} + \text{Time value}$$

The intrinsic value of an option is equal to its in-the-money amount. If the option is out-of-the-money, it has no intrinsic or in-the-money value. The intrinsic value is equivalent, and may be explained, by reference to the option's *terminal value*. The terminal value of an option is the price the option would command just as it is about to expire (see Figures 1–3 and 1–4).

When an option is about to expire, an option holder has two alternatives available to him: He may exercise the option or permit it to expire unexercised. Because he cannot continue to hold the option in the hopes that the premium will appreciate and the option may be sold for a profit, the option is worth whatever profit it may generate upon exercise.

This raises an important question: Is the option in- or out-of-the-money? If the option is out-of-the-money, then it will be unprofitable to exercise, and the holder will permit it to expire unexercised or abandon the option.

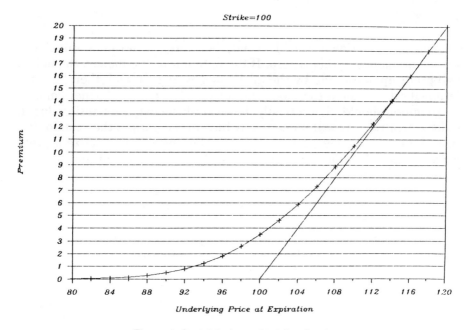

Figure 1–3   Intrinsic and total call value.

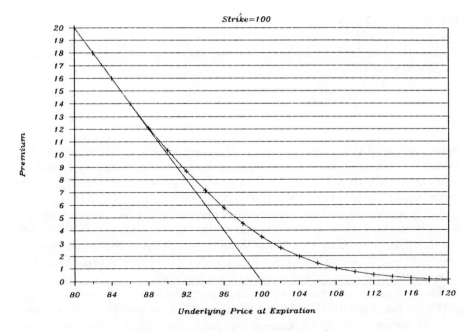

Figure 1–4   Intrinsic and total put value.

An abandoned option is worthless and, therefore, the terminal value of an out-of-the-money option is zero. If the option is in-the-money, the holder will profit upon exercise by the in-the-money amount and, therefore, the terminal value of an in-the-money option equals the in-the-money amount.

An option should, theoretically, never trade below its intrinsic value. If it does, arbitrageurs will immediately buy all the options they can for less than the in-the-money amount, exercise the option, and realize a profit equal to the difference between the in-the-money amount and the premium paid for the option.

An option contract often trades at a level in excess of its intrinsic value. This excess is referred to as the option's time value or sometimes as its extrinsic value.

When an option is about to expire, its premium is reflective solely of intrinsic value. But when there is some time until option expiration, there exists some probability that market conditions will change such that the option may become profitable (or more profitable) to exercise (see Figure 1–5). Time value reflects the probability of a favorable development in terms of prevailing market conditions which might permit a profitable exercise.

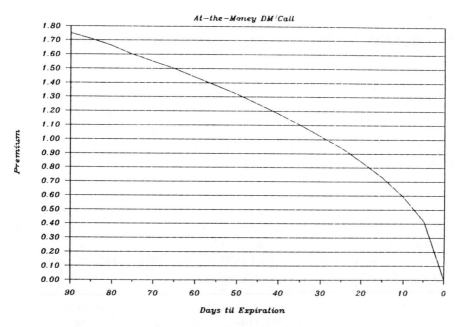

Figure 1–5   Time value decay.

Generally, an option's time value will be greatest when the option is at-the-money. In order to understand this point, consider options which are deep in- or out-of-the-money. When an option is deep out-of-the-money, the probability that the option will ever trade in-the-money becomes remote. Thus the option's time value becomes negligible or even zero.

When an option trends deep in-the-money, the leverage associated with the option declines. Leverage is the ability to control a large amount of resources with a relatively modest investment.

Consider the extraordinary case where a call option has a strike price of zero. Under these circumstances, the option's intrinsic value equals the outright purchase price of the instrument. There is no leverage associated with this option; therefore, the option trader might as well simply buy the underlying instrument outright. Thus there is no time value associated with the option.

A number of different factors impact on an option on futures' time value in addition to the in- or out-of-the-money amount. These include: (1) term until option expiration, (2) market volatility, and (3) short-term interest rates. Options exercisable for actual commodities or financial instruments are also affected by any other cash flows such as dividends (in the case of stock) or coupon payments (bonds).

Term until Expiration

An option's extrinsic value is most often referred to as time value for the simple reason that the term until option expiration has perhaps the most significant and dramatic effect upon the option premium. All other things being equal, premiums will always diminish over time until option expiration.

In order to understand this phenomenon, consider that options perform two basic functions: (1) they permit commercial interests to hedge or off-set the risk of adverse price movement; and (2) they permit traders to speculate on anticipated price movements.

The first function suggests that options represent a form of price insurance. The longer the term of any insurance policy, the more it costs. The longer the life of an option, the greater the probability that adverse events will occur—hence, the value of this insurance is greater.

Likewise, when there is more time left until expiration, there is more time during which the option could potentially move in-the-money. Therefore, speculators will pay more for an option with a longer life.

Not only will the time value of an option decline over time, but that time value decay or erosion may accelerate as the option approaches expiration. Be cautioned: accelerated time value decay is a phenomenon that is characteristic of at- or near-the-money options only. Deep in- or out-of-the-money options tend to exhibit a linear pattern of time value decay.

Volatility

Option holders can profit when options trend into-the-money. If gold prices are expected to move upwards by 10 percent, option traders become more inclined to buy calls. But if gold prices are expected to move upwards by 20 percent over the same time period, traders become even more anxious to buy calls, bidding the premium up in the process.

It is not always easy to predict the direction in which prices will move, but it may be possible to measure volatility nonetheless. Market volatility is often thought of as price movement in either direction, up or down. In this sense, it is the magnitude, not the direction, of the movement that counts.

Standard deviation is a statistic that is often employed to measure volatility. For example, you may see a volatility assessed at 10, 15, 20 percent, and so forth. The use of this statistic implies that commodity price movements may be modeled by the *normal price distrib ition.* The normal distribution is represented by the familiar bell shaped curve.

To interpret a volatility of 19 percent, for example, you can say with approximately 68 percent certainty that the price of the underlying instrument will be within plus or minus 19 percent of where it is now at the conclusion of a year. Or you can say with a probability of 95 percent that the price of the underlying instrument will be within plus or minus 38 percent (2 × 19%) of where the price lies now at the conclusion of a year. A rule of thumb is: The greater the price volatility, the more the option is worth.

Short-Term Rates

Whenever someone invests funds in any venture, some positive return is expected. When an option is purchased, there is an investment equal to the premium. (An option purchased on domestic exchanges cannot by current regulation be margined.)

Since the option is paid for up front and in cash, a return is expected on the investment. This implies that premiums must be discounted to reflect the lost opportunity represented by an investment in options.

When the opportunity cost rises, as reflected in the rate at which funds may alternately be invested on a short-term basis, the price of an option is discounted accordingly. When the opportunity cost decreases, the premium appreciates.

These remarks must be qualified by the following considerations. First, the effect described is applicable only to options on futures and not to options exercisable for actual instruments. In fact, rising short-term rates will tend to increase call premiums and decrease put premiums for options exercisable for actual instruments.

Secondly, these remarks apply holding all other considerations equal. But of course, we know that all else is never held equal. For example, if short-term rates are rising or falling, this suggests that bond futures prices will be affected. This consideration will also have an impact often much greater in magnitude than the impact of fluctuating short-term rates.

Delta

When the price of the underlying instrument rises, call premiums rise and put premiums fall. But by how much? The change in the premium relative to the change in the underlying commodity price is measured by a common option statistic known as *delta.*

Delta is *generally* expressed as a number from zero to 1.0. Deep in-the-money deltas will approach 1.0. Deep out-of-the-money deltas will approach zero. Finally, at- or near-the-money deltas will run at about 0.50.

Delta

Deep In-the-Money $\longrightarrow$ 1.00
At-the-Money $\longrightarrow$ 0.50
Deep Out-of-the-Money $\longrightarrow$ 0.00

It is easy to understand why a deep in- or out-of-the-money option may have a delta equal to 1.0 or zero, respectively. A deep in-the-money premium is reflective solely of intrinsic or in-the-money value. If the option moves slightly more or less in-the-money, its time value may not be affected. Its intrinsic value, however, reflects the relationship between the market price and the fixed strike price, hence a delta of 1.0. A deep out-of-the-money option has no value and is completely unaffected by slightly fluctuating market prices, hence a delta of zero.

A call delta of 0.50 suggests that if the value of the underlying instrument advances by $1, the premium will advance by 50 cents. A put delta of 0.50 suggests that if the value of the underlying instrument advances by $1, the premium will *fall* by 50 cents.

It is probably more appropriate, therefore, to express the delta associated with a (bullish) long call or short put position as a positive number and to express the delta associated with a (bearish) long put or short call position as a negative number.

Delta is a dynamic concept. It will change as the market price moves upwards or downwards. If an at-the-money call starts trending into-the-money, its delta will start to climb, or if the market starts falling, the call delta will likewise fall.

QUESTIONS

1. A call option . . .
   (a) Represents the right to buy on the part of the option writer.
   (b) May be purchased at a fixed cost with a particular strike price.
   (c) Entails the transfer of real property.
   (d) Grants the buyer or holder the right to buy while the writer accepts the obligation to sell.
   (e) Is sold for a profit when the underlying market declines.
2. The option premium . . .
   (a) Is negotiated between buyer and seller at the time the option is written.
   (b) Rises when the underlying price advances.
   (c) Represents the price at which the put or call option may be exercised.

(d) Can be considerably more than the intrinsic plus the time value associated with an option.

(e) None of the above.

3. A call option on bond futures is purchased for 1 ^{32}/$_{64}$ths ($1,500) with a strike price of 84 ^{00}/$_{32}$ds. The breakeven point equals . . .

(a) The exercise price less the option premium.

(b) 84 ^{16}/$_{64}$ths.

(c) The point at which the buyer will find it profitable to exercise the option.

(d) 85 ^{16}/$_{32}$ds.

(e) Cannot be found without more information.

4. A put option is in-the-money when . . .

(a) The holder can realize a profit by exercising it now after deducting the initial cost of the option (the premium).

(b) The exercise price is less than or equal to the current market price.

(c) The market price is less than the option strike price.

(d) The market is trading at a point less than the strike price minus the premium.

(e) The strike price equals the exercise price.

5. A call holder can realize a profit . . .

(a) When the option expires in-the-money.

(b) When the loss on exercise is cushioned by the initial receipt of the option premium.

(c) Whenever the underlying market advances.

(d) Even if the writer exercises the option prior to expiration.

(e) If the option can be offset at a premium in excess of the initial purchase price.

6. A put option on Eurodollar futures is sold at 0.21 with a strike price of 92.00. The breakeven point may be calculated as _____ index points (fill in the blank).

7. (a) March West German mark futures are priced at 0.4173. A 0.4200 call is purchased at a 0.0036 premium. If the market advances to 0.4245 by expiration, the call may be exercised for a *gross* profit of _____ and a *net* profit of _____ cents/mark (fill in the blanks).

(b) The writer of this option will realize a profit as long as the DM remains under _____ dollars/mark (fill in the blank).

8. An option may be fully identified . . .

(a) By reference to its type, strike price, and expiration.

(b) When you know the option series.

(c) By its exercise price and expiration date.

(d) (a) and (b) above.

(e) All of the above.

9. The two elements which comprise an option premium are . . .

(a) In-the-money and intrinsic value.

(b) Intrinsic and time value.

(c) The market price, the strike price, volatility, term until expiration and short-term interest rates.

     (d) Extrinsic value and time value.

     (e) All of the above.

10. A 92.50 put on Eurodollar futures is purchased at 0.35. At expiration, the futures contract is trading at 92.15. The terminal value of this option equals _____ (fill in the blank).

11. Factors which affect an option on T-bond futures premium do *not* include . . .

     (a) The relationship between the market and exercise price.

     (b) The coupon income which accrues on the bond.

     (c) Short-term interest rates and market volatility.

     (d) The number of days until the option expires.

     (e) Option term, volatility, short-term rates.

12. All else being equal, rising short-term interest rates . . .

     (a) Tend to cause options on futures premiums to move up.

     (b) Do not affect options on securities.

     (c) Will cause call options on stock to fall in price and put options on stock to rise in price.

     (d) Mean that at-the-money put and call premiums for options on futures will be roughly equal.

     (e) Tend to diminish the value of options on futures.

13. Which statement is false?

     (a) Volatility and term until expiration tend to have similar effects upon the option premium.

     (b) An option may be considered a form of insurance policy.

     (c) The farther an option is in-the-money, the greater the "deductible" associated with the option.

     (d) An option which is deep out-of-the-money may have little probability of running in-the-money to permit a profitable exercise.

     (e) Delta reflects the expected change in the option premium given a change in the price of the underlying instrument.

2
Option Pricing Concepts

Options are available on instruments as diverse as stock indexes, debt securities, currencies, and futures on all these types of financial instruments. As different as these options are, the most frequently asked question about these markets is: How should they be expected to price?

It is relatively easy to get a "feel" for where a stock or debt security price *should* be. It is far more difficult if not impossible to get an intuitive feel for where an option premium should be.

Fortunately, there are ways to evaluate the fair-market value of any particular option. In practice, many of these methods represent the proverbial "black box." The purpose of this section is to unlock that black box and show how these pricing models work.

We will discuss two of the most commonly used models: the Black-Scholes and the Cox-Ross-Rubinstein models. We will also discuss how these formulas must be modified to price options on futures, options on securities, and options on physical commodities. Finally, we will discuss the most elusive input which must be known in order to utilize these models: market volatility.

BLACK-SCHOLES VERSUS COX-ROSS-RUBINSTEIN

Professors Black and Scholes of the University of Chicago introduced what was to become the most commonly cited option pricing model in 1973. This was a fortuitous date because it coincided roughly with the introduction of exchange-traded stock options on the CBOE, the CBOE experience providing the model upon which modern exchange-traded options are based. A few years later, Professors Cox, Ross, and Rubinstein introduced another pricing model which now enjoys popularity second only to the Black-Scholes model.

19

Both models produce similar results because they are very similar. In fact, the Cox-Ross-Rubinstein model represents a logical precursor to the Black-Scholes model, despite the fact that the Black-Scholes model was introduced earlier in a chronological sense. In order to gain an intuitive understanding of the Black-Scholes model, we will start by describing the concepts underlying the Cox-Ross-Rubinstein model.

Underlying Price Distribution

Assume that the price of bonds is at 100 percent of par. What is the fair-market value of a call struck at 100? In order to address that question, let us review the concept of fair-market value:

> The *fair-market value* of an option is the premium at which both buyer and seller expect to break even in a statistical sense, that is, over a large number of trials.

To make an assessment regarding the probability of a profit or loss, one needs to know the expected pricing behavior of the instrument for which the option may be exercised or the underlying price distribution.

Let us make a very simplifying assumption: the market price will move either up or down by 5 points from its current level of 100 by the time option expiration rolls around with a 50:50 probability. Thus, the market may assume values of either 95 or 105.

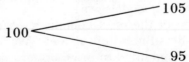

(The assumption that prices will move up or down by a fixed amount in accordance with a known probability is the fundamental concept associated with a "binomial" price distribution. Binomial means two numbers—the price may assume one of two values.)

Having assessed the possible price levels and the probabilities of achieving those levels, one needs to identify the value of the option at each price level. The value of an option at expiration, its *terminal value*, is simply a reflection of its in-the-money amount. If the option is out-of-the-money at expiration, it is worthless. Thus the terminal value of a call (C) is the greater of the underlying price (U) less the exercise price (E), or U − E, and zero:

$$C = \text{Max}\,[(U - E),\, 0]$$

The terminal value of a put (P) is the greater of the exercise price less the underlying price and zero:

$$P = \text{Max}[(E - U), 0]$$

If the market rallies to 105, the terminal value of the call equals the maximum of $5 = (105 - 100)$ and zero—or 5 percent of par. If the market falls to 95, the terminal value of the call equals the maximum of $-5 = (95 - 100)$ and zero—or zero.

Given a 50:50 probability of achieving either result, the fair value of the option equals 2.5 percent of par:

$$C = 0.50 \, \text{Max}[(105 - 100), 0] + 0.50 \, \text{Max}[(95 - 100), 0]$$

$$= (0.50 \times 5) + (0.50 \times 0)$$

$$= 2.5 \text{ percent of par.}$$

If the market may "rachet" up or down 5 points when it is initially at 100, it may likewise rachet up or down 5 points when it has achieved a value of 105 or 95:

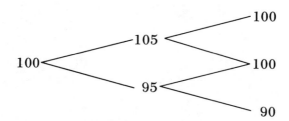

The market may continue to display this form of price dispersion for multiple periods:

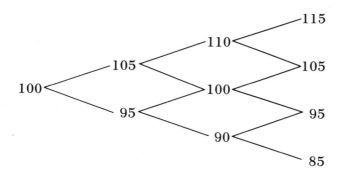

The Cox-Ross-Rubinstein model requires you to work backwards to assess the value of the option at each branch of our tree. For example, when the price has achieved a value of 110 one period prior to expiration, we know that the option must be worth 10 points. (You have a 50 percent probability that the market will advance to 115 where the option will be worth 15 points, a 50 percent probability that the market will fall to 105 where the option is worth 5 points.)

Working backwards in this manner, we can identify the value of the option at any given branch. The following table displays the underlying market price and the option price in parentheses:

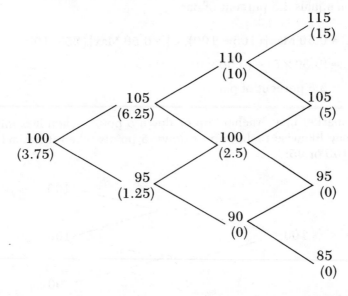

The option should be priced at 3.75 percent of par in accordance with this procedure.

Delta

Delta, which represents the expected change in the premium given a particular change in the value of the underlying instrument, may likewise be modeled with the use of this binomial model.

Return now to our simple example where the current price of 100 may appreciate to 105 or fall to 95 by expiration. The initial value of the premium is 2.5 percent of par. If the market rises to 105, the terminal value of the option equals 5; if the market falls to 95, the option value is zero.

The delta may be found by taking the difference in premiums at the next step along the tree divided by the difference in underlying values:

$$\text{Delta} = (5 - 0)/(105 - 95)$$

$$= 5/10$$

$$= 0.50$$

The delta of 0.50 may be confirmed by noting that if the market rises from 100 to 105, the premium will rise from its initial value of 2.5 to 5. Thus the premium rises by 2.5 points, one half the advance in the underlying market. If the market falls to 95, the premium falls to zero, a decline of 2.5 over a 5 point decline in the underlying instrument.

Delta may likewise be derived assuming a more complex probability tree. The following table shows the underlying price, the premium in parentheses and the delta in brackets:

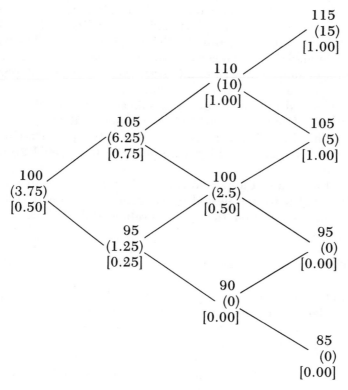

To this point we have ignored the fact that when you buy an option, you pay cash. This is cash you might otherwise invest elsewhere, in T-bills for example, and it represents a lost opportunity which impacts upon the option premium. In particular, you must discount the premium at any given point in time by some applicable short-term interest rate over the life of the option.

Assume that rates are at 8 percent and the option has a half year (0.50 years) to expiration. You can discount the 3.75 premium by using the following formula:

$$C = e^{-rt} [3.75]$$
$$= e^{-(.08)(.5)} [3.75]$$
$$= 3.60$$

Our limited consideration of the binomial pricing model has already reaped some significant benefits because our probability tree confirms many pricing characteristics associated with options. For example, our tree illustrates how a call premium advances or declines as the underlying market fluctuates, driving the option into- or out-of-the-money.

Time value decay is likewise illustrated. Holding the market constant at 100, the market declines from 3.75 to 2.5 from the first period to the third. Of course, if the market remains at 100 by expiration, it will be worthless. This is accelerated time value decay as the option would experience a minor decline in premium from 3.75 to 2.5 over two periods (a 1.25 point drop) and a 2.5 drop over the last period to expiration.

But accelerated time-value decay is indicative only of at- or near-the-money options. Holding the market in-the-money at 105, the premium declines from 6.25 to 5, a 1.25 point drop over two periods. Holding the option out-of-the-money at 95, a 1.25 point decline from 1.25 to zero is experienced.

Finally, the greater the period is to expiration, the greater is the premium. Our call with one period to expiration was valued at 2.5. With three periods to expiration, the option is valued at 3.75.

Black-Scholes

In the limit, as the number of periods utilized in our pricing model becomes very large, the binomial distribution assumes characteristics of the normal distribution. Thus the Cox-Ross-Rubinstein model generates results which are similar to those generated with the Black-Scholes model presuming that you use a relatively large number of intervals. (For practical purposes, this number is probably somewhere near 25 or 30 intervals minimum.)

Rather than attempting to derive the model, let us provide the pricing model for options on futures contracts:

$$C = e^{-rt} [UN(d_1) - EN(d_2)]$$
$$d_1 = [\ln(U/E) + 0.5tv^2] / v \sqrt{(t)}$$
$$d_2 = d_1 - v \sqrt{(t)}$$

Where: C = Call premium.

      r = Short-term interest rate.

      t = Term until expiration, expressed in years, *e.g.*, 91 days/365 days in year equals 0.25 years.

      v = Volatility expressed on an annualized basis.

      U = Underlying price.

      E = Exercise price.

      N = Cumulative normal probability (see Table 2–1 to match up d_1 or d_2 to values in table).

The call delta (for options of futures) may be derived as:

$$\text{Delta} = e^{-rt}N(d_1)$$

Finally, the "put-call parity" formula allows us to identify the value of a put with the same strike price:

$$C - P = e^{-rt}[U - E]$$

or:

$$P = C - e^{-rt}[U - E]$$

The put delta (for options on futures) equals:

$$\text{Delta} = e^{-rt}[N(d_1) - 1]$$

Example: A Japanese yen call option is struck at 60 cents (per 100 yen). The futures market is at 61, there are 91 days to expiration, volatility is at 16 percent, and domestic short-rates are at 8 percent. Find the price of the call:

$$C = e^{-(.08)(.25)}[61(.5987) - 60(.5675)]$$
$$= 2.42$$
$$d_1 = [\ln(61/60) + 0.5(.25)(.16)^2]/(.16)\sqrt{(.25)}$$
$$= .2466$$
$$N(.2466) = .5987$$
$$d_2 = .2466 - (.16)\sqrt{(.25)}$$
$$= .1666$$
$$N(.1666) = .5675$$

Find the call delta:

$$\text{Delta} = e^{-(.08)(.25)}(.5987)$$
$$= .5868$$

Find the value of the put with the same strike:

$$P = 2.42 - e^{-(.08)\,(.25)}[61 - 60]$$
$$= 1.44$$

Find the put delta:

$$Delta = e^{-(.08)\,(.25)}(.5987 - 1)$$
$$= -.3933$$

Model Comparison

Our analysis thus far has been based upon the assumption that the option will be held until expiration, at which point a decision is made to exercise or abandon the option. But is this assumption valid? European-style options only permit exercise of the option on the expiration date, but American-style options permit the exercise of an option at any time prior to the option's expiration.

Table 2–1   Cumulative Normal Probability Distribution

	.00	.01	.02	.03	.04	.05	.06	.07	.08	.09
0.00/	.5000	.5040	.5080	.5120	.5159	.5199	.5239	.5279	.5319	.5358
0.10/	.5398	.5438	.5478	.5517	.5557	.5596	.5636	.5675	.5714	.5753
0.20/	.5793	.5832	.5871	.5909	.5948	.5987	.6026	.6064	.6103	.6141
0.30/	.6179	.6217	.6255	.6293	.6331	.6368	.6406	.6443	.6480	.6517
0.40/	.6554	.6591	.6628	.6664	.6700	.6736	.6772	.6808	.6844	.6879
0.50/	.6915	.6950	.6985	.7019	.7054	.7088	.7123	.7157	.7190	.7224
0.60/	.7257	.7291	.7324	.7356	.7389	.7421	.7454	.7486	.7517	.7549
0.70/	.7580	.7611	.7642	.7673	.7703	.7734	.7764	.7793	.7823	.7852
0.80/	.7881	.7910	.7939	.7967	.7995	.8023	.8051	.8078	.8106	.8133
0.90/	.8159	.8186	.8212	.8238	.8264	.8289	.8315	.8340	.8365	.8389
1.00/	.8413	.8437	.8461	.8485	.8508	.8531	.8554	.8577	.8599	.8621
1.10/	.8643	.8665	.8686	.8708	.8729	.8749	.8770	.8790	.8810	.8830
1.20/	.8849	.8869	.8888	.8906	.8925	.8943	.8962	.8980	.8997	.9015
1.30/	.9032	.9049	.9066	.9082	.9099	.9115	.9131	.9147	.9162	.9177
1.40/	.9192	.9207	.9222	.9236	.9251	.9265	.9279	.9292	.9306	.9319
1.50/	.9332	.9345	.9357	.9370	.9382	.9394	.9406	.9418	.9429	.9441
1.60/	.9452	.9463	.9474	.9484	.9495	.9505	.9515	.9525	.9535	.9545
1.70/	.9554	.9564	.9573	.9582	.9591	.9599	.9608	.9616	.9625	.9633
1.80/	.9641	.9649	.9656	.9664	.9671	.9678	.9686	.9693	.9699	.9706
1.90/	.9713	.9719	.9726	.9732	.9738	.9744	.9750	.9756	.9761	.9767
2.00/	.9772	.9778	.9783	.9788	.9793	.9798	.9803	.9808	.9812	.9817

Table 2-1 *(Continued)*

	.00	.01	.02	.03	.04	.05	.06	.07	.08	.09
2.10/	.9821	.9826	.9830	.9834	.9838	.9842	.9846	.9850	.9854	.9857
2.20/	.9861	.9864	.9868	.9871	.9875	.9878	.9881	.9884	.9887	.9890
2.30/	.9893	.9896	.9898	.9901	.9904	.9906	.9909	.9911	.9913	.9916
2.40/	.9918	.9920	.9922	.9925	.9927	.9929	.9931	.9932	.9934	.9936
2.50/	.9938	.9940	.9941	.9943	.9945	.9946	.9948	.9949	.9951	.9952
2.60/	.9953	.9955	.9956	.9957	.9959	.9960	.9961	.9962	.9963	.9964
2.70/	.9965	.9966	.9967	.9968	.9969	.9970	.9971	.9972	.9973	.9974
2.80/	.9974	.9975	.9976	.9977	.9977	.9978	.9979	.9979	.9980	.9981
2.90/	.9981	.9982	.9982	.9983	.9984	.9984	.9985	.9985	.9986	.9986
3.00/	.9986	.9987	.9987	.9988	.9988	.9989	.9989	.9989	.9990	.9990
−3.00/	.0014	.0013	.0013	.0012	.0012	.0011	.0011	.0011	.0010	.0010
−2.90/	.0019	.0018	.0018	.0017	.0016	.0016	.0015	.0015	.0014	.0014
−2.80/	.0026	.0025	.0024	.0023	.0023	.0022	.0021	.0021	.0020	.0019
−2.70/	.0035	.0034	.0033	.0032	.0031	.0030	.0029	.0028	.0027	.0026
−2.60/	.0047	.0045	.0044	.0043	.0041	.0040	.0039	.0038	.0037	.0036
−2.50/	.0062	.0060	.0059	.0057	.0055	.0054	.0052	.0051	.0049	.0048
−2.40/	.0082	.0080	.0078	.0075	.0073	.0071	.0069	.0068	.0066	.0064
−2.30/	.0107	.0104	.0102	.0099	.0096	.0094	.0091	.0089	.0087	.0084
−2.20/	.0139	.0136	.0132	.0129	.0125	.0122	.0119	.0116	.0113	.0110
−2.10/	.0179	.0174	.0170	.0166	.0162	.0158	.0154	.0150	.0146	.0143
−2.00/	.0228	.0222	.0217	.0212	.0207	.0202	.0197	.0192	.0188	.0183
−1.90/	.0287	.0281	.0274	.0268	.0262	.0256	.0250	.0244	.0239	.0233
−1.80/	.0359	.0351	.0344	.0336	.0329	.0322	.0314	.0307	.0301	.0294
−1.70/	.0446	.0436	.0427	.0418	.0409	.0401	.0392	.0384	.0375	.0367
−1.60/	.0548	.0537	.0526	.0516	.0505	.0495	.0485	.0475	.0465	.0455
−1.50/	.0668	.0655	.0643	.0630	.0618	.0606	.0594	.0582	.0571	.0559
−1.40/	.0808	.0793	.0778	.0764	.0749	.0735	.0721	.0708	.0694	.0681
−1.30/	.0968	.0951	.0934	.0918	.0901	.0885	.0869	.0853	.0838	.0823
−1.20/	.1151	.1131	.1112	.1094	.1075	.1057	.1038	.1020	.1003	.0985
−1.10/	.1357	.1335	.1314	.1292	.1271	.1251	.1230	.1210	.1190	.1170
−1.00/	.1587	.1563	.1539	.1515	.1492	.1469	.1446	.1423	.1401	.1379
−0.90/	.1841	.1814	.1788	.1762	.1736	.1711	.1685	.1660	.1635	.1611
−0.80/	.2119	.2090	.2061	.2033	.2005	.1977	.1949	.1922	.1894	.1867
−0.70/	.2420	.2389	.2358	.2327	.2297	.2266	.2236	.2207	.2177	.2148
−0.60/	.2743	.2709	.2676	.2644	.2611	.2579	.2546	.2514	.2483	.2451
−0.50/	.3085	.3050	.3015	.2981	.2946	.2912	.2877	.2843	.2810	.2776
−0.40/	.3446	.3409	.3372	.3336	.3300	.3264	.3228	.3192	.3156	.3121
−0.30/	.3821	.3783	.3745	.3707	.3669	.3632	.3594	.3557	.3520	.3483
−0.20/	.4207	.4168	.4129	.4091	.4052	.4013	.3974	.3936	.3897	.3859
−0.10/	.4602	.4562	.4522	.4483	.4443	.4404	.4364	.4325	.4286	.4247
−0.00/	.5000	.4960	.4920	.4880	.4841	.4801	.4761	.4721	.4681	.4642

In the context of the option on futures markets, early exercise is practiced with frequency. The reason is made clear when one considers the leverage value associated with an option on a futures contract.

Futures positions, either long or short, may be margined initially with securities on which the futures trader continues to earn the float. Thus there are no explicit opportunity costs associated with the initial placement of a futures position. (Of course, subsequent variation margins are paid or received in cash.) By contrast, option buyers are required to pay cash to secure their positions upon purchase. This means there is actually *negative leverage* associated with an option on futures relative to the underlying futures contract itself.

At some point, as an option falls deeper and deeper in-the-money, the option may be worth more "dead than alive;" it may be worthwhile to exercise the option despite the fact that it has some term until expiration. This is due to the fact that a deep in-the-money option has little or no time value. In fact, its price behavior will approximate that of a futures contract since delta will approximate 1.0. The holder of this deep in-the-money option will want to recover the intrinsic value to invest those funds elsewhere. Because the market for "deep ins" may be quite thin, the buyer is forced to exercise in order to recover that value.

Clearly, an American-style option which provides the holder the flexibility to exercise early is worth more than a European-style option which cannot be exercised early. The upshot of this is that the Black-Scholes model cannot account for the possibility of early exercise while the Cox-Ross-Rubinstein model is in fact capable of handling early exercise!

Thus, the Black-Scholes model may tend to underprice in-the-money options by a tick or two (relative to results from the Cox-Ross-Rubinstein model). This phenomenon is illustrated in Tables 2–2 and 2–3. (Sometimes out-of-the-moneys are priced differently by these two models. This is due more to rounding procedures than any difference in the models.) As expiration approaches or as the option goes out-of-the-money, the difference in values generated by the two models becomes less obvious.

While the Cox-Ross-Rubinstein model is conceptually superior to the Black-Scholes model (as it accounts for the possibility of early exercise), there are some disadvantages. Specifically, the model is computationally inefficient.

In other words, your desktop computer may take more time to compute fair premiums using the Cox-Ross-Rubinstein model (upwards to perhaps one to two seconds) than the Black-Scholes derivation. The speed issue is particularly important when using a large number of intervals and may prove troublesome when generating large tables of premiums or working with large-scale simulations. This consideration, however, becomes irrelevant when using a fast mainframe computer where the computation may take but a few nanoseconds.

Table 2–2 Black-Scholes Pricing Model
Option Theoretical Premium/Delta Matrix

Options on Sep. '86 Bond Futures

Today's Date: 7/7/86   Volatility: 17.00%
Expiration Date: 8/23/86   Short-Term Rate: 6.00%

Underlying/		Exercise Price				
		96.00	98.00	100.00	102.00	104.00
98.00	CALL	3.30	2.23	1.34	0.60	0.34
	Delta	0.6388	0.5082	0.3789	0.2638	0.1714
	PUT	1.31	2.23	3.33	4.58	6.31
	Delta	0.3535	0.4841	0.6134	0.7285	0.8209
99.00	CALL	4.09	2.58	1.60	1.14	0.47
	Delta	0.6982	0.5736	0.4432	0.3207	0.2168
	PUT	1.10	1.59	2.60	4.13	5.44
	Delta	0.2941	0.4187	0.5491	0.6716	0.7755
100.00	CALL	4.55	3.33	2.27	1.37	0.62
	Delta	0.7521	0.6363	0.5082	0.3814	0.2680
	PUT	0.57	1.34	2.27	3.36	4.60
	Delta	0.2402	0.3560	0.4841	0.6109	0.7243
101.00	CALL	5.41	4.11	2.61	1.63	1.17
	Delta	0.7997	0.6947	0.5723	0.4444	0.3241
	PUT	0.43	1.13	1.62	2.63	4.16
	Delta	0.1926	0.2976	0.4200	0.5479	0.6682
102.00	CALL	6.29	4.58	3.36	2.30	1.40
	Delta	0.8406	0.7479	0.6338	0.5082	0.3838
	PUT	0.32	0.60	1.37	2.30	3.39
	Delta	0.1517	0.2444	0.3585	0.4841	0.6085

Table 2–3 Cox-Ross-Rubinstein Pricing Model
Option Theoretical Premium/Delta Matrix

Options on Sep. '86 Bond Futures

Today's Date: 7/7/86

Volatility: 17.00%

Expiration Date: 8/23/86

Short-Term Rate: 6.00%

Underlying/		Exercise Price				
		96.00	98.00	100.00	102.00	104.00
98.00	CALL	3.31	2.25	1.35	0.59	0.33
	Delta	0.6405	0.5096	0.3801	0.2626	0.1678
	PUT	1.32	2.25	3.34	4.58	6.32
	Delta	0.3545	0.4852	0.6150	0.7332	0.8292
99.00	CALL	4.10	2.58	1.60	1.15	0.48
	Delta	0.7015	0.5761	0.4433	0.3209	0.2176
	PUT	1.11	1.58	2.59	4.14	5.46
	Delta	0.2938	0.4188	0.5517	0.6745	0.7786
100.00	CALL	4.56	3.34	2.28	1.38	0.62
	Delta	0.7564	0.6380	0.5096	0.3826	0.2664
	PUT	0.57	1.35	2.28	3.37	4.60
	Delta	0.2394	0.3570	0.4852	0.6125	0.7294
101.00	CALL	5.43	4.13	2.61	1.63	1.18
	Delta	0.8032	0.6978	0.5748	0.4446	0.3245
	PUT	0.44	1.14	1.61	2.63	4.17
	Delta	0.1930	0.2975	0.4201	0.5504	0.6708
102.00	CALL	6.29	4.58	3.37	2.31	1.41
	Delta	0.8495	0.7526	0.6356	0.5096	0.3849
	PUT	0.31	0.59	1.38	2.31	3.40
	Delta	0.1476	0.2432	0.3595	0.4852	0.6102

Fortunately, there is no reason for an individual to attempt to calculate premiums by hand. A number of commercially available computer programs may be used to cut this work down to size.

OPTIONS ON DIFFERENT UNDERLYING INSTRUMENTS

Computing premiums for options on futures is the most straightforward premium calculation one may employ. This is intuitive in that options share many similarities with futures.

Both options and futures call for the deferred delivery of a particular instrument. Futures call for the obligatory delivery of a particular instrument (this obligation may be offset by an offsetting market transaction, of course). Options call for the contingent delivery, upon exercise, of a given instrument. That contingency is at the discretion of the long and is usually determined by reference to the in- or out-of-the-money amount of the option.

Computing premiums for options on other types of instruments is slightly more complicated. Still, the basic option on futures pricing model presented in the prior section is of use.

Forward Pricing Model

Two complications arise when trying to calculate premiums for options on actual financial instruments such as options on stock, bonds, or foreign currency:

1. Futures are relatively straightforward in that the only cash flows associated with the instrument come as a result of its fluctuating price. (These cash flows, incidentally, are generally ignored when pricing these options.) Other investment instruments entail cash flows. For example, a leveraged buyer of bonds pays interest to finance the purchase, presumably at the term repo rate. Moreover, the buyer of bonds receives periodic coupon payments. Likewise, the buyer of stock receives dividend payments; when you buy foreign currency, you invest it at the Eurocurrency rate.
2. It is difficult to compare a spot price to a futures or forward price. In order to use the option on futures pricing model to evaluate options on alternate instruments, you must reconcile the spot to a forward price.

These considerations are accounted for by referencing short-term interest rate levels and any "payouts" associated with the underlying instrument to construct a forward price.

Given a simple interest assumption, the forward price (F) may be represented as:

$$F = S[1 + (r - d)t]$$

Where: F = Forward price.
   S = Spot price.
   r = Short-term financing rate.
   d = Payouts such as dividends, coupon income, etc., expressed as an annual percentage of the spot price.
   t = Term until option expiration expressed in years, *e.g.*, 1/2 year equals 0.50.

(A 360-day year is generally used in the context of short-term interest rate instruments and currencies. It may be more appropriate to use a 365-day year assumption in the context of note and bond markets.)

Representing the payouts as an annualized percentage implies a continuous accrual of the amount. This may be appropriate in the context of a foreign currency option where you invest the currency at the foreign rate (which is used directly as "d").

It may be inappropriate to do so when evaluating options on stocks paying periodic dividends or bonds paying specific coupon payments. These payouts (D) are independent of the spot price level. In that case, you may use the following formula to find the forward price:

$$F = S(1 + rt) - D$$

In any case, you can simply calculate the forward value and substitute the same for the underlying price (U) in the premium evaluation formula provided above. The formula for delta provided above is likewise subtly different. For calls, the delta is:

$$Delta = e^{-dt} N(d_1)$$

For puts, the formula becomes:

$$Delta = e^{-dt} [N(d_1) - 1]$$

Example: Find the premiums and deltas for a put and call as described in the prior example except that it is an option on actual yen. The options are struck at 60 cents (per 100 yen). The spot market is at 61, there are 90 days to expiration, volatility is at 16 percent, domestic short-term or Eurodollar rates are at 8 percent, and Japanese short-term or Euroyen rates are at 4 percent. First, find the forward rate:

$$F = 61[1 + (.08 - .04)(.25)]$$
$$= 61.61$$

The yen forward price is higher than spot because yen exhibits "negative carry." When the forward price exceeds the spot price, the currency is generally referred to as a "premium" currency in the interbank or foreign exchange market (FX). Should the forward price fall short of the spot price, the currency may be referred to as a "discount" currency.

Find the price of the call:

$$C = e^{-(.08)(.25)}[(61.61)(.6443) - 60(.6141)]$$

$$= 2.79$$

$$d_1 = [\ln(61.61/60) + 0.5(.25)(.16)^2]/(.16)\sqrt{(.25)}$$

$$= .3710$$

$$N(.3716) = .6443$$

$$d_2 = .3710 - (.16)\sqrt{(.25)}$$

$$= .2910$$

$$N(.2910) = .6141$$

Find the call delta:

$$Delta = e^{-(.04)(.25)}(.6443)$$

$$= .6379$$

Find the value of the put with the same strike:

$$P = 2.79 - e^{-(.08)(.25)}[61.6131 - 60]$$

$$= 1.21$$

Find the put delta:

$$Delta = e^{-(.04)(.25)}(.6443 - 1)$$

$$= -.3522$$

Pricing Characteristics

Several interesting points are apparent when you consider the pricing characteristics of options on securities versus options on futures.

A common myth in the option markets is that the (absolute value of the) put and call deltas for the same strike must add up to 1.0. This is *not true*. In our example pertaining to the option on yen futures, the deltas of .5868 and .3933 add up to .9801. For options on actual yen, the deltas of .6379 and .3522 add up to .9901. Option deltas only add up to 1.0 for options on securities when there are no payouts. They always fall slightly short of 1.0 for options on futures except when there is no time to expiration or if short-term rates are zero.

Secondly, it is clear from inspection of the put-call parity relationship that at-the-money puts and calls for options on futures should trade at equivalent levels. But the relative premium levels for puts and calls on securities vary depending upon whether the security exhibits positive or negative carry.

Positive carry is a condition where the payouts exceed the short-term financing costs. Negative carry is the reverse: where short-term financing costs exceed the payouts. Carry relationships will determine whether the forward price is greater than or less than the spot price. Positive carry suggests that forwards in successively deferred months will price and lower levels (discount currency); negative carry suggests that forwards in successively deferred months will price at higher and higher levels (premium currency).

As a result, an at-the-money call on a security with positive carry is effectively "pushed" out-of-the-money and a put in-the-money. Where negative carry prevails, calls are pushed in-the-money and puts out-of-the-money. For example, yen in our previous example exhibits negative carry. The call option on yen futures was priced at 2.42—the call option on actual yen was priced higher at 2.79. Likewise, the put on yen futures was priced at 1.46—the put on actual yen was priced at 1.21.

A third point which is highly related to the second is that short-term rates impact upon options on futures and options on actuals in different ways. The effect upon options on futures is simple. Rising short-term rates uniformly dampen both put and call premiums for options on futures. This is attributed to the opportunity cost associated with committing funds to an option purchase. The absolute effect of this consideration is, however, minimal.

The effect upon options on securities is compound. Similar to options on futures, the "opportunity cost effect" slightly diminishes option premiums. By far the more significant consideration may be referred to as the "carry effect." The higher the short-term rate, the lower the positive carry or the greater the negative carry. The effect on forward prices and, consequently, on option premiums is discussed above.

MEASURING VOLATILITY

A number of variables impact on the option price: (1) underlying prices, (2) exercise prices, (3) term until expiration, (4) volatility, (5) short-term rates, and (6) in the case of options on securities, any dividends, coupons, investment income, and such.

All of these variables are readily observable with one exception, volatility. Volatility is perhaps the most illusive input into an option pricing model.

Moreover, it is one of the most significant variables which impact upon the premium.

Many analysts spend much of their time trying to fine-tune a pricing model by developing an algorithm which utilizes a probability distribution which may conform more closely to reality than the binomial or normal distributions. Other analysts feel that studying volatility may provide more significant rewards.

What Does Volatility Mean?

Volatility, in the context of the option market, refers to the potential dispersion of the underlying instrument over the option life. Thus, volatility is nondirectional. It does *not* refer to the potential for either bullish or bearish price movement.

Volatility is usually measured statistically as a variance, or more commonly, as a standard deviation (square root of the variance) of returns, expressed on an annual percentage basis. This is useful because a normal distribution may be fully defined by reference to its mean and standard deviation.

> *Volatility* represents the annualized standard deviation of the log of price relatives. A price relative is equal to today's price divided by yesterday's price.

Volatilities may be interpreted insofar as we can assign a probability that an underlying price may assume a value within a given range. For example, a volatility of 19 percent suggests that there is an approximate 68 percent probability that the price will remain within a range bounded by the current price (the mean of the distribution) plus or minus 19 percent. It suggests further that there is a 95 percent probability the price will remain within a range bounded by the current price plus or minus 2 times the volatility or 38 percent.

By taking the 19 percent volatility divided by the square root of 365 ($19\% / \sqrt{365}$ = approximately 1%), we can say with 68 percent confidence that the underlying price should fall within a range bounded by the current price plus and minus 1 percent at the conclusion of one day. These confidence levels are discernible by studying the cumulative normal probability distribution table (Table 2–1).

Historic Volatility

A historic volatility, as its name implies, represents the volatility actually observed in the recent past. For example, you may take prices over the last n days and calculate an annualized standard deviation (see Figure 2–1).

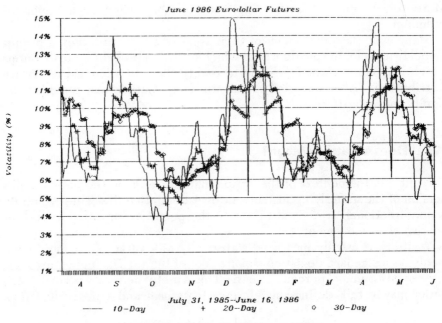

Figure 2-1   10-, 20-, 30-Day volatility.

The first step is to convert raw price levels observed in the market to returns. The following formula is typically used:

$$R_t = \ln (P_t/P_{t-1})$$

Example: On June 12, 1986, September 1986 Eurodollars were at 92.88. On the 13th, the market advanced to 93.14. The return may be calculated as:

Return = ln(93.14/92.88)
       = .002795 or 0.28% advance

Significant problems may arise if your data series is incomplete. For example, you may have observations for Monday, Tuesday, Wednesday, and Friday but no observation for Thursday. Of course, this problem is encountered every weekend and over holidays as well.

It is a safe assumption that a $1 price movement from Monday to Tuesday is more significant than a $1 price movement from Monday to Friday. Obviously, the longer the period is between two dates, the wider is the average dispersion that may be expected in the price of a particular instrument. Consequently, an adjustment is called for: We discount the return calculated as above by the square root of the number of days between the current and previous observation.

Example: On Friday, June 13th, September Eurodollars were at 93.14. By Monday the 16th, they were at 93.18. The adjusted return is calculated as:

$$\text{Return} = \ln(93.18/93.14)/\sqrt{(3)}$$
$$= .000248 \text{ or } 0.025\% \text{ advance}$$

Once a series of adjusted, logged returns is constructed, one may calculate historic volatility by taking the sample standard deviation multiplied by the square root of 365 (days in a year):

$$\text{Volatility} = \sqrt{(365)} \times \text{SD}(\text{Returns}_{t \,\ldots\, t-n})$$

The sample standard deviation may be found by use of the following formula:

$$\text{Sample SD} = \sqrt{\sum_{t=1}^{n}(\text{Return}_t - \text{Average Return})^2/n - 1]}$$

Example: Study the September Eurodollar futures market from June 6 to June 19, 1986:

	Settlement Price	Adjusted Return	$(R_t - \text{Ave R})^2$
6/06/86	92.92		
6/09/86	92.77	−0.000933	0.000001656
6/10/86	92.80	0.000323	0.000000001
6/11/86	92.80	0.000000	0.000000125
6/12/86	92.88	0.000862	0.000000258
6/13/86	93.14	0.002795	0.000005959
6/16/86	93.18	0.000248	0.000000011
6/17/86	93.25	0.000751	0.000000157
6/18/86	93.26	0.000107	0.000000061
6/19/86	93.17	−0.000966	0.000001742
		Mean = 0.000354	
		Sum =	0.000009971

$$\text{Sample SD} = \sqrt{[0.000009971/(9-1)]}$$
$$= 0.001116414$$

$$\text{Volatility} = \sqrt{(365)} \times 0.001116414$$
$$= 2.13\%$$

For those familiar with Eurodollar futures volatility, this volatility of 2.13 percent looks rather low. Typically, volatilities will be posted at much higher levels—in the 20–30 percent range, for example. What accounts for this discrepancy?

This volatility was calculated based on the IMM index (100 less the yield). Typically, however, volatilities and option premiums for both options on Eurodollar and T-bill futures are calculated based on yields rather than index levels. (Although strikes are invariably quoted on the basis of the index.) Thus 2.01 percent of 93.00 equals 28.29 percent of 7.00.

Implied Volatility

Volatility is one of the most significant inputs for an option pricing model. Surprisingly, it is also one of the most important *outputs* from a pricing model! This is in reference to the practice of using "implied" volatilities for the purpose of identifying fair-market option premiums.

A number of variables must be input into an option (on futures) pricing model including: (1) the underlying futures price (U), (2) the exercise price (E), (3) term until expiration (t), (4) volatility (v), and (5) short-term interest rates (r). These inputs are used to calculate the option premium and delta:

$$\text{Premium} = f(U, E, t, v, r)$$

All of these inputs are readily observable in the marketplace with the notable exception of marketplace volatility. In fact, the option premium is readily observable and (presumably) efficiently priced in liquid markets.

The implied volatility is calculated using those readily observable variables plus the prevailing premium level:

$$\text{Volatility} = f(\text{Premium, U, E. t, r})$$

Unfortunately, if you attempt to solve the Black-Scholes pricing formula for volatility, you get an unsolvable polynomial making it necessary to use an "iterative" method to solve for volatility.

An iterative technique requires an initial estimate of volatility to serve as a "seed" value. This seed value is plugged into a pricing model, and the resulting premium is compared to the prevailing option premium. If the resulting premium is less than the market premium, the estimate of volatility is increased. If the resulting premium is more than the market premium, the estimate is decreased. This procedure is repeated until the resulting premium is reasonably close to the market premium (within some predefined tolerance level).

Which Volatility Is Best?

Many analysts ask: should I use a historic or an implied volatility for the purpose of identifying fair-market option premiums. The answer is neither!

You should use the actual volatility that will be observed between the current date and the option expiration date. Unfortunately, this information is not available, so you are forced to estimate this volatility with either a historic or an implied method.

If you are using a historic method, the obvious question is: how many data points should be used? In general, the use of approximately 15–20 data points should produce an estimate which approximates the volatility that you would calculate with an implied method.

This reasoning, however, implicitly assumes that the implied volatility is superior! In general, conventional wisdom holds that one should rely upon an implied volatility unless the market is extremely illiquid or thin.

QUESTIONS

1. Which statement is false?
   (a) The Black-Scholes model assumes that prices are distributed log-normally.
   (b) The Cox-Ross-Rubinstein model assumes that prices follow a distribution which assumes the properties of the normal distribution in the limit.
   (c) The Black-Scholes model is designed to evaluate American-style options.
   (d) The Cox-Ross-Rubinstein model is based upon a binomial pricing distribution.
   (e) The Cox-Ross-Rubinstein model will generally value in-the-money options higher than does the Black-Scholes model.
2. Delta . . .
   (a) Is valid over very small price movements and over short periods of time.
   (b) Equals 1.0 for in-the-money options.
   (c) Equals 1.0 for out-of-the-money options.
   (d) Does not change over time.
   (e) Is frequently represented as a negative number for long calls.
3. (a) There is a 50:50 probability that the market value of gold will be at $325 or $375 by option expiration. You own a call struck at $350. Without considering time value of money, how much is this call worth?
   (b) What is the delta of this option?
   (c) What would the value of this option be given a 10 percent short-term rate and a one-half year term. (You will need your calculator.)

4. (a) Consider the following probability tree. There is a 50:50 probability that the market will rise or fall at each branch of the tree. You have a call struck at $350. Without considering the time value of money, find the option premium at each branch.

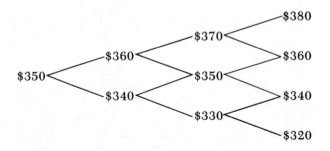

(b) What is the delta at each branch?

5. Implied volatility . . .
   (a) Represents the actual volatility observed in the marketplace over the last n days.
   (b) Can be used to identify the option delta.
   (c) Will fall within one standard deviation of historic volatility with a 68 percent probability.
   (d) Can be found essentially by running the pricing model backwards to solve for volatility.
   (e) None of the above.

6. (a) Use the Black-Scholes model to find the value of a call on deutsche mark futures. The market (U) is at .4280, the call has an exercise price (E) of .4200, there are 120 days until expiration (t = 120/365), short-term rates (r) are at 7.5 percent, market volatility (v) is at 11 percent. You will need a calculator and a normal probability table.

   Reminder:

   $$\text{Call Premium} = e^{-rt}[UN(d_1) - EN(d_2)]$$

   where: $d_1 = [\ln(U/E) + 0.5v^2 t]/v\sqrt{(t)}$
   $$d_2 = d_1 - v\sqrt{(t)}$$

   (b) What is the delta associated with this option?
   (c) Find the value of the put option (P) with the same strike using the put/call parity formula.

      Reminder:

      $$P = C - e^{-rt}(U - E)$$

3
Risk, Reward, and Probability

Risk and reward always tend to balance. Where a business proposition entails high risk, relatively high rewards are generally expected. A low risk venture usually entails reduced reward potential.

This section addresses these issues in the context of outright option buy and sell strategies. In addition, we consider the opportunity to create market positions using a combination of futures and options or options and options which resemble outright buy or sell strategies using either futures or options.

MEASURING MARKET RISK

Many traders spend a great deal of time studying the potential risks and returns associated with an option strategy. For example, you know that when you buy an option your maximum risk equals the premium paid up front to secure your purchase. But it is often difficult to assess the probability that you will be faced with the full loss of the premium or the probability that you will buy a call, and the market will trade over the breakeven to permit a profitable exercise at expiration.

However, with the aid of a calculator and a normal probability distribution table, you can assess these odds. This section will describe that process and make a few observations about the relative risks and rewards associated with in-, at-, and out-of-the-money options.

Market Volatility and Movement

If you toss a "fair" coin in the air, the probability that it will come up heads or tails should be 50:50. This is a very simple probability distribution. In order to assess the odds associated with an option strategy, you must attempt to identify the pricing distribution associated with the underlying instrument. As discussed earlier, many analysts believe that the distribution of percentage price returns on a financial instrument may be approximated adequately through the use of the normal probability distribution.

Note that analysts believe that *returns* (the percentage price change from day to day) may be normally distributed. What about prices? If one is satisfied that returns may be approximated with a normal distribution, then mathematically it may be proven that prices are "log-normally" distributed.

Whereas the normal distribution is symmetric about its mean, average, the log-normal distribution is asymmetric, which means there is a greater probability of a high rather than a low price. This makes sense in that all financial instruments have a very strong support level—they can not fall below zero! On the other hand, there is no absolute impediment to upward price movement.

Measuring Volatility

A normal or log-normal distribution is fully defined by reference to the mean and standard deviation. You can use the current underlying price as the mean for your distribution. Identifying the standard deviation or volatility is more tricky.

A *historic volatility* may be calculated using a time series of past observations of the commodity. For example, you can use 10, 20, 30, and so forth past observations. Technically, this calculation involves taking the annualized sample standard deviation of the log of today's price divided by yesterday's price.

Most option traders, however, prefer an *implied volatility*. This volatility is implicit in the option premium. Given information about the market price, strike price, option term, short-term rates, and volatility, you can calculate an option premium using various computer models. If you know the option premium but not the volatility, you can essentially run the option pricing model backwards to solve for volatility.

Calculating the Odds

You can find the probability the market will be under some "target price" (P) at the conclusion of any given number of days (d) by using the following formula:

$$N = \ln(P/C)/v \sqrt{(d/365)}$$

Where:

        N = Value of the standard normal random variable.

        P = Target price level.

        C = Current price level.

        v = Market volatility.

        d = Days you will hold position.

The best way to describe the use of this method is with an illustration.

Example: On June 6, 1986, September deutsche mark futures were trading at 45.29 cents per mark. The at-the-money (or nearest-to-the-money) call struck at 45 was trading at 1.51 cents per mark with an implied volatility of 15.42 percent. A buyer of this option may well ask: What is the probability that the market will run over the breakeven point of 46.51 (strike price plus premium) by expiration 91 days hence?

In order to answer that question, you need a calculator and the cumulative normal probability distribution Table 3–1. First, you need to solve for N in our equation. Substituting for these variables, we may calculate:

Table 3–1   Cumulative Normal Probability Distribution

	.00	.01	.02	.03	.04	.05	.06	.07	.08	.09
0.00/	.5000	.5040	.5080	.5120	.5159	.5199	.5239	.5279	.5319	.5358
0.10/	.5398	.5438	.5478	.5517	.5557	.5596	.5636	.5675	.5714	.5753
0.20/	.5793	.5832	.5871	.5909	.5948	.5987	.6026	.6064	.6103	.6141
0.30/	.6179	.6217	.6255	.6293	.6331	.6368	.6406	.6443	.6480	.6517
0.40/	.6554	.6591	.6628	.6664	.6700	.6736	.6772	.6808	.6844	.6879
0.50/	.6915	.6950	.6985	.7019	.7054	.7088	.7123	.7157	.7190	.7224
0.60/	.7257	.7291	.7324	.7356	.7389	.7421	.7454	.7486	.7517	.7549
0.70/	.7580	.7611	.7642	.7673	.7703	.7734	.7764	.7793	.7823	.7852
0.80/	.7881	.7910	.7939	.7967	.7995	.8023	.8051	.8078	.8106	.8133
0.90/	.8159	.8186	.8212	.8238	.8264	.8289	.8315	.8340	.8365	.8389
1.00/	.8413	.8437	.8461	.8485	.8508	.8531	.8554	.8577	.8599	.8621
1.10/	.8643	.8665	.8686	.8708	.8729	.8749	.8770	.8790	.8810	.8830
1.20/	.8849	.8869	.8888	.8906	.8925	.8943	.8962	.8980	.8997	.9015
1.30/	.9032	.9049	.9066	.9082	.9099	.9115	.9131	.9147	.9162	.9177
1.40/	.9192	.9207	.9222	.9236	.9251	.9265	.9279	.9292	.9306	.9319
1.50/	.9332	.9345	.9357	.9370	.9382	.9394	.9406	.9418	.9429	.9441
1.60/	.9452	.9463	.9474	.9484	.9495	.9505	.9515	.9525	.9535	.9545
1.70/	.9554	.9564	.9573	.9582	.9591	.9599	.9608	.9616	.9625	.9633
1.80/	.9641	.9649	.9656	.9664	.9671	.9678	.9686	.9693	.9699	.9706
1.90/	.9713	.9719	.9726	.9732	.9738	.9744	.9750	.9756	.9761	.9767

Table 3–1 *(Continued)*

	.00	.01	.02	.03	.04	.05	.06	.07	.08	.09
2.00/	.9772	.9778	.9783	.9788	.9793	.9798	.9803	.9808	.9812	.9817
2.10/	.9821	.9826	.9830	.9834	.9838	.9842	.9846	.9850	.9854	.9857
2.20/	.9861	.9864	.9868	.9871	.9875	.9878	.9881	.9884	.9887	.9890
2.30/	.9893	.9896	.9898	.9901	.9904	.9906	.9909	.9911	.9913	.9916
2.40/	.9918	.9920	.9922	.9925	.9927	.9929	.9931	.9932	.9934	.9936
2.50/	.9938	.9940	.9941	.9943	.9945	.9946	.9948	.9949	.9951	.9952
2.60/	.9953	.9955	.9956	.9957	.9959	.9960	.9961	.9962	.9963	.9964
2.70/	.9965	.9966	.9967	.9968	.9969	.9970	.9971	.9972	.9973	.9974
2.80/	.9974	.9975	.9976	.9977	.9977	.9978	.9979	.9979	.9980	.9981
2.90/	.9981	.9982	.9982	.9983	.9984	.9984	.9985	.9985	.9986	.9986
3.00/	.9986	.9987	.9987	.9988	.9988	.9989	.9989	.9989	.9990	.9990
−3.00/	.0014	.0013	.0013	.0012	.0012	.0011	.0011	.0011	.0010	.0010
−2.90/	.0019	.0018	.0018	.0017	.0016	.0016	.0015	.0015	.0014	.0014
−2.80/	.0026	.0025	.0024	.0023	.0023	.0022	.0021	.0021	.0020	.0019
−2.70/	.0035	.0034	.0033	.0032	.0031	.0030	.0029	.0028	.0027	.0026
−2.60/	.0047	.0045	.0044	.0043	.0041	.0040	.0039	.0038	.0037	.0036
−2.50/	.0062	.0060	.0059	.0057	.0055	.0054	.0052	.0051	.0049	.0048
−2.40/	.0082	.0080	.0078	.0075	.0073	.0071	.0069	.0068	.0066	.0064
−2.30/	.0107	.0104	.0102	.0099	.0096	.0094	.0091	.0089	.0087	.0084
−2.20/	.0139	.0136	.0132	.0129	.0125	.0122	.0119	.0116	.0113	.0110
−2.10/	.0179	.0174	.0170	.0166	.0162	.0158	.0154	.0150	.0146	.0143
−2.00/	.0228	.0222	.0217	.0212	.0207	.0202	.0197	.0192	.0188	.0183
−1.90/	.0287	.0281	.0274	.0268	.0262	.0256	.0250	.0244	.0239	.0233
−1.80/	.0359	.0351	.0344	.0336	.0329	.0322	.0314	.0307	.0301	.0294
−1.70/	.0446	.0436	.0427	.0418	.0409	.0401	.0392	.0384	.0375	.0367
−1.60/	.0548	.0537	.0526	.0516	.0505	.0495	.0485	.0475	.0465	.0455
−1.50/	.0668	.0655	.0643	.0630	.0618	.0606	.0594	.0582	.0571	.0559
−1.40/	.0808	.0793	.0778	.0764	.0749	.0735	.0721	.0708	.0694	.0681
−1.30/	.0968	.0951	.0934	.0918	.0901	.0885	.0869	.0853	.0838	.0823
−1.20/	.1151	.1131	.1112	.1094	.1075	.1057	.1038	.1020	.1003	.0985
−1.10/	.1357	.1335	.1314	.1292	.1271	.1251	.1230	.1210	.1190	.1170
−1.00/	.1587	.1563	.1539	.1515	.1492	.1469	.1446	.1423	.1401	.1379
−0.90/	.1841	.1814	.1788	.1762	.1736	.1711	.1685	.1660	.1635	.1611
−0.80/	.2119	.2090	.2061	.2033	.2005	.1977	.1949	.1922	.1894	.1867
−0.70/	.2420	.2389	.2358	.2327	.2297	.2266	.2236	.2207	.2177	.2148
−0.60/	.2743	.2709	.2676	.2644	.2611	.2579	.2546	.2514	.2483	.2451
−0.50/	.3085	.3050	.3015	.2981	.2946	.2912	.2877	.2843	.2810	.2776
−0.40/	.3446	.3409	.3372	.3336	.3300	.3264	.3228	.3192	.3156	.3121
−0.30/	.3821	.3783	.3745	.3707	.3669	.3632	.3594	.3557	.3520	.3483
−0.20/	.4207	.4168	.4129	.4091	.4052	.4013	.3974	.3936	.3897	.3859
−0.10/	.4602	.4562	.4522	.4483	.4443	.4404	.4364	.4325	.4286	.4247
−0.00/	.5000	.4960	.4920	.4880	.4841	.4801	.4761	.4721	.4681	.4642

$$N = \ln(46.51/45.29)/.1542 \sqrt{(91/365)}$$
$$= 0.3452$$

To find the probability associated with N, you must refer to the cumulative normal probability distribution table and look up the figure for 0.3452 (rounded to 0.35). You will find that this number equals 0.6368. This suggests that there is approximately a 64 percent probability that the market will remain *under* the breakeven point by the time expiration rolls around. It follows that there is about a 36 percent probability that the market will run over the breakeven point.

Assessing Probabilities for Different Struck Options

Out-of-the-money options generally attract a substantially greater interest than do in-the-money options. The reason is simple: Out-of-the-money options will always cost less than comparable in-the-money options. Because the risk associated with buying an option is reflected directly in the premium, many option traders prefer to trade almost exclusively out-of-the-moneys.

A smart option trader will consider not only the maximum risk associated with trading an option, but the probability associated with that risk. Upon examination you will find that risk must balance with reward. Where the option trader takes on a relatively large dollar risk, a relatively large dollar reward is inherent in the position. Small risks are associated with relatively smaller potential rewards. If this were not true, it would suggest that the market is mispriced and that arbitrage opportunities exist.

In other words, the option premium is negotiated to balance risk and reward and the asymmetry between risk and reward levels associated with long and short options. Note that in our prior example, there was only a 36 percent chance that the call buyer would show a profit by expiration. Thus there was a 64 percent probability that the call *seller* would show a profit!

Example: Consider the risks and rewards associated with the in-, at-, and out-of-the-money *calls* on September 1986 deutsche mark futures on June 6th (see Figure 3–1). September 1986 futures were at 45.29 at the time.

	Premium	Strike	Vol.	Prob < Strike	B/E	Prob > B/E
In-Mny	2.07	44.00	15.35%	35%	46.07	41%
At-Mny	1.51	45.00	15.42%	47%	46.51	36%
Out-Mny	1.08	46.00	15.68%	58%	47.08	31%

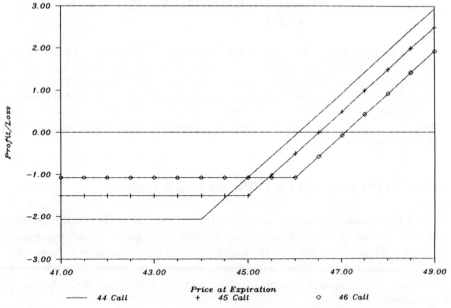

Figure 3–1   In-, at-, out-money DM calls.

Clearly, the in-the-money 44 call, by virtue of its relatively large premium, entails greater risk than the out-of-the-money 46 call. However, the probability that the maximum loss associated with the in-the-money option will be realized (if the market runs below the 44 strike) is relatively small at 35 percent compared to the probability of losing the entire 46 call premium at 58 percent. Moreover, the probability of realizing a profit is greater with the in-the-money option, by virtue of its lower breakeven point, than with the out-of-the-money option.

Example: Consider the risks and rewards associated with the in-, at-, and out-of-the-money *puts* on September 1986 deutsche mark futures on June 6th (see Figure 3–2). September 1986 futures were at 45.29 at the time.

	Premium	Strike	Vol.	Prob > Strike	B/E	Prob < B/E
In-Mny	1.78	46.00	15.45%	42%	44.22	38%
At-Mny	1.22	45.00	15.36%	53%	43.78	33%
Out-Mny	0.81	44.00	15.70%	64%	43.19	27%

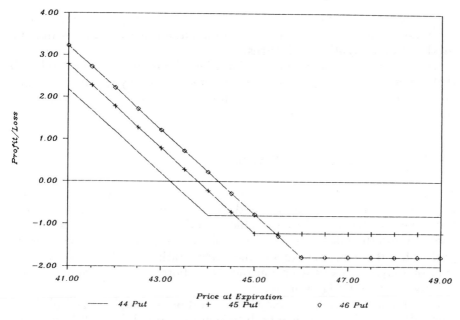

Figure 3–2   In-, at-, out-money DM puts.

The same rationale applies with put options; the in-the-money option entails greater maximum risk. But the probability of realizing the maximum loss is low at 42 percent relative to the probability of losing the entire premium (64 percent) associated with the cheap out-of-the-money option. The probability of realizing a profit is also greater with the in-the-money option (?8 percent) than it is with the out-of-the-money option (27 percent). This suggests that when you buy options, you get what you pay for. If you buy an expensive option, you get more risk, but you also buy more profit potential.

Remember: Options can be thought of as forms of insurance policies; if you pay more for the option, you get more. The farther the option is out-of-the-money, the less profit potential it will provide (and the less protection if it is used as a hedge vehicle). The degree to which the option is out-of-the-money is analogous to the deductible component of an insurance policy.

SYNTHETIC FUTURES, SYNTHETIC OPTIONS

It is clear from the previous discussion that outright option strategies, either buys or sells, may be used to create very different risk/reward scenarios. Surprisingly, a combination of futures and options may be used to create "synthetic" options, or a combination of two options may be used to create "synthetic" futures.

These strategies may be interesting when the market is mispriced such that a synthetic may be established to slant the odds to your favor, or when you already hold a futures or option position and wish to alter your risk/reward scenario quickly and efficiently.

Double- and Single-Edged Blades

The best way to understand the concept of synthetic futures and options is to use the analogy of double- and single-edged blades. A futures contract may be thought of as a double-edged blade: If you buy a futures contract and the market moves favorably, rallies, you can realize sizable profits; but if you are wrong and the market falls, large losses can accrue very quickly. Thus a futures contract "cuts both ways" and may be compared to a double-edged blade.

By comparison, an option may be thought of as a single-edged blade. A long call and a short put may both be considered mildly bullish positions (as opposed to a strongly bullish long futures position). If you buy a call and the market rallies, you may realize large profits limited only to the extent of the option premium paid up front. If the market declines, your loss is limited to the premium. A short put entails a limited profit opportunity (the premium) if the market rallies and open-ended loss if the market declines.

A long put and a short call may be considered mildly bearish positions (as opposed to a strongly bearish short futures position). If you buy a put, you realize an open-ended gain if the market falls or a limited loss should the market advance. A short call may yield a limited gain in a bear market but also open-ended losses if the market advances.

Long futures	strongly bullish	(++)
Long call or short put	mildly bullish	(+)
Long put or short call	mildly bearish	(−)
Short futures	strongly bearish	(−−)

Let us represent mildly bullish and mildly bearish positions with a plus sign (+) and minus sign (−), respectively. Strongly bullish and strongly bearish positions may be represented with two signs (++) and (−−), respectively.

By combining a bullish or bearish futures position with an option of the opposite orientation, you create synthetic options. For example, by combining a strongly bullish long futures position with a mildly bearish long put, you create a mildly bullish long call. In effect, the strongly bullish character of the long futures overcomes the mild bearishness of the long put, resulting in a mildly bullish position.

Synthetic Option

Long Futures (++)	+ Long Put (−)	= Long Call (+)
Long Futures (++)	+ Short Call (−)	= Short Put (+)
Short Futures (−−)	+ Short Put (+)	= Short Call (−)
Short Futures (−−)	+ Long Call (+)	= Long Put (−)

Likewise, by combining two mildly bullish (long call and short put) or two mildly bearish (long put and short call) option positions, you can create a position which resembles a strongly bullish long futures or strongly bearish short futures position, respectively.

Synthetic Futures

Long Call (+)	+ Short Put (+)	= Long Futures (++)
Long Put (−)	+ Short Call (−)	= Short Futures (−−)

Synthetic Options

In order to understand how synthetic options are created, we can dissect the component futures and option positions by examining several examples.

Example: A synthetic long call is created by going long Swiss franc futures at 56 cents per franc and buying a 56 put for 1.50 (see Figure 3–3). A synthetic long call struck at 56 is thereupon created.

Futures @ Expiration	Long Futures	+	Long Put	=	Synthetic Long Call
60	4.00		(1.50)		2.50
58	2.00		(1.50)		0.50
56	—		(1.50)		(1.50)
54	(2.00)		0.50		(1.50)
52	(4.00)		2.50		(1.50)

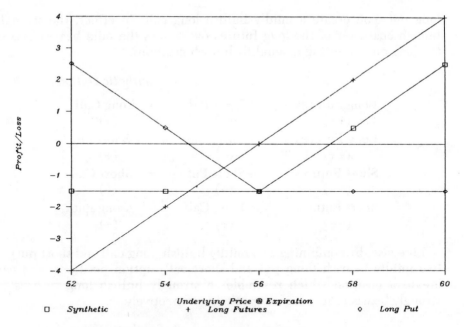

Figure 3–3   Synthetic long 56 call.

Example: A synthetic short put is created by going long Swiss franc futures at 56 cents per franc and selling a 56 call for 1.50 (see Figure 3–4). A synthetic short put struck at 56 is thereupon created.

Futures @ Expiration	Long Futures	+	Short Call	=	Synthetic Short Put
60	4.00		(2.50)		1.50
58	2.00		(0.50)		1.50
56	—		1.50		1.50
54	(2.00)		1.50		(0.50)
52	(4.00)		1.50		(2.50)

Example: A synthetic short call is created by going short Swiss franc futures at 56 cents per franc and selling a 56 put for 1.50 (see Figure 3–5). A synthetic short call struck at 56 is thereupon created.

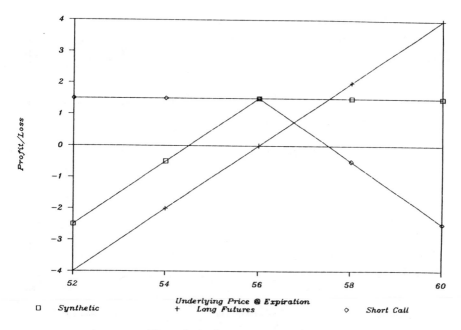

| □ | Synthetic | + | Long Futures | ◊ | Short Call |

Underlying Price @ Expiration

Figure 3–4   Synthetic short 56 put.

Futures @ Expiration	Short Futures	+	Short Put	=	Synthetic Short Call
60	(4.00)		1.50		(2.50)
58	(2.00)		1.50		(0.50)
56	—		1.50		1.50
54	2.00		(0.50)		1.50
52	4.00		(2.50)		1.50

Example: A synthetic long put is created by going short Swiss franc futures at 56 cents per franc and buying a 56 call for 1.50 (see Figure 3–6). A synthetic long put struck at 56 is created.

Futures @ Expiration	Short Futures	+	Long Call	=	Synthetic Long Put
60	(4.00)		2.50		(1.50)
58	(2.00)		0.50		(1.50)
56	—		(1.50)		(1.50)
54	2.00		(1.50)		0.50
52	4.00		(1.50)		2.50

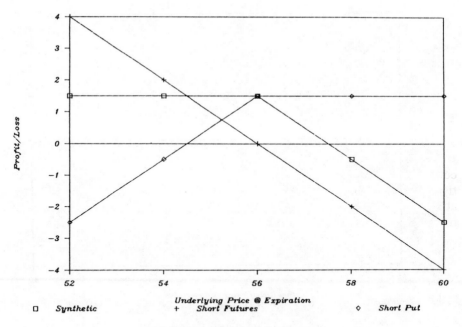

Figure 3–5   Synthetic short 56 call.

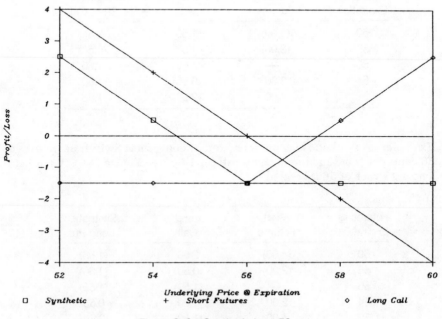

Figure 3–6   Synthetic long 56 put.

In-, At-, Out-of-the-Moneys

By combining an at-the-money long put with a long futures contract, one creates a synthetic at-the-money long call. But what happens if one buys an in- or out-of-the-money put against that long futures contract?

For example, if one were to buy a put struck in-the-money at 57 against those Swiss franc futures at 56, one would create a synthetic long call struck *over* the market at 57. In other words, you would create a synthetic out-of-the-money long call. Similarly, by buying an out-of-the-money put struck at 55, you would create an in-the-money synthetic long call! You could take a very aggressive in-the-money put and convert it into a relatively conservative synthetic out-of-the-money long call or take a conservative out-of-the-money long put and convert it into a relatively aggressive in-the-money long call!

Example: A synthetic long call is created by going long Swiss franc futures at 56 cents per franc and buying an in-the-money 58 put for 2.70. A synthetic long call struck out-of-the-money at 58 is created (see Figure 3–7). This synthetic long call is purchased at a price of 0.70.

Futures @ Expiration	Long Futures	+	Long Put	=	Synthetic Long Call
60	4.00		(2.70)		1.30
58	2.00		(2.70)		(0.70)
56	—		(0.70)		(0.70)
54	(2.00)		1.30		(0.70)
52	(4.00)		3.30		(0.70)

Example: A synthetic long call is created by going long Swiss franc futures at 56 cents per franc and buying an out-of-the-money 54 put for 0.70. A synthetic long call struck in-the-money at 54 is thereupon created (see Figure 3–8). Effectively, this synthetic long call is purchased at a price of 2.70.

Futures @ Expiration	Long Futures	+	Long Put	=	Synthetic Long Call
60	4.00		(0.70)		3.30
58	2.00		(0.70)		1.30
56	—		(0.70)		(0.70)
54	(2.00)		(0.70)		(2.70)
52	(4.00)		1.30		(2.70)

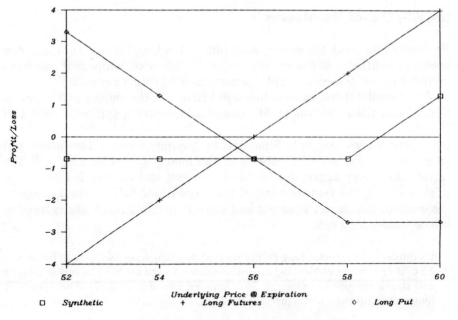

□ Synthetic	+ Long Futures	◇ Long Put

Figure 3–7   Synthetic long 58 call.

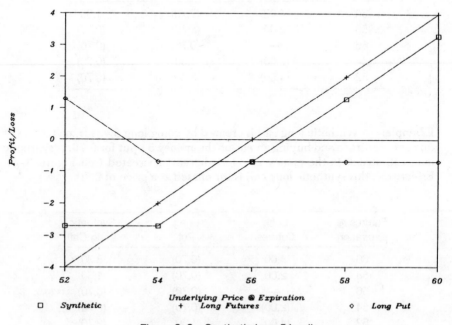

□ Synthetic	+ Long Futures	◇ Long Put

Figure 3–8   Synthetic long 54 call.

The out-of-the-money synthetic call is effectively purchased at the put premium *less* the in-the-money amount of the put. The in-the-money synthetic call is effectively purchased at the put premium *plus* the out-of-the-money amount of the put. As a general rule, the synthetic price may be determined as shown next.

If the natural option is in-the-money ⇒

   Synthetic Premium = Natural Premium − (In-the-Money Amount)

If the natural option is out-of-the-money ⇒

Synthetic Premium = Natural Premium + (Out-of-the-Money Amount)

Example: A synthetic short put is created by going long Swiss franc futures at 56 cents per franc and selling an out-of-the-money 58 call for 0.75. A synthetic short put struck in-the-money at 58 is created. This synthetic short put is sold at a price of 2.75.

Futures @ Expiration	Long Futures	+	Short Call	=	Synthetic Short Put
60	4.00		(1.25)		2.75
58	2.00		0.75		2.75
56	—		0.75		0.75
54	(2.00)		0.75		(1.25)
52	(4.00)		0.75		(3.25)

Example: A synthetic short put is created by going long Swiss franc futures at 56 cents per franc and selling an in-the-money 54 call for 2.70. A synthetic short put struck in-the-money at 54 is thereupon created. Effectively, this synthetic short put is sold at a price of 0.70.

Futures @ Expiration	Long Futures	+	Short Call	=	Synthetic Short Put
60	4.00		(3.30)		0.70
58	2.00		(1.30)		0.70
56	—		0.70		0.70
54	(2.00)		2.70		0.70
52	(4.00)		2.70		(1.30)

Synthetic Futures

Synthetic futures are just as easy to construct. Simply take two mildly bullish options (long call and short put) with the same strike price to create a strongly bullish long futures contract or take two mildly bearish options (long put and short call) to create a strongly bearish short futures contract.

Example: You buy a 56 call for 1.50 and sell a 56 put for 1.50 when Swiss franc futures are trading at 56 (see Figure 3–9). This is equivalent to buying futures at 56.

Futures @ Expiration	Long Call	+	Short Put	=	Synthetic Long Futures
60	2.50		1.50		4.00
58	0.50		1.50		2.00
56	(1.50)		1.50		—
54	(1.50)		(0.50)		(2.00)
52	(1.50)		(2.50)		(4.00)

Example: You buy a 56 put for 1.50 and sell a 56 call for 1.50 when Swiss franc futures are trading at 56 (see Figure 3–10). This is equivalent to selling futures at 56.

Futures @ Expiration	Long Put	+	Short Call	=	Synthetic Short Futures
60	(1.50)		(2.50)		(4.00)
58	(1.50)		(0.50)		(2.00)
56	(1.50)		1.50		—
54	0.50		1.50		2.00
52	2.50		1.50		4.00

Similarly, you can use in- or out-of-the-money options to create synthetic long or short futures. For example, you can buy an in-the-money call and sell an out-of-the-money put or buy an out-of-the-money call and sell an in-the-money put.

Example: You buy a 58 call for .75 and sell a 58 put for 2.70 when Swiss franc futures are trading at 56 (see Figure 3–11). This is equivalent to buying futures at 56.05.

Futures @ Expiration	Long Call	+	Short Put	=	Synthetic Long Futures
60	1.25		2.70		3.95
58	(0.75)		2.70		1.95
56	(0.75)		0.70		(0.05)
54	(0.75)		(1.30)		(2.05)
52	(0.75)		(3.30)		(4.05)

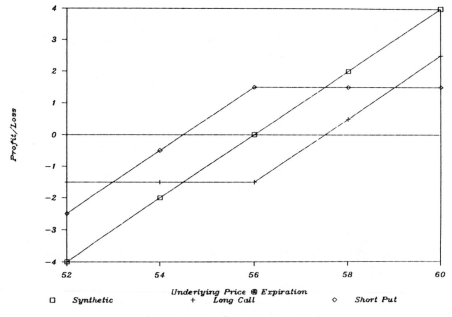

Figure 3-9   Synthetic long futures.

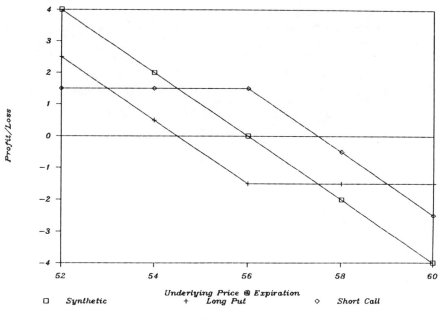

Figure 3-10   Synthetic short futures.

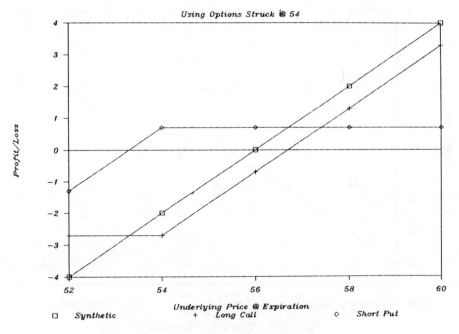

Figure 3–11   Synthetic long futures.

Example: You buy a 54 call for 2.70 and sell a 54 put for 0.70 when Swiss franc futures are trading at 56 (see Figure 3–12). This is equivalent to buying futures at 56.

Futures @ Expiration	Long Call	+	Short Put	=	Synthetic Long Futures
60	3.30		0.70		4.00
58	1.30		0.70		2.00
56	(0.70)		0.70		—
54	(2.70)		0.70		(2.00)
52	(2.70)		(1.30)		(4.00)

Here the rule is that the effective purchase or sale price of a synthetic long futures equals the option strike price adjusted by the net premium paid or received:

	Net Debit	*Net Credit*
Synthetic Long Futures Price	Strike + Debit	Strike − Credit
Synthetic Short Futures Price	Strike − Debit	Strike + Credit

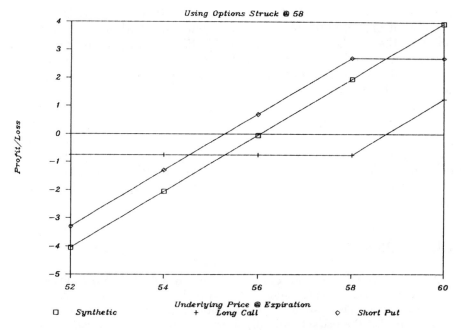

Figure 3-12   Synthetic long futures.

Why Synthetics?

Why would an option trader ever wish to trade synthetic options or synthetic futures? Clearly, these strategies require taking two positions rather than a single position; therefore, they entail two commissions rather than one.

Most synthetics are created when a trader initially takes one position, and then something happens to cause the trader to change his market position. He alters that original position with the placement of another order. For example, a trader may have originally been very bullish and bought futures. Subsequently, he begins to believe that the market may become mildly bullish to neutral, so he sells a call, creating a synthetic short put. This practice may be simpler than liquidating the original long futures contract and reestablishing a new short put position.

Synthetics may also be attractive when they may be placed such that the trader's risk/reward profile and probabilities of gain versus loss are more attractive using the synthetic than the outright position. In our example above, a trader may sell a 58 put for 2.70 or establish a synthetic short 58 put at an effective price of 2.75 by buying Swiss franc futures at 56 and selling a 58 call at 0.75.

Clearly, the risk/reward profile of the synthetic is superior. The break-even point on the outright short put equals 55.30 while the breakeven point on the *synthetic* short put is at 55.25. Given a volatility of 13.85 percent over 90 days, this suggests that there is a 44 percent probability of loss with the outright put and only a 43 percent chance of loss with the synthetic short put!

Superficially, the synthetic appears to be the superior investment, but this analysis disregards another important factor: By selling the outright put you bring in 2.75 cents per franc which may be invested at prevailing short-term rates over the life of the option. By entering the synthetic, you only have 0.75 cents per franc to invest! This underscores the point that in an efficiently priced option market, quasi-arbitrage opportunities are rare indeed.

QUESTIONS

1. March West German mark futures are priced at 0.4173. A 0.4200 call is purchased at a 0.36 premium. Volatility in the DM market is calculated at 15 percent. There are 30 days until option expiration. What is the probability that the market will rally over the B/E point by expiration? (You will need a calculator with a natural logarithm function and a normal distribution table to perform this calculation.)

2. Bond volatility is at 12 percent; bond futures are at $83\,24/32$ds. You sell an 84 put for $1\,16/64$ths ($1,250) with 60 days to expiration. Assuming that the option will be held until term, what is the probability you will retain the entire premium? What is the probability of a loss? What is the probability you will make a profit less than the premium?

3. T-bond futures are at 87–06 and there are 92 days until option expiration. Given the information provided below, find the probability of making a profit assuming you buy the puts and buy the calls (under the breakeven for puts, over the breakeven for calls).

		Prem.	Vol.	B/E	Prob.
In-Mny	84 Calls	$4\,01/64$ths	12.6%		
In-Mny	86 Calls	$2\,41/64$ths	12.1%		
Out-Mny	88 Calls	$1\,42/64$ths	12.1%		
Out-Mny	90 Calls	$1\,01/64$ths	12.5%		
In-Mny	90 Puts	$3\,48/64$ths	12.2%		
In-Mny	88 Puts	$2\,33/64$ths	12.5%		
Out-Mny	86 Puts	$1\,37/64$ths	12.7%		
Out-Mny	84 Puts	$60/64$ths	13.2%		

4. When you sell an in-the-money call, your position is more _____ _____ (aggressive or conservative) than an out-of-the-money short call.

5. Which statement is false?
    (a) The combination of a long futures contract and a short call creates a synthetic short put.
    (b) The combination of a long call and short put creates a synthetic long futures.
    (c) The combination of a short futures contract and a long put creates a synthetic long call.
    (d) An out-of-the-money short put and a short futures contract creates a synthetic in-the-money short call.
    (e) An in-the-money long put and an out-of-the-money short call creates a synthetic short futures contract.
6. (a) You buy bond futures at 96.16/32ds and sell a 98 call for 48/64ths. You have created a _____ (in-the-money/out-of-the-money) synthetic _____.
    (b) What is the effective breakeven point on this synthetic option?

4
Option Spreads

Perhaps the most attractive feature of options is their flexibility. One may go long or short futures in anticipation of a strongly bullish or strongly bearish market scenario, respectively, but options permit you to capitalize on much more subtle market forecasts.

This chapter will focus on option spreads. An option spread is a strategy which requires you to buy and sell options of the same type: to buy a call and sell a call or to buy a put and sell a put.

> An *option spread* entails the simultaneous purchase and sale of options of the same type: to buy a call and sell a call or to buy a put and sell a put. These options differ with respect to strike price, expiration date, or both.

As you will see, spreads are quite flexible. They may be used to take advantage of strongly bull or strongly bear markets. They also may be used to capitalize on mildly trending markets or even neutral markets.

This chapter will review the fundamentals and some of the finer points of trading vertical, horizontal, and diagonal spreads. Further, ratio or weighted spreads and backspreads will be considered. Before reviewing the specific strategies, let us review a particular market philosophy of spread trading.

TWO-DIMENSIONAL TRADING

Implicit in any option strategy is a forecast, not only regarding price direction (of the instrument for which the option may be exercised), but also with respect to other variables which impact upon an option premium.

Most notable among these variables is time or term to expiration. Options, therefore, may be said to trade in at least two dimensions: *price* and *time!* A smart option trader will attempt to make all the variables which impact upon an option premium and consequently, upon an option strategy, work to his benefit.

Differential Rates of Decay

The term until option expiration plays an important role in defining the time value associated with an option. As discussed in a prior chapter, the longer the term until expiration, the greater will be the time value associated with the option. The shorter the term until expiration, the lower the time value will be.

Moreover, time value tends to erode at an accelerating pace, meaning a near-term option experiences more decay than a long-term option, for equal periods of time. But many option traders ignore or are unaware of the fact that time value decay impacts differently upon in-, at-, and out-of-the-money options.

In particular, an in- or an out-of-the-money option has less time value at the start relative to an at- or near-the-money option. All else being equal, the decay pattern associated with an in- or an out-of-the-money option tends to be much more linear than that displayed by at- or near-the-money options which tend to accelerate (see Figure 4–1).

Moreover, the time value of an in- or an out-of-the-money option may drop to zero well before option expiration. This is especially true when (1) the option is "deep" in- or out-of-the-money, (2) there is a short term until expiration, or (3) volatility is low. Options experience differential rates of decay depending upon whether they are (1) near-term or long-term and (2) in- or out-of-the-money versus at- or near-the-money.

This suggests that option traders may wish to take short positions in options which will expire soon and long positions in longer-term options which will not experience accelerated decay. This also suggests that short positions should be concentrated in at- or near-the-money options while long positions are better placed with in- or out-of-the-money options.

Rates of Decay

	Near-Term	*Long-Term*
At- or Near-the-Money	Rapid Acceleration	Slight Acceleration
In- or Out-of-the-Money	Time Value May Bottom Out	Linear Decay

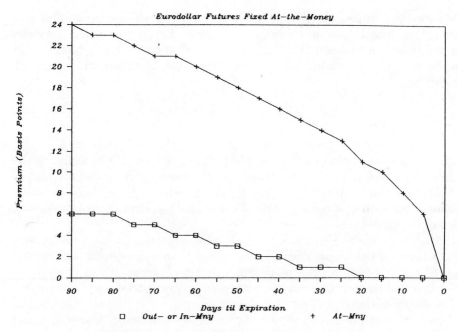

Figure 4-1 Differential rates of time value decay.

Option Trading Rules

A first rule of option trading is: Take advantage of the natural phenomenon of time value decay.

(1) Make time value decay work for you!

Time is on your side or can be on your side even when your option strategy involves buying as well as selling options (such as an option spread).

Rules two and three also emphasize the special character of options.

(2) Know your risks!

Carefully study the risk/reward profile associated with an option strategy. Most option spreads allow limiting your risk to known parameters. Many of these strategies further entail strictly limited reward potential.

Many option traders will identify the ratio between potential reward and risk (maximum reward/maximum risk). But, as discussed in a previous chapter, one must be cognizant of the probability of achieving any particular profit or loss. In general, these probabilities will balance out any asymmetry between risk and reward.

A strategy with a high reward/risk ratio means that you have a low probability of large profit and a relatively high probability of a relatively small loss. A strategy with a low reward/risk ratio means that you have a high probability of small profit and a relatively low probability of large loss.

When trying to take advantage of time value decay, you pursue strategies of the latter nature: strategies where you have a high probability of small profit, low probability of large loss. Fortunately, an astute option trader can often trade out of a situation where a large loss is imminent in order to limit the loss. There is very little an option trader can do, however, to stop the forward march of time.

(3)   **Know when to hold and when to liquidate!**

This is a corollary to the idea of "let your profits run and cut your losses short." By being familiar with the dynamics of an option strategy, you can tell when it is best advised to hold or fold an option strategy. The dynamics of an option strategy reflect the possible movements not only over the first very important dimension, price, but also over the second dimension, time.

The high-probability strategy discussed above relies more on one's judgment regarding when to hold and when to liquidate than does the low-probability strategy. This is because the latter strategy usually requires more active management than the former strategy. The option trader who pursues the former strategy must be prepared to trade the position frequently.

(4)   **Use commissions wisely!**

Because a spread entails at least two positions relative to a single outright option position, more commissions are generally incurred. Find strategies with high payoff probabilities to guarantee that commissions are wisely spent.

VERTICAL SPREADS

A vertical spread entails the purchase of a put and the sale of a put or the purchase of a call and the sale of a call. The two options which comprise a vertical spread share a common expiration (are exercisable for the same futures contract). What distinguishes the two is that they differ with respect to strike price.

A *vertical spread* entails the purchase of a call and the sale of a call or the purchase of a put and the sale of a put. These options share a common expiration date but differ with respect to strike prices.

These strategies are referred to as *vertical* spreads because of the way options are quoted in the financial press. Option months are quoted horizontally in columns across the page. Strike prices are quoted vertically in rows. Consequently, you can scan a page vertically to identify options which comprise a vertical spread. Because the options which comprise the spread differ with respect to the amount by which they are in- or out-of-the-money, these spreads are also sometimes referred to as "money spreads."

Bull and Bear Spreads

Vertical spreads may be classified on the basis of whether they permit the trader to take advantage of an essentially bullish or an essentially bearish market scenario. These spreads may be put on with equal ease using either puts or calls.

The feature that binds bullish spreads—either call or put—together is the fact that you buy the lower-struck option and sell the upper-struck option. Bearish spreads are distinguished by the fact that you must buy the upper-struck option and sell the lower-struck option.

Bull and Bear Vertical Spreads

	Low-Struck Option	High-Struck Option
Bull Spread	Buy	Sell
Bear Spread	Sell	Buy

Example: On July 9, 1986, you could have purchased a 93.00 call exercisable for September 1986 Eurodollar futures for 0.52 or $1,300 (see Figure 4–2). By concurrently selling a 93.50 September call for 0.22 ($550), you will have created a vertical bull call spread.

Long 1 Sep. 93.00 Call(s)	@ 0.52	=	– $1,300
Imp. Volatility = 18.33% Delta = 0.79			
Short 1 Sep. 93.50 Call(s) @ 0.22	@ 0.22	=	$550
Imp. Volatility = 21.15% Delta = – 0.46			
NET DEBIT			– $750
NET DELTA			0.33

This spread entails an initial net debit of $750. What would happen if the strategy were held 69 days to expiration on September 15, 1986?

If the price falls to 92.50:

Abandon 1 Sep. 93.00 Call(s)	@ 0.00	=	$0
Abandon 1 Sep. 93.50 Call(s)	@ 0.00	=	$0
Original Net Debit/Credit		=	– $750
TOTAL PROFIT/LOSS			– $750

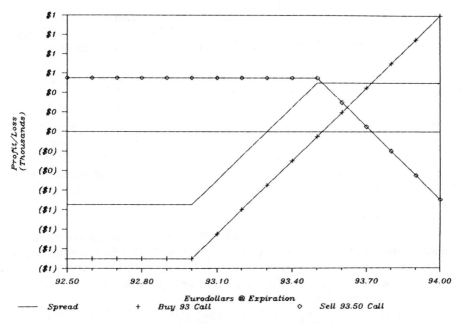

Figure 4–2   93.00/93.50 vertical bull call spread.

If the price falls to 93.00:

Abandon 1 Sep. 93.00 Call(s)	@ 0.00	=	$0
Abandon 1 Sep. 93.50 Call(s)	@ 0.00	=	$0
Original Net Debit/Credit		=	– $750
TOTAL PROFIT/LOSS			– $750

If the price trades to 93.50:

Exercise 1 Sep. 93.00 Call(s)	@ 0.50	=	$1,250
Abandon 1 Sep. 93.50 Call(s)	@ 0.00	=	$0
Original Net Debit/Credit		=	– $750
TOTAL PROFIT/LOSS			$500

If the price rises to 94.00:

Exercise 1 Sep. 93.00 Call(s)	@ 1.00	=	$2,500
Exercise 1 Sep. 93.50 Call(s)	@ 0.50	=	– $1,250
Original Net Debit/Credit		=	– $750
TOTAL PROFIT/LOSS			$500

The trader loses the entire net debit of $750 if the market falls to or below the lower of the two strikes (93.00) by expiration. If the market rallies to the upper of the two strikes (93.50) or beyond, the trader's profit equals $500.

Because this spread results in an initial net debit (that is, the long call is worth more than the short call), it is referred to as a "debit spread."

The previous example illustrates that, like an outright long call position, the *bullish* vertical call spread entails strictly limited risk. Under no circumstances can the trader lose more than the net debit (analogous to the premium on an outright long position) required to enter the spread. However, the spread is comprised of a short as well as a long option, which means a vertical spread entails elements of both a long option (limited risk) *and* a short option (limited profit potential). As illustrated, the vertical spread limits profit to a fixed amount.

The profit/loss potential associated with a spread illustrated previously may be defined with respect to the initial net debit and the relationship between the two strike prices. Similar to an outright long call, the maximum risk is the net debit. The maximum return equals the difference in strikes less the net debit.

In our previous example, if the market rallies to the upper of the two strikes by expiration, the 93.00 call is 50 basis points in-the-money. This equates to the difference in strikes. The 93.50 call is at-the-money and worthless. Thus the profit equals 50 basis points less the initial debit of 30 basis points or 20 basis points ($500 at $25 per basis point).

If the market rallies above the upper of the two strikes, profit accruing on the in-the-money value of the long 93.00 call is offset by loss on the in-the-money value of the short 93.50 call. Profit is limited to $500. The breakeven point (B/E) at which both buyer and seller earn zero profit and zero loss equals the lower strike of 93.00 plus the debit of 30 basis points or 93.30.

Bull Call Spread:

Maximum Loss = Net Debit

Maximum Profit = Difference in Strikes − Net Debit

B/E Point = Low Strike + Maximum Loss

What if you do the opposite? *Sell* the spread by selling the lower-struck option and buying the upper-struck option, rather than buy the spread? In that case, you create a *bearish* vertical call spread. The risks and rewards are opposite that of the *bull* call spread; the maximum reward is the net *credit* while the maximum risk is the difference in strikes less the net credit.

Example: On July 9, 1986, you could have created a vertical bear call spread by selling the 93.00 call exercisable for September 1986 Eurodollar futures for 0.52 ($1,300) and buying the 93.50 September call for 0.22 ($550) (see Figure 4–3).

Short 1 Sep. 93.00 Call(s)	@ 0.52	=	$1,300
Imp. Volatility = 18.33% Delta = − 0.79			
Long 1 Sep. 93.50 Call(s) @ 0.22	@ 0.22	=	− $550
Imp. Volatility = 21.15% Delta = 0.46			
NET CREDIT			$750
NET DELTA			− 0.33

This spread entails an initial net credit of $750. Holding the position for 69 days to expiration on September 15, 1986, would mean a profit of $750 if the market trades at or below the lower of the two strikes (93.00). A loss of $500 would result if the market trades at or above the upper of the two strikes (93.50).

Similar to selling a call, the bear call spread means that the trader will retain the entire premium if both options fall out-of-the-money. The maximum profit thus equals the initial net credit.

If, however, the market rallies to the upper strike or beyond, the short lower-struck option is exercised against the bear call spreader. As the long

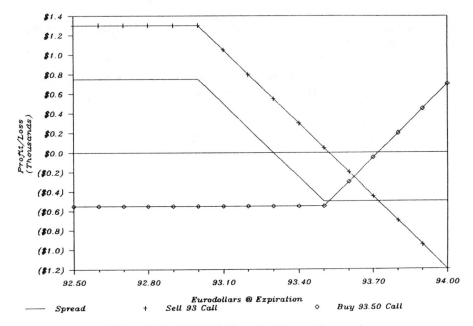

Figure 4–3   93.00/93.50 vertical bear call spread.

upper-struck call goes into-the-money, it too will be exercised. Losses accruing on the short call will, however, always be greater than any profits accruing on the long call by the difference in strikes.

The maximum loss equals the difference in strikes less the net credit. The breakeven point equals the lower strike plus the maximum profit (net credit).

Bear Call Spread:

Maximum Loss = Difference in Strikes − Net Credit

Maximum Profit = Net Credit

B/E Point = Low Strike + Maximum Profit

Debit and Credit Spreads

Vertical spreads are distinguished on the basis of whether they are essentially bullish or bearish and on the basis of whether they result in an initial net debit or an initial net credit. As discussed before, a bull call spread results in an initial net debit while a bear call spread results in an initial net credit. This is intuitive when you consider whether the options involved in the spreads illustrated previously are in-, at-, or out-of-the-money.

In the prior example, Eurodollars were at 93.48, meaning the 93.50 call was near- or essentially at-the-money. By contrast, the 93.00 call was approximately 50 basis points in-the-money. An in-the-money option always commands a greater premium than a comparable at- or out-of-the-money option.

By buying the in-the-money and selling the at-the-money call (to create a bull call spread), you buy more premium than you sell, resulting in a net debit. By selling the in-the-money and buying the at-the-money call (to create a bear call spread), you sell more premium than you buy, which results in a net credit. By similar reasoning, a *bear* put spread results in an initial net debit while a *bull* put spread results in an initial net credit.

	Debit Spreads	*Credit Spreads*
Bull Spreads	Call	Put
Bear Spreads	Put	Call

Example: On July 9, 1986, you could have purchased a 93.00 put exercisable for September 1986 Eurodollar futures for 0.06 or $150. By concurrently selling a 93.50 September put for 0.22 ($550), you have created a vertical bull put spread (see Figure 4–4).

Short 1 Sep. 93.50 Put(s) @ 0.22   = $550

Imp. Volatility = 18.47%   Delta = 0.53

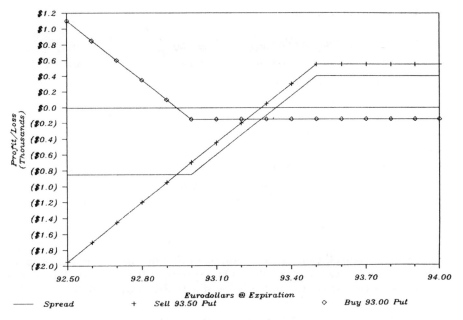

Figure 4–4   93.00/93.50 vertical bull put spread.

Long 1 Sep. 93.00 Put(s) @ 0.06	=	– $150
Imp. Volatility = 18.93% Delta = – 0.21		
NET CREDIT		$400
NET DELTA		0.33

This spread entails an initial net credit of $400. What would happen if the strategy were held 69 days to expiration on September 15, 1986?

If price falls to 92.50:

Exercise 1 Sep. 93.50 Put(s)	@ – 1.00	=	– $2,500
Exercise 1 Sep. 93.00 Put(s)	@ 0.50	=	$1,250
Original Net Debit/Credit		=	$400
TOTAL PROFIT/LOSS			– $850

If price falls to 93.00:

Exercise 1 Sep. 93.50 Put(s)	@ 0.50	=	– $1,250
Abandon 1 Sep. 93.00 Put(s)	@ 0.00	=	$0
Original Net Debit/Credit		=	$400
TOTAL PROFIT/LOSS			– $850

If price trades to 93.50:

Abandon 1 Sep. 93.50 Put(s)	@ 0.00	=	$0
Abandon 1 Sep. 93.00 Put(s)	@ 0.00	=	$0
Original Net Debit/Credit		=	$400
TOTAL PROFIT/LOSS			$400

If price rises to 94.00:

Abandon 1 Sep. 93.50 Put(s)	@ 0.00	=	$0
Abandon 1 Sep. 93.00 Put(s)	@ 0.00	=	$0
Original Net Debit/Credit		=	$400
TOTAL PROFIT/LOSS			$400

The trader retains the entire net credit of $400 if the market rises to or above the upper of the two strikes (93.50) by expiration. If the market falls to the lower of the two strikes (93.00) or below, the trader's loss equals $850.

Like selling a put, the maximum profit equals the initial net credit of $400. The maximum profit equals the difference in strikes (50 basis points) less the net credit (16 basis points) or $400 (34 basis points). The breakeven point equals the upper strike (93.50) less the net credit (16 basis points) or 93.34.

> Bull Put Spread:
>
> Maximum Loss = Difference in Strikes – Net Credit
>
> Maximum Profit = Net Credit
>
> B/E Point = High Strike – Maximum Profit

If one were to pursue the opposite strategy, buy the put spread by buying the 93.50 put and selling the 93.00 put (a bear put spread), a net debit would result (see Figure 4–5). The maximum risk is reflected in the net debit; the maximum profit equals the difference in strikes less the net debit; the breakeven equals the high strike less the net debit.

> Bear Put Spread:
>
> Maximum Loss = Net Debit
>
> Maximum Profit = Difference in Strikes – Net Debit
>
> B/E Point = High Strike – Maximum Loss

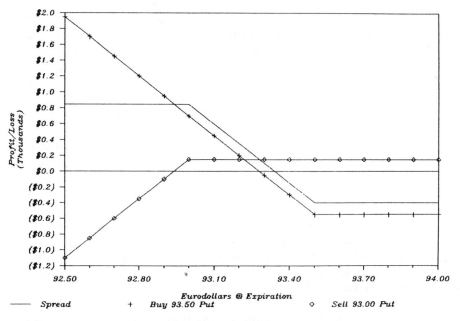

Figure 4–5   93.00/93.50 vertical bear put spread.

Which is better suited to take advantage of a bullish market, a bull (debit) call spread or a bull (credit) put spread? Consider the risks and rewards associated with the 93.00/93.50 bull call and bull put spreads described previously.

	Risk	Reward	B/E	Ratio Reward/Risk
Bull call	$750	$500	93.30	0.67
Bull put	$850	$400	93.34	0.47

The potential magnitude of profit and loss is similar with both bull spreads. In fact, we could expect that under most circumstances, the risk/reward structures of two vertical spreads with the same bullish or bearish orientation would have almost identical risks and rewards.

The fact that these risk/reward structures are somewhat different represents a slight market inefficiency. This is apparent given that the 93.50 call has an implied volatility of 21.15 percent.

In this case, the bull call spread is much more attractive. Note that the ratio of reward to risk is superior with the bull call spread. Further, the breakeven is much lower. The bull call spread provides a relatively high probability of a large reward and a reduced probability of a relatively small loss (vis-a-vis the bull put spread).

Even in a more efficiently priced market, however, there are other issues:

1. *Credit versus debit.* The credit put spread means that you receive $400 up front. Many investors regard this as an interest-free loan over the life of the option. By contrast, the debit call spread means that you may have to finance the $750 debit over the life of the options. Clearly, the credit spread appears to be superior in this respect. However, the market generally compensates you for incurring a debit and penalizes you for a credit position.

   Think of the market as a bank. If you lend money to the bank, you expect to be paid interest. If you borrow, you must pay interest. Thus even if the implied volatilities are all identical with the put and call spreads, you expect the reward/risk ratio to be slightly more favorable with the call spread.

2. *Control.* If the market is trading between the two strike prices, the credit spreader will be short an in-the-money option and long an out-of-the-money option. By contrast, the debit spreader will be long an in-the-money and short an out-of-the-money option.

   Because the short gives up control regarding the timing of a possible exercise, the credit spreader may find his strategy disrupted prematurely by exercise of the short option at a time when the long option is out-of-the-money. This is particularly true when the short is trading near its intrinsic value, when term to expiration is short, volatility is low, or the option is relatively deep in-the-money. By contrast, the debit spreader is more in control of what happens to the spread.

High-Probability Trading

Which is more attractive: buying a 93.00/93.50 bull call spread or buying a 93.50/94.00 bull call spread?

	Risk	Reward	B/E	Ratio Reward/Risk
93.00/93.50 Bull call spread	$750	$500	93.30	0.67
93.50/94.00 Bull call spread	$425	$825	93.67	1.94

At the time the 93.00/93.50 spread could have been placed for a 30 basis point debit, you could have purchased the 93.50 call for 22 basis points and sold a 94.00 call for 5 basis points. Compare the risks and rewards associated with both strategies.

Given a 19 percent volatility over the 69 days until expiration, we may calculate a 63 percent probability that the market will trade above the 93.30 breakeven point on the 93.00/93.50 spread. Likewise, we may calculate a probability of only 36 percent that the market will trade above the 93.67 breakeven on the 93.50/94.00 spread.

The 93.00/93.50 spread has a high probability of a relatively low profit and a low probability of a relatively large loss. The 93.50/94.00 spread has a low probability of a large profit and a relatively high probability of a small loss. However, if the market remains perfectly stable at around 93.50 (actually, the market was trading at 93.47 at the time), the 93.00/93.50 spread will realize its maximum profit. By contrast, if the market remains stable, the 93.50/94.00 spread realizes its maximum loss.

The 93.00/93.50 spread means that you sell a near-the-money and buy an out-of-the-money option. Thus you take advantage of the accelerated time value decay associated with at- or near-the-money options. The 93.50/94.00 spread means you buy an at-the-money and sell an out-of-the-money option; therefore, time value decay works against this spread. This phenomenon is illustrated in Figures 4–6, 4–7, and 4–8.

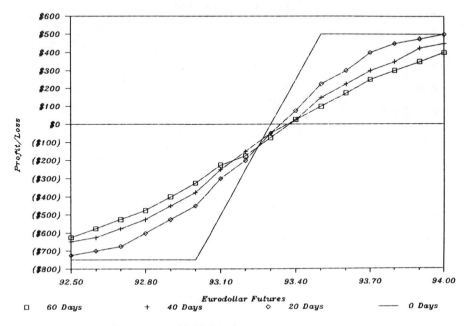

Figure 4–6   93.00/93.50 vertical bull call spread.

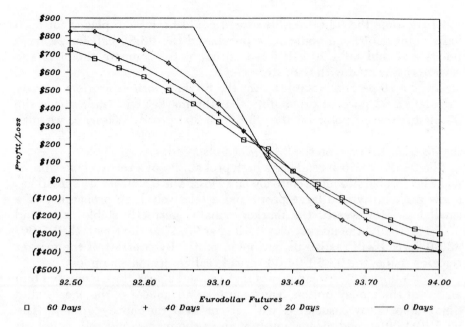

Figure 4–7   93.00/93.50 vertical bear put spread.

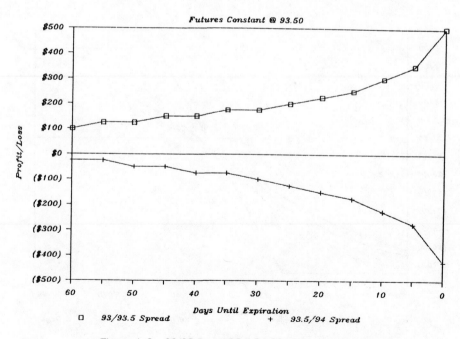

Figure 4–8   93/93.5 and 93.5/94.00 bull call spreads.

HORIZONTAL SPREADS

A horizontal spread entails the purchase of a put and the sale of a put or the purchase of a call and the sale of a call. The two options which comprise a horizontal spread share a common strike price. The two options are distinguished in that they differ with respect to expiration dates.

> A *horizontal spread* entails the purchase of a call and the sale of a call or the purchase of a put and the sale of a put. These options share a common strike price but differ with respect to expiration dates.

You can scan option quotations on the pages of the financial press horizontally to identify options which comprise horizontal spreads. Option months are normally quoted horizontally in columns across the page. Strike prices are normally quoted vertically in rows.

Because the options which comprise the spread have different terms to expiration, these spreads are also sometimes referred to as "time" or "calendar spreads."

Debit Horizontal

We are interested primarily in a single type of horizontal spread, a *debit horizontal.* This spread is characterized by the sale of a shorter-term option (generally in the nearby month) and the purchase of a longer-term option (a deferred option).

This spread almost invariably results in an initial net debit because long-term options command greater premiums than do short-term options with the same strike. (However, the spread does not *necessarily* result in a debit when you are trading options on futures. This is due to the fact that the options are exercisable for futures in two different months. This fact has significant implications discussed later.) The idea is to capitalize on the fact that short-term options display more pronounced time value decay characteristics than do longer-term options.

> **Example:** On July 9, 1986, you could have sold a 93.50 call exercisable for September 1986 (with 69 days to expiration) Eurodollar futures for 0.22 points or $550. By concurrently buying a 93.50 December 1986 (160 days to expiration) call for 0.31 ($775), you will have created a debit horizontal call spread (see Figure 4–9). September futures were at 93.47 while December futures were at 93.48. Thus the Sep/Dec spread may be quoted at − .01 (September price less December price).

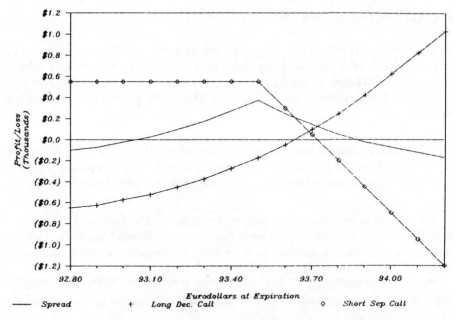

Figure 4–9   Sep/Dec 93.50 debit horizontal spread.

Long 1 Dec. 93.50 Call(s)	@ 0.31	=	− $775
Imp. Volatility = 19.15% Delta = 0.45			
Short 1 Sep. 93.50 Call(s)	@ 0.22	=	$550
Imp. Volatility = 21.15% Delta = − 0.46			
NET DEBIT			− $225
NET DELTA			− 0.01

This spread entails an initial net debit of $225. What would happen if the strategy were held 69 days to expiration on September 15, 1986? Assume that the December long call is liquidated at that point at the prevailing market price given a volatility of 19 percent and that the − .01 Sep/Dec spread is maintained.

If September falls to 92.80:

Sell 1 Dec. 93.50 Call(s)	@ 0.05	=	$125
Abandon 1 Sep. 93.50 Call(s)	@ 0.00	=	$0
Original Net Debit/Credit		=	− $225
TOTAL PROFIT/LOSS		− $100	

If September trades to 93.50:

Sell 1 Dec. 93.50 Call(s)	@ 0.24	=	$600
Abandon 1 Sep. 93.50 Call(s)	@ 0.00	=	$0
Original Net Debit/Credit		=	− $225
TOTAL PROFIT/LOSS			$375

If September rises to 94.20:

Sell 1 Dec. 93.50 Call(s)	@ 0.72	=	$1,800
Exercise 1 Sep. 93.50 Call(s)	@ 0.69	=	− $1,725
Original Net Debit/Credit		=	− $225
TOTAL PROFIT/LOSS			− $150

Profit is maximized in a horizontal spread when the market trades at or near the common strike price around the expiration date. Because the profit is contingent upon the sale price of the long deferred call at expiration of the nearby call, there is no convenient formula you can use to estimate the maximum profit. Rather, the profit must be approximated by simulation as shown above. In the foregoing example, the maximum profit was approximated at 15 basis points or $375.

Because profit is maximized at the common strike, it is advisable to use strikes near the area in which you believe the market may be trading at expiration of the nearby option. If you are mildly bearish, set the strikes slightly below the market. If your are mildly bullish, set the strikes slightly above the market.

This approach is illustrated in Figure 4–10, showing the spread value at 60, 40, and 20 days to expiration. Holding futures at or near the 93.50 strike means that the value of the spread increases over time. This advance becomes increasingly dramatic as the expiration date draws near.

Do not attempt to set the strikes too far away from the money. Remember: This spread is intended to capitalize on the differential time value decay associated with short-term and long-term near-the-money options. It will not work if you are using in- or out-of-the-money options which experience linear decay or which bottom out in terms of time value well before expiration.

This fact is also illustrated in Figure 4–10 as the value of the spread declines over time when the market is well below or above the 93.50 strike.

Just as the maximum profit cannot be calculated in a straightforward manner, the breakeven points can likewise only be approximated through the process of simulation. In this case, the breakevens are located around

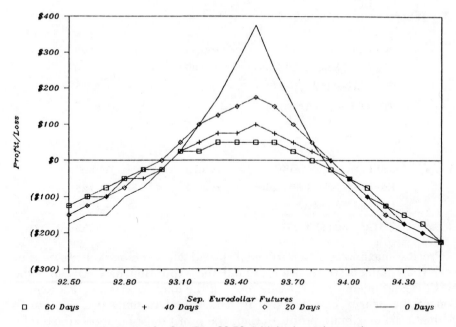

Figure 4–10   Sep/Dec 93.50 debit horizontal spread.

92.95 and 94.05 (for the September contract holding the Sep/Dec spread constant). The prospective maximum loss may be estimated as the initial net debit of $225. This is intuitive.

If the market declines significantly by expiration of the September contract, it is clear that the short Sep call is worthless. Likewise, as the December futures price declines, the long Dec call is driven deep out-of-the-money. At some point, it too becomes worthless, and the spread results in the loss of the initial net debit.

Approximate Maximum Loss = Net Debit

Profit Maximized: At the Common Strike Price

If the market advances significantly, losses accrue on the short Sep call equal to the in-the-money amount. As the market advances, the long Dec call moves deep in-the-money as well. At some point, a deep in-the-money option is worth nothing more than its intrinsic value. The loss on the short option is offset by profit on exercise of the long option, and the spreader is left with a loss equal to the initial net debit.

Horizontal Put Spread

You can place a horizontal spread using either calls as illustrated earlier or by using puts. In either case, the results are quite similar.

Example: On July 9, 1986, you could have sold a 93.50 put exercisable for September 1986 (with 69 days to expiration) Eurodollar futures for 0.22 or $550. By concurrently buying a 93.50 December 1986 (160 days to expiration) put for 0.33 ($825), you will have created a debit horizontal put spread. September futures were at 93.47 while December futures were at 93.48. The Sep/Dec spread may be quoted at − .01 (September price less December price).

Long 1 Dec. 93.50 Put(s)	@ 0.33	= − $825
Imp. Volatility = 19.19% Delta = − 0.52		
Short 1 Sep. 93.50 Put(s)	@ 0.22	= $550
Imp. Volatility = 18.47% Delta = 0.53		
NET DEBIT/CREDIT		− $275
NET DELTA		0.01

This spread entails an initial net debit of $275. What would happen if the strategy were held 69 days until expiration on September 15, 1986? Assume that the December long put is liquidated at that point at the prevailing market price given a volatility of 19 percent and that the − .01 Sep/Dec spread is maintained.

If September falls to 92.80:

Sell 1 Dec. 93.50 Put(s)	@ 0.73	= $1,825
Exercise 1 Sep. 93.50 Put(s)	@ 0.70	= − $1,750
Original Net Debit/Credit		= − $275
TOTAL PROFIT/LOSS		− $200

If September trades to 93.50:

Sell 1 Dec. 93.50 Put(s)	@ 0.24	= $600
Abandon 1 Sep. 93.50 Put(s)	@ 0.00	= $0
Original Net Debit/Credit		= − $275
TOTAL PROFIT/LOSS		$325

If September rises to 94.20:

Sell 1 Dec. 93.50 Put(s)	@ 0.03	= $75
Abandon 1 Sep. 93.50 Put(s)	@ 0.00	= $0
Original Net Debit/Credit		= − $275
TOTAL PROFIT/LOSS		− $200

The maximum profit and breakeven points may be approximated through simulation. The estimate is dependent on what you estimate the long-term put will be worth at expiration of the near-term put (see Figures 4–11 and 4–12). This value can be estimated with the use of an option pricing model; however, this requires that you estimate the long-term option's volatility at the time the near-term expires.

The maximum risk may be approximated as the initial net debit. If the market rallies sharply, both options fall deep out-of-the-money and at some point become worthless.

If the market declines sharply, both options fall deep in-the-money. A loss equal to the in-the-money amount of the short put upon exercise is offset by the profit on exercise of the long put. This assumes that the long put will be worth only its in-the-money amount, which is typical for deep in-the-money options.

Underlying Futures Spread

We have indicated that the maximum risk associated with a horizontal call or put spread is approximately equal to the initial net debit. Why only approximately?

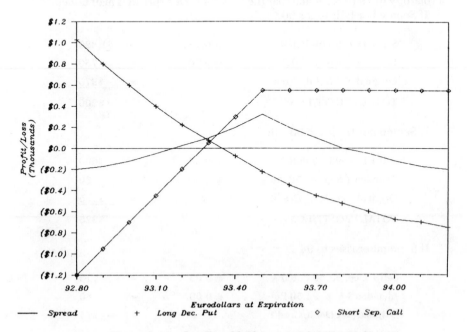

Figure 4–11   Sep/Dec 93.50 horizontal put spread.

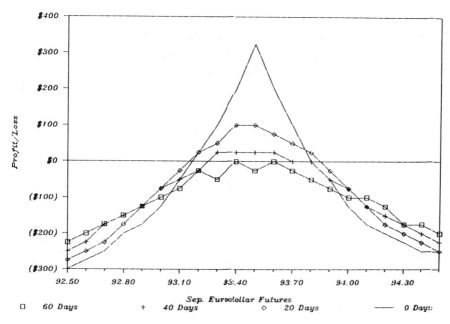

Figure 4–12   Sep/Dec 93.50 put horizontal spread.

Evaluating calendar spreads is a more complicated task for options on futures relative to stock options. The reason is that the two legs of a horizontal spread using options on futures are exercisable for two different contracts.

A 100 share lot of IBM is a 100 share lot of IBM no matter whether an IBM option expires in September or December. But a September futures contract is not the same as a December futures contract. In our previous example, September was trading at 93.47 while December was trading at 93.48 for a – 1 basis point spread. What happens if the spread rallies or declines?

Example: The debit 93.50 horizontal call spread previously illustrated is strung out between September and December Eurodollar futures (see Figure 4–13). The current Sep/Dec spread is – 0.01. What happens if the spread falls 20 basis points to – 0.21?
 If Sep falls to 92.80, Dec to 93.01:

Sell 1 Dec. 93.50 Call(s)	@ 0.08	=	$200
Abandon 1 Sep. 93.50 Call(s)	@ 0.00	=	$0
Original Net Debit/Credit		=	– $225
TOTAL PROFIT/LOSS			– $25

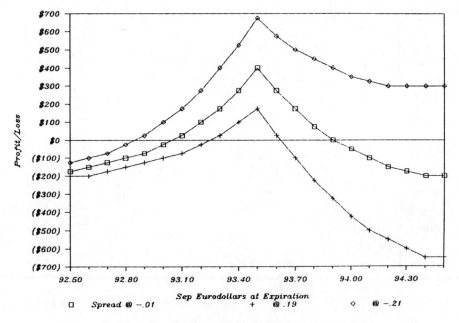

Figure 4–13   Sep/Dec 93.50 debit horizontal spread.

If Sep trades to 93.50, Dec to 93.71:

Sell 1 Dec. 93.50 Call(s)	@ 0.36	=	$900
Abandon 1 Sep. 93.50 Call(s)	@ 0.00	=	$0
Original Net Debit/Credit		=	− $225
TOTAL PROFIT/LOSS			$675

If Sep trades to 94.20, Dec to 94.41:

Sell 1 Dec. 93.50 Call(s)	@ 0.91	=	$2,275
Exercise 1 Sep. 93.50 Call(s)	@ 0.70	=	− $1,750
Original Net Debit/Credit		=	− $225
TOTAL PROFIT/LOSS			$300

What if the spread rallies 20 basis points to 0.19?
If Sep falls to 92.80, Dec to 92.61:

Sell 1 Dec. 93.50 Call(s)	@ 0.03	=	$75
Abandon 1 Sep. 93.50 Call(s)	@ 0.00	=	$0
Original Net Debit/Credit		=	− $225
TOTAL PROFIT/LOSS			− $150

If Sep trades to 93.50, Dec to 93.31:

Sell 1 Dec. 93.50 Call(s)	@ 0.16	=	$400
Abandon 1 Sep. 93.50 Call(s)	@ 0.00	=	$0
Original Net Debit/Credit		=	− $225
TOTAL PROFIT/LOSS			$175

If Sep trades to 94.20, Dec to 94.01:

Sell 1 Dec. 93.50 Call(s)	@ 0.57	=	$1,425
Exercise 1 Sep. 93.50 Call(s)	@ 0.70	=	− $1,750
Original Net Debit/Credit		=	− $225
TOTAL PROFIT/LOSS			− $550

Thus if the Sep/Dec spread declines (December rallies relative to September), the call spreader can earn a larger profit. If the Sep/Dec spread advances (December falls relative to September), the call spreader is worse off.

This is intuitive. The call spreader is long a December call (a bullish position) and short a September call (an essentially bearish position). Consequently, if December rallies relative to September, the call spreader's profits are augmented and losses are limited. If December falls relative to September, the call spreader's profits are limited and potential losses are increased.

On the other hand, if the horizontal spread were placed using puts instead of calls, the bias would be reversed (see Figure 4–14). The profit potential associated with a horizontal put spread is augmented when the deferred futures price falls relative to the nearby futures price (the spread rallies). Profit potential is diminished with a horizontal put spread when the deferred futures contract rallies relative to the nearby futures price (the spread falls).

Futures Spread Impact on Calendar Option Spread

	Horizontal Call Spread	Horizontal Put Spread
Futures Spread Rallies	(−)	(+)
Futures Spread Declines	(+)	(−)

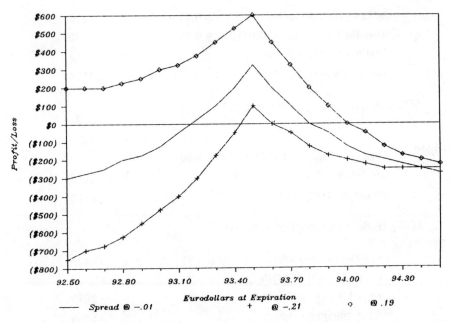

Figure 4–14   Sep/Dec 93.50 horizontal put spread.

DIAGONAL SPREADS

A diagonal spread entails the purchase of a put and the sale of a put or the purchase of a call and the sale of a call. The two options which comprise a diagonal spread differ with respect to both strike price and expiration dates.

A *diagonal spread* entails the purchase of a call and the sale of a call or the purchase of a put and the sale of a put. These options differ with respect to strike price and expiration dates.

Because this spread involves options which differ with respect to both strike and expiration, it incorporates elements of both the vertical and horizontal spread. Several rules of thumb are used to trade diagonal spreads:

1. Sell the nearby and buy the deferred option. This allows you to capitalize on the accelerated time value decay associated with near-term options.
2. Sell an at- or near-the-money option and buy a low-struck option to enter a mildly bullish position.

3. Sell an at- or near-the-money option and buy a high-struck option to enter a mildly bearish position.

Diagonal Bull Call Spread

The vertical bull call spread allows you to profit as long as the market rises above a breakeven point by expiration, a bullish position. The horizontal call spread allows you to capitalize on a neutral trading range. The diagonal call spread allows you to profit in a mildly bullish range.

Example: On July 9, 1986, you could have sold a 93.50 call exercisable for September 1986 (with 69 days to expiration) Eurodollar futures for 0.22 or $550. By concurrently buying a 93.00 December 1986 (160 days to expiration) call for 0.65 ($1,625), you have created a diagonal call spread. September futures were at 93.47 while December futures were at 93.48.

Long 1 Dec. 93.00 Call(s)	@ 0.65	= − $1,625
Imp. Volatility = 21.37% Delta = 0.65		
Short 1 Sep. 93.50 Call(s)	@ 0.22	= $550
Imp. Volatility = 21.15% Delta = − 0.46		
NET DEBIT/CREDIT		− $1,075
NET DELTA		0.19

This spread entails an initial net debit of $1,075. What would happen if the strategy were held 69 days until expiration on September 15, 1986? Assume that the December long call is liquidated at that point at the prevailing market price given a volatility of 19 percent and the −.01 Sep/Dec spread is maintained.
     If Sep falls to 92.80, Dec to 92.81:

Sell 1 Dec. 93.00 Call(s)	@ 0.18	= $450
Abandon 1 Sep. 93.50 Call(s)	@ 0.00	= $0
Original Net Debit/Credit		= − $1,075
TOTAL PROFIT/LOSS		− $625

If Sep trades to 93.50, Dec to 93.51:

Sell 1 Dec. 93.00 Call(s)	@ 0.58	= $1,450
Abandon 1 Sep. 93.50 Call(s)	@ 0.00	= $0
Original Net Debit/Credit		= − $1,075
TOTAL PROFIT/LOSS		$375

If Sep rises to 94.20, Dec to 94.21:

Sell 1 Dec. 93.00 Call(s)	@ 1.21	= $3,025
Exercise 1 Sep. 93.50 Call(s)	@ 0.70	= − $1,750
Original Net Debit/Credit		= − $1,075
TOTAL PROFIT/LOSS		$200

Like the horizontal spread, the diagonal spread has uncertainty regarding the maximum possible profit and breakeven point(s). You must simulate the possible sale price of the long low-struck deferred call in order to assess possible outcomes (see Figures 4–15 and 4–16). Also similar to a horizontal spread, you can approximate the maximum potential loss of a diagonal spread by reference to the initial net debit. In the foregoing case, the maximum you can lose is approximately $1,075.

If the market falls dramatically, both options fall out-of-the-money and are worthless. Even the long-term December 93.00 call will be worthless by expiration of the September 93.50 call if it is deep out-of-the-money. Thus the spread trader is left with the initial net debit.

If the market rallies sharply, both options are driven deep in-the-money. The short 93.50 option will generate a loss equal to its in-the-money

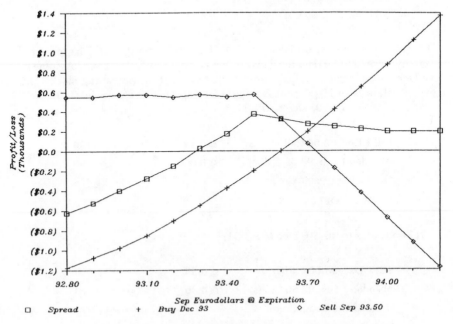

Figure 4–15   93/93.50 Sep/Dec diagonal call spread.

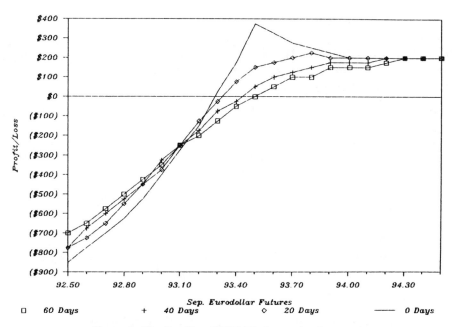

Figure 4–16   Sep/Dec 93/93.50 diagonal call spread.

amount at expiration. Likewise, the deep in-the-money long 93.00 call will be worth its intrinsic value.

The long call, however, has 50 basis points ($1,250) more intrinsic value than the short (given the assumption that the futures underlying both options are trading at equivalent levels). Therefore, the returns associated with the spread in the event of a substantial rally equal the difference in strike prices less the initial debit. In the foregoing case that translates to a $175 ($1,250 less $1,075) profit! Because the return on the "downside" (in the event of a market advance) is much worse than the return on the "upside" (in the event of a market decline), this strategy is clearly somewhat bullish.

The maximum profit, however, is realized at the short strike price (93.50 in the foregoing case). This is attributed to the accelerated time value decay associated with near- or at-the-money options. As expiration approaches, holding September futures constant at 93.50, it is clear that the value of the spread appreciates at an accelerated pace.

Diagonal Call Spread:

Approximate "Downside" Loss = Initial Net Debit

Approximate "Upside" Return = Difference in Strikes – Initial Net Debit

Profit Maximized: At the Short Strike Price

Diagonal Put Spread

By selling a nearby, near-the-money call and buying a deferred, in-the-money call, you can create a diagonal call spread as illustrated previously. What if you used puts instead of calls?

Example: On July 9, 1986, you could have sold a 93.50 put exercisable for September 1986 (with 69 days to expiration) Eurodollar futures for 0.22 or $550. By concurrently buying a 94.00 December 1986 (160 days to expiration) put for 0.70 ($1,750), you have created a diagonal put spread. September futures were at 93.47 while December futures were at 93.48.

Long 1 Dec. 94.00 Put(s)	@ 0.70	= − $1,750
Imp. Volatility = 24.72% Delta = − 0.70		
Short 1 Sep. 93.50 Put(s)	@ 0.22	= $550
Imp. Volatility = 18.47% Delta = 0.53		
NET DEBIT/CREDIT		− $1,200
NET DELTA		− 0.17

This spread entails an initial net debit of $1,200. What would happen if the strategy were held 69 days until expiration on September 15, 1986? Assume that the December long put is liquidated at that point at the prevailing market price given a volatility of 19 percent and that the −.01 Sep/Dec spread is maintained.

If Sep falls to 92.80, Dec to 92.81:

Sell 1 Dec. 94.00 Put(s)	@ 1.19	= $2,975
Exercise 1 Sep. 93.50 Put(s)	@ 0.70	= − $1,750
Original Net Debit/Credit		= − $1,200
TOTAL PROFIT/LOSS		$25

If Sep trades to 93.50, Dec to 93.51:

Sell 1 Dec. 94.00 Put(s)	@ 0.55	= $1,375
Abandon 1 Sep. 93.50 Put(s)	@ 0.00	= $0
Original Net Debit/Credit		= − $1,200
TOTAL PROFIT/LOSS		$175

If Sep trades to 94.20, Dec to 94.21:

Sell 1 Dec. 94.00 Put(s)	@ 0.13	= $325
Abandon 1 Sep. 93.50 Put(s)	@ 0.00	= $0
Original Net Debit/Credit		= − $1,200
TOTAL PROFIT/LOSS		− $875

Like the diagonal call spread, you can approximate the maximum loss of a diagonal put spread by reference to the initial net debit (see Figures 4–17 and 4–18). In the foregoing case, the maximum you can lose is approximately $1,200.

If the market rises dramatically, both options fall out-of-the-money and are worthless. Even the long-term December 94.00 put will be worthless by expiration of the September 93.50 put if it is sufficiently out-of-the-money, and the spread trader will be left with the initial net debit.

If the market declines sharply, both options are driven deep in-the-money. The short 93.50 option will generate a loss equal to its in-the-money amount by expiration. Likewise, the deep in-the-money long 94.00 put will also be worth its intrinsic value.

If the Sep/Dec futures spread is at zero, the long put has 50 basis points ($1,250) more intrinsic value than the short put. In the event of a substantial decline, the diagonal put spread returns equal the difference in strike prices less the initial debit. That translates to a $50 ($1,250 less $1,200) profit. Because the return on the "upside" (in the event of a market advance) is much worse than the return on the "downside" (in the event of a market advance), this strategy is clearly somewhat bearish.

The maximum profit, however, is realized at the short strike price (93.50 in the foregoing case). This is attributed to the accelerated time value decay associated with near- or at-the-money options. As expiration

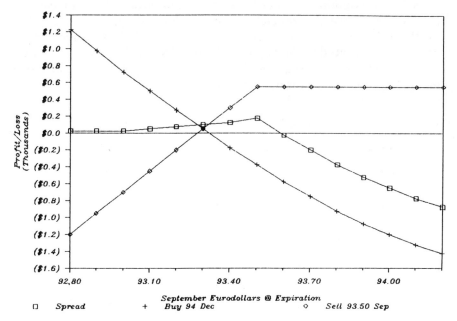

Figure 4–17   Sep/Dec 93.50/94.00 diagonal put spread.

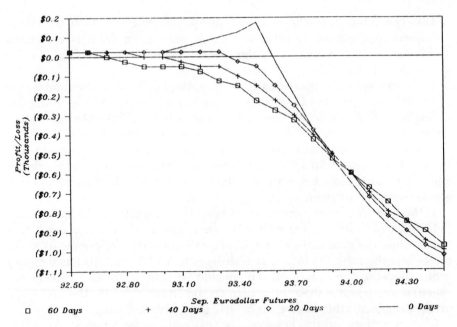

Figure 4–18   Sep/Dec 93.50/94.00 diagonal put spread.

approaches, holding September futures constant at 93.50, it is clear that the value of the spread appreciates at an accelerated pace.

In this case, the maximum profit simulated at $175 is rather limited. This can be attributed to the fact that the implied volatility was quite high on the long option and relatively low on the short option. This disparity suggests that the long put is overpriced.

> Diagonal Put Spread:
>
> Approximate "Upside" Loss = Initial Net Debit
>
> Approximate "Downside" Return = Difference in Strikes
>   – Initial Net Debit
>
> Profit Maximized: At the Short Strike Price

Futures Spread Movement

The returns modeled previously are based on the assumption that the spread between September and December remains constant. But of course, the spread may fluctuate dramatically.

The effect of futures spread movement has a similar impact on the diagonal spread as it has on a horizontal spread. If the futures spread should decline (December rallies relative to September), this has a positive impact on the diagonal call spread and a negative impact on the diagonal put spread. If the spread should rally (December falls relative to September), this has a negative impact on the call spread and a positive impact on the put spread.

Example: Consider the Sep/Dec 93.00/93.50 diagonal call spread illustrated earlier (see Figure 4–19). What happens if December rallies 20 basis points relative to September such that the spread may be quoted as −.21?
  If Sep falls to 92.80, Dec to 93.01:

Sell 1 Dec. 93.00 Call(s)	@ 0.27	=	$675
Abandon 1 Sep. 93.50 Call(s)	@ 0.00	=	$0
Original Net Debit/Credit		=	− $1,075
TOTAL PROFIT/LOSS			− $400

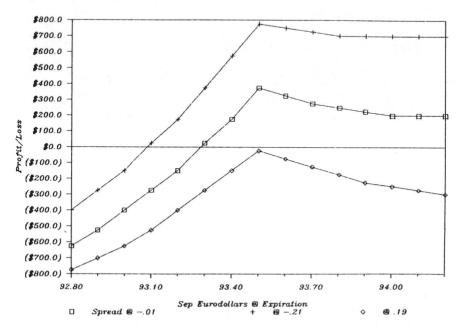

Figure 4–19   93/93.50 Sep/Dec diagonal call spread.

If Sep trades to 93.50, Dec to 93.71:

Sell 1 Dec. 93.00 Call(s)	@ 0.74	= $1,850
Abandon 1 Sep. 93.50 Call(s)	@ 0.00	= $0
Original Net Debit/Credit		= – $1,075
TOTAL PROFIT/LOSS		$775

If Sep trades 94.20, Dec to 94.41:

Sell 1 Dec. 93.00 Call(s)	@ 1.41	= $3,525
Exercise 1 Sep. 93.50 Call(s)	@ 0.70	= – $1,750
Original Net Debit/Credit		= – $1,075
TOTAL PROFIT/LOSS		$700

What happens if December falls relative to September such that the spread may be quoted as .19?
If Sep falls to 92.80, Dec to 92.61:

Sell 1 Dec. 93.00 Call(s)	@ 0.12	= $300
Abandon 1 Sep. 93.50 Call(s)	@ 0.00	= $0
Original Net Debit/Credit		= – $1,075
TOTAL PROFIT/LOSS		– $775

If Sep trades to 93.50, Dec to 93.31:

Sell 1 Dec. 93.00 Call(s)	@ 0.44	= $1,100
Abandon 1 Sep. 93.50 Call(s)	@ 0.00	= $0
Original Net Debit/Credit		= – $1,075
TOTAL PROFIT/LOSS		$25

If Sep rises to 94.20, Dec to 94.01:

Sell 1 Dec. 93.00 Call(s)	@ 1.01	= $2,525
Exercise 1 Sep. 93.50 Call(s)	@ 0.70	= – $1,750
Original Net Debit/Credit		= – $1,075
TOTAL PROFIT/LOSS		– $300

Example: Consider the Sep/Dec 94.00/93.50 diagonal put spread illustrated earlier (see Figure 4–20). What happens if December rallies 20 basis points relative to September such that the spread may be quoted as –.21?
If Sep falls to 92.80, Dec to 93.01:

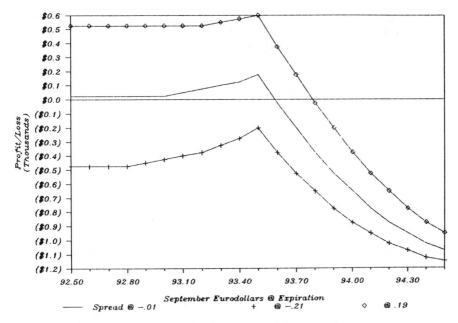

Figure 4–20   Sep/Dec 93.50/94.00 diagonal put spread.

Sell 1 Dec. 94.00 Put(s)	@ 0.99	=	$2,475
Exercise 1 Sep. 93.50 Put(s)	@ 0.70	=	− $1,750
Original Net Debit/Credit		=	− $1,200
TOTAL PROFIT/LOSS			− $475

If Sep trades to 93.50, Dec to 93.71:

Sell 1 Dec. 94.00 Put(s)	@ 0.40	=	$1,000
Abandon 1 Sep. 93.50 Put(s)	@ 0.00	=	$0
Original Net Debit/Credit		=	− $1,200
TOTAL PROFIT/LOSS			− $200

If Sep rises to 94.20, Dec to 94.41:

Sell 1 Dec. 94.00 Put(s)	@ 0.07	=	$175
Abandon 1 Sep. 93.50 Put(s)	@ 0.00	=	$0
Original Net Debit/Credit		=	− $1,200
TOTAL PROFIT/LOSS			− $1,025

What happens if December falls relative to September such that the spread may be quoted as .19?

If Sep falls to 92.80, Dec to 92.61:

Sell 1 Dec. 94.00 Put(s)	@ 1.39	=	$3,475
Exercise 1 Sep. 93.50 Put(s)	@ 0.70	=	− $1,750
Original Net Debit/Credit		=	− $1,200
TOTAL PROFIT/LOSS			$525

If Sep trades to 93.50, Dec to 93.31:

Sell 1 Dec. 94.00 Put(s)	@ 0.72	=	$1,800
Abandon 1 Sep. 93.50 Put(s)	@ 0.00	=	$0
Original Net Debit/Credit		=	− $1,200
TOTAL PROFIT/LOSS			$600

If Sep rises to 94.20, Dec to 93.50:

Sell 1 Dec. 94.00 Put(s)	@ 0.22	=	$550
Abandon 1 Sep. 93.50 Put(s)	@ 0.00	=	$0
Original Net Debit/Credit		=	− $1,200
TOTAL PROFIT/LOSS			− $650

Comparing Verticals, Horizontals, and Diagonals

Let us compare the estimated risks and rewards associated with a vertical bull call spread, a horizontal debit call spread, and a diagonal call spread. The vertical call spread may be characterized as the most bullish of the three. (However, it is only mildly bullish relative to a long futures contract.) The horizontal spread is quite neutral, while the diagonal call spread is somewhere between, mildly bullish.

This is illustrated clearly in the net delta associated with the initial placement of these three spreads:

	Initial Net Delta
Vertical	0.33
Horizontal	− 0.01
Diagonal	0.19

A vertical spread is roughly equivalent to buying 0.33 futures. The horizontal spread is quite neutral as evidenced by the delta of −0.01. Finally, the diagonal spread is somewhere between—equivalent to 0.19 long futures.

These net deltas may be calculated by examining the deltas associated with all four options which are referenced in the three spreads:

	Strike	
	93.00	93.50
Sep Call	0.79	0.46
Dec Call	0.65	0.45

As expiration approaches, in-the-money deltas approach 1.0, out-of-the-money deltas approach zero. Holding futures constant, the net deltas on the vertical and horizontal spreads become more positive. This means that the spreads become more bullish over time. Looking at it another way, the spreads become less stable as expiration approaches.

This phenomenon is sometimes referred to as "convexity." Our discussion has centered upon high probability strategies, strategies with a high probability of modest profit, low probability of relatively larger loss. Generally this means taking advantage of time value decay. Strategies that take advantage of time value decay are subject to the risks of convexity, a phenomenon that will be examined in greater detail in a subsequent chapter.

WEIGHTED SPREADS

Weighted spreads represent a variation on the vertical spread. A vertical spread entails the purchase of one call and the sale of one call or the purchase of one put and the sale of one put.

A *ratio* spread means that you sell more options than you buy. A *backspread* is just the opposite: you buy more options than you sell.

A weighted spread is a special case of the vertical spread. A *ratio* spread entails the sale of more options than are purchased. A *backspread* entails the purchase of more options than are sold.

Because the ratio spread allows you to capitalize on time value decay while a backspread depends upon market volatility in order to realize a profit, we will focus on the ratio spreads.

Two-for-One Ratio Spread

The *two-for-one* is the most commonly practiced ratio spread. This strategy calls for the purchase of one option (put or call) and the sale of two options (puts or calls). Like a vertical spread, the long and short legs of the spread share a common expiration but differ with respect to strike prices.

Example: It is July 9, 1986. A ratio call spread could be placed by buying a September 93.50 call for 22 basis points ($550) and selling two 93.75 calls for 12 basis points each or $600 in total (see Figures 4–21 and 4–22). (September Euros are trading at 93.47.)

Long 1 Sep. 93.50 Call(s)	@ 0.22	=	– $550
Imp. Volatility = 21.15% Delta = 0.46			
Short 2 Sep. 93.75 Call(s)	@ 0.12	=	$600
Imp. Volatility = 21.09% Delta = – 0.30			
NET DEBIT/CREDIT			$50
NET DELTA			– 0.14

What happens at expiration on September 15, 1986, assuming that the market falls, remains relatively stable, or advances?
    If the market falls to 93.40:

Abandon 1 Sep. 93.50 Call(s)	@ 0.00	=	$0
Abandon 2 Sep. 93.75 Call(s)	@ 0.00	=	$0
Original Net Debit/Credit		=	$50
TOTAL PROFIT/LOSS			$50

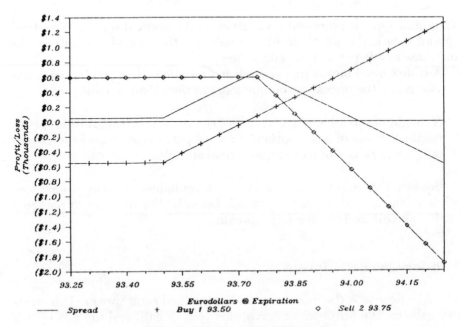

Figure 4–21   2-for-1 ratio call spread.

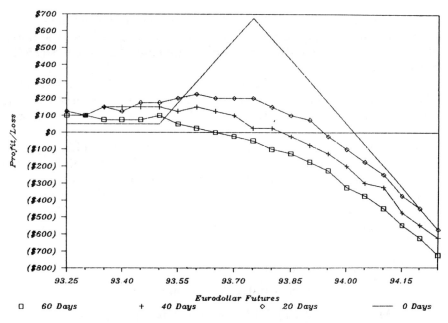

Figure 4–22   2-for-1 ratio call spread.

If the market trades to 93.75:

Exercise 1 Sep. 93.50 Call(s)	@ 0.25	=	$625
Abandon 2 Sep. 93.75 Call(s)	@ 0.00	=	$0
Original Net Debit/Credit		=	$50
TOTAL PROFIT/LOSS			$675

If the market rises to 94.10:

Exercise 1 Sep. 93.50 Call(s)	@ 0.60	=	$1,500
Exercise 2 Sep. 93.75 Call(s)	@ 0.35	=	– $1,750
Original Net Debit/Credit		=	$50
TOTAL PROFIT/LOSS			– $200

If the market is at the lower strike or below by expiration, both calls fall out-of-the-money, and the trader is left with the original net debit or net credit. In this case, the initial placement of the spread results in the receipt of a modest credit of $50.

Profit is maximized at the upper of the two strike prices. Here the single long call is 25 basis points in-the-money, and it is worth $625. The two short higher-struck calls are at-the-money and worthless. Thus the profit equals the in-the-money amount of the long call plus the initial net credit or minus the initial net debit. In this case, that equals $675 (27 basis points).

If the futures price rises above the upper strike price, the two short calls will be in-the-money. At some point, the losses which accrue from the exercise of the short options offset the profit from the single in-the-money long option.

The losses associated with one of the two short calls offsets profits from the single long call. If the futures price rises above the higher strike price as expiration approaches, it is as if you short one futures contract in a rising market. The breakeven point is identified as the upper strike price plus the maximum profit. In this case, that equals 93.75 plus 27 basis points of 94.02.

> 2-for-1 Ratio Call Spread:
>
> Downside Return = Initial Net Debit or Credit
>
> Maximum Return = Difference in Strikes plus or minus
>   Initial Net Credit or Net Debit
>
> Upper B/E = Upper Strike + Maximum Return

Because you sell more options than are purchased, this strategy may permit you to take advantage of time value decay. The value of the spread advances dramatically when the market is at or near the upper of the two strike prices. Normally, the spread is placed when the market is near or even under the lower of the two strikes. The idea is to find a situation where the market may be expected to gradually trade toward the short strike price by expiration.

If the market price does not move upwards, however, the loss is limited to any initial net debit. Of course, in this case the placement of the spread results in an initial net credit. The prospect of a flat market is not at all bothersome. The risk is that the market will rally rapidly up to and through the upper strike price level. This could leave the spreader with large losses.

Just as you can place a two-for-one ratio call spread in anticipation of a mildly bullish market, you can place a two-for-one ratio put spread in anticipation of a mildly bearish market.

Example: It is July 9, 1986. A two-for-one ratio put spread is placed by buying a September 93.50 Eurodollar futures put for 22 basis points ($550)

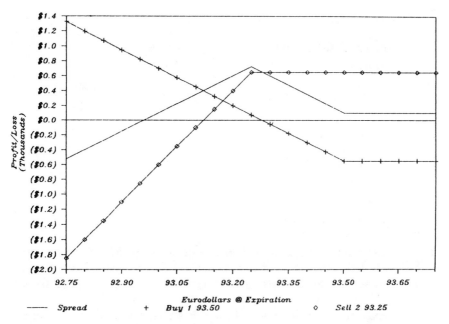

Figure 4–23   2-for-1 ratio put spread.

and selling two 93.25 calls for 13 basis points each or $650 in total (see Figure 4–23). (September Euros are trading at 93.47.)

Long 1 Sep. 93.50 Put(s)	@ 0.22	=	– $550
Imp. Volatility = 18.47% Delta = – 0.53			
Short 2 Sep. 93.25 Put(s)	@ 0.13	=	$650
Imp. Volatility = 19.65% Delta = 0.36			
NET DEBIT/CREDIT			$100
NET DELTA			0.19

What happens at expiration on September 15, 1986, if the market falls, remains relatively stable, or advances?

If the market falls to 92.90:

Exercise 1 Sep. 93.50 Put(s)	@ 0.60	=	$1,500
Exercise 2 Sep. 93.25 Put(s)	@ 0.35	=	– $1,750
Original Net Debit/Credit		=	$100
TOTAL PROFIT/LOSS			– $150

If the market trades to 93.25:

Exercise 1 Sep. 93.50 Put(s)	@ 0.25	=	$625
Abandon 2 Sep. 93.25 Put(s)	@ 0.00	=	$0
Original Net Debit/Credit		=	$100
TOTAL PROFIT/LOSS			$725

If the market rises to 93.60:

Abandon 1 Sep. 93.50 Put(s)	@ 0.00	=	$0
Abandon 2 Sep. 93.25 Put(s)	@ 0.00	=	$0
Original Net Debit/Credit		=	$100
TOTAL PROFIT/LOSS			$100

If the market price is at the upper strike or above at expiration, both puts fall out-of-the-money, and the trader is left with either the original net debit or net credit. In this case, the initial placement of the spread results in a $100 credit.

Profit is maximized at the lower of the two strike prices. Here, the single long put falls 25 basis points in-the-money and is worth $625. The two short lower-struck puts are at-the-money and worthless. Thus the profit equals the in-the-money amount of the long put plus the initial net credit or minus the initial net debit. In this case, that equals $725 (29 basis points).

If the market price is lower than the upper strike price level, the two short puts fall in-the-money. At some point, losses which accrue from the exercise of the short options offset the profit from the single in-the-money long option.

The loss associated with one of the two short puts offsets the profit from the single long put. Under the lower of the two strikes, it is as if you long one futures contract in a falling market. The lower breakeven profit is identified as the lower strike price less the maximum profit. In this case, this equals 93.25 less 29 basis points of 92.96.

2-for-1 Ratio Put Spread:

Upside Return = Initial Net Debit or Credit

Maximum Return = Difference in Strikes plus or minus
Initial Net Credit or Net Debit

Lower B/E = Lower Strike − Maximum Return

Analogous to the ratio call spread, the ratio put spread is normally placed when the market is around or above the upper of the two strikes. Hopefully, the market will gradually trade toward the short strike price by expiration. The risk is that the market will decline rapidly down to and through the area surrounding the lower strike price.

Three-for-One and Three-for-Two Ratios

Although the two-for-one ratio is the most common, other ratios are sometimes employed, such as the three-for-one or the three-for-two ratios.

> **Example:** It is July 9, 1986. A three-for-one ratio call spread is placed by buying a September 93.50 call for 22 basis points ($550) and selling three 93.75 calls for 12 basis points each or $900 in total. (September Euros are trading at 93.47.)

Long 1 Sep. 93.50 Call(s)	@ 0.22	=	− $550
Imp. Volatility = 21.15% Delta = 0.46			
Short 3 Sep. 93.75 Call(s)	@ 0.12	=	$900
Imp. Volatility = 21.09% Delta = − 0.30			
NET DEBIT/CREDIT			$350
NET DELTA			− 0.45

What happens at expiration on September 15, 1986, assuming that the market falls, remains relatively stable, or advances?

If the market falls to 93.40:

Abandon 1 Sep. 93.50 Call(s)	@ 0.00	=	$0
Abandon 3 Sep. 93.75 Call(s)	@ 0.00	=	$0
Original Net Debit/Credit		=	$350
TOTAL PROFIT/LOSS			$350

If the market trades to 93.75:

Exercise 1 Sep. 93.50 Call(s)	@ 0.25	=	$625
Abandon 3 Sep. 93.75 Call(s)	@ 0.00	=	$0
Original Net Debit/Credit		=	$350
TOTAL PROFIT/LOSS			$975

If the market rallies to 94.10:

Exercise 1 Sep. 93.50 Call(s)	@ 0.60	=	$1,500
Exercise 3 Sep. 93.75 Call(s)	@ 0.35	=	− $2,625
Original Net Debit/Credit		=	$350
TOTAL PROFIT/LOSS			− $775

The risks and rewards associated with the three-for-one are similar to those associated with the two-for-one. The notable difference is that above the upper of the two strike prices, it is as if you are short *two* futures rather than one in a rising market. The upper breakeven point equals the upper strike price plus one half of the maximum profit. Because you sell three rather than two calls, this trade almost invariably results in a nice initial credit.

The maximum profit, equal to the difference in strikes plus the initial net credit, is larger than the maximum profit associated with the two-for-one trade. (The two-for-one spread compensates you in that the upper breakeven point is pushed up somewhat.)

3-for-1 Ratio Call Spread:

Downside Return = Initial Net Debit or Credit

Maximum Return = Difference in Strikes plus or minus
Initial Net Credit or Net Debit

Upper B/E = Upper Strike + One-Half of the Maximum Return

Example: It is July 9, 1986. A three-for-two ratio call spread is placed by buying two September 93.50 calls for 22 basis points each ($1,100) and selling three 93.75 calls for 12 basis points each or $900 in total. (September Euros are trading at 93.47.)

Long 2 Sep. 93.50 Call(s)	@ 0.22	=	− $1,100
Imp. Volatility = 21.15% Delta = 0.46			
Short 3 Sep. 93.75 Call(s)	@ 0.12	=	$900
Imp. Volatility = 21.09% Delta = − 0.30			
NET DEBIT/CREDIT			− $200
NET DELTA			0.01

What happens by expiration on September 15, 1986, assuming that the market falls, remains relatively stable, or advances?
If the market falls to 93.40:

Abandon 2 Sep. 93.50 Call(s)	@ 0.00	=	$0
Abandon 3 Sep. 93.75 Call(s)	@ 0.00	=	$0
Original Net Debit/Credit		=	− $200
TOTAL PROFIT/LOSS			− $200

If the market trades to 93.75:

Exercise 2 Sep. 93.50 Call(s)	@ 0.25	=	$1,250
Abandon 3 Sep. 93.75 Call(s)	@ 0.00	=	$0
Original Net Debit/Credit		=	– $200
TOTAL PROFIT/LOSS			$1,050

If the market rises to 94.10:

Exercise 2 Sep. 93.50 Call(s)	@ 0.60	=	$3,000
Exercise 3 Sep. 93.75 Call(s)	@ 0.35	=	– $2,625
Original Net Debit/Credit		=	– $200
TOTAL PROFIT/LOSS			$175

Here the major difference is that you can exercise two options at the short strike price level rather than one. You earn the difference in strikes twice. However, this spread usually results in an initial net debit insofar as you are short only 1.5 options for every option you are long.

3-for-2 Ratio Call Spread:

Downside Return = Initial Net Debit or Credit

Maximum Return = Twice the Difference in Strikes plus or minus Initial Net Credit or Net Debit

Upper B/E = Upper Strike + Maximum Return

Which of the three strategies (two-for-one, three-for-one, three-for-two) is superior? No single strategy dominates (see Figure 4–24). Risk and return always tend to balance. If they did not, arbitrage opportunities would exist.

	Downside Return	*Maximum Return*	*Upper B/E*
2-for-1	$50	$675	94.02
3-for-1	$350	$975	93.95
3-for-2	– $200	$1,050	94.17

Backspreads

If you do the opposite of a ratio spread—buy more options than are sold—you create a *backspread*. The risks and rewards associated with these strategies are the exact opposite of those associated with similarly weighted ratio spreads.

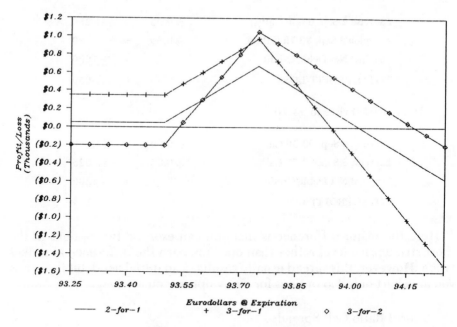

Figure 4–24   Ratio call spreads.

The risk/reward profiles are also comparable. In fact, if you simply rotate the ratio spread diagrams along a horizontal axis, you create a diagram illustrating an option strategy of the opposite orientation; you change a long strategy into a short strategy or vice versa (see Figure 4–25).

Similarly, you can rotate these graphics along a vertical axis and change the orientation from a put to a call or a call to a put. This is illustrated nicely by comparing the two-for-one ratio put and two-for-one ratio call spread diagrams (see Figures 4–26 and 4–27).

Rotate on a Vertical Axis: Put   <= => Call
Rotate on a Horizontal Axis: Long <= => Short

QUESTIONS

1. An option spread . . .
   (a) Is the purchase and sale of two options of the same type and strike price.
   (b) Is the same as an option straddle.

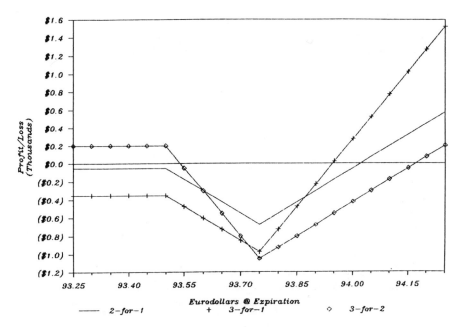

Figure 4-25   Call backspreads.

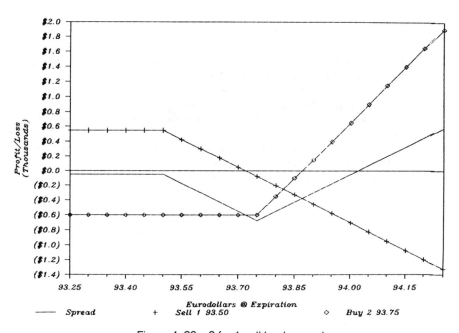

Figure 4-26   2-for-1 call backspread.

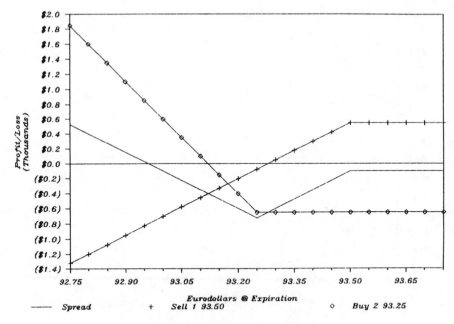

Figure 4–27   2-for-1 put backspread.

(c) Means that you buy or sell two puts or two calls.
(d) Involves unlimited risk.
(e) Does not constrain one's potential profits.
2. Which statement is false?
(a) A vertical spread is also referred to as a money spread.
(b) A vertical spread involves two options with the same expiration date but with different strike prices.
(c) A horizontal spread involves two options with different expiration dates but with the same strike price.
(d) Elements of a vertical and horizontal spread are reflected in the performance of a diagonal spread.
(e) A vertical spread is also referred to as a time spread.
3. (a) An 84/86 bull call spread is executed when T-bond futures are at 86–00. The 84 call is trading at $2\,^{48}/_{64\text{ths}}$; the 86 call is at $1\,^{32}/_{64\text{ths}}$. What is the initial net debit or credit?
(b) What is the maximum risk associated with this strategy?
(c) What is the maximum potential reward associated with this strategy?
(d) Where is the B/E point?
(e) What is the probability that the spreader will breakeven or better? (Volatility is at 12 percent and there are 60 days until expiration. You will need a calculator and a normal probability table.)

4. A horizontal spread . . .
   (a) Yields the maximum profit when the market trades at or near the common strike price.
   (b) Can be put on only with call options.
   (c) Always results in an initial net debit.
   (d) Has a risk/reward scenario that may be skewed upwards or downwards depending on whether you put the spread on using calls or puts.
   (e) None of the above.
5. If you believe that nearby futures will decline slightly relative to deferred futures but that the market will otherwise remain relatively stable, you should . . .
   (a) Buy the futures spread.
   (b) Buy a diagonal put spread.
   (c) Enter a debit horizontal spread using calls.
   (d) Enter a debit horizontal spread using puts.
   (e) Buy a vertical bull call spread where the upper strike is near the current market price.
6. Which statement is false?
   (a) The risk associated with a debit horizontal spread may be estimated as the initial debit.
   (b) The B/E points associated with a debit horizontal spread equal the common strike price plus or minus the debit.
   (c) A diagonal spread involves options with different strikes and expiration dates.
   (d) The maximum risk associated with a debit diagonal spread is different depending upon whether the market moves up or down.
   (e) A bear put spread may be put on at a net debit.
7. A ratio spread . . .
   (a) Is the same as a backspread.
   (b) Means that you sell more options than you buy.
   (c) Is done on a two-for-one basis.
   (d) References the conversion factor associated with the cheapest to deliver bond.
   (e) Means that you sell more options than you write.
8. (a) You buy a diagonal put spread by buying a September 88–00 put on bond futures for $3\,^{20}/_{64ths}$ and selling a June 86–00 put for $1\,^{40}/_{64ths}$. Assuming that the June/September futures spread remains stable, what is the maximum risk if the market advances sharply?
   (b) What is the maximum risk if the market declines sharply?
9. (a) You buy one call on DM futures struck at 0.4200 for 1.72 and sell two 0.4400 calls for 0.74 a piece. What is the initial net debit?
   (b) What is the maximum profit and at what price could it be realized?

5
Three-Dimensional Option Trading

Option prices are affected by a number of market-driven variables. The relationship of market price relative to a fixed exercise price (*price*) is the most commonly referenced of these variables. The term until option expiration (*time*) is a second very significant variable which impacts upon an option value. A third especially significant variable is expected marketplace variability (*volatility*).

Because all of these variables impact upon the option premium, they all impact to one degree or another upon option strategies. This chapter discusses the measurement and impact of price, time, and volatility on an option premium and, consequently, on an option strategy.

Because our intent is to highlight the effect of the third significant variable, volatility, we will illustrate the impact of all three variables in the context of *volatility plays*, strategies usually thought of as methods to take advantage of anticipated changes in marketplace volatility such as straddles, strangles, guts, butterflies, and condors.

PRICING FORMULA DERIVATIVES

Prior to studying the impact of price, time, and volatility upon option strategies, let us reexamine the Black-Scholes option pricing formula. It is clear that this formula is capable of yielding some valuable insights with respect to the anticipated movement of option premiums given changes in some other variable. In particular, the formula may be used to identify the sensitivity of the option premium to various market conditions. This is accomplished by applying a little calculus and taking a derivative of the option premium with respect to the variable of interest (holding all other variables constant).

Delta

The price movement of the instrument for which an option may be exercised is the most frequently watched element which impacts on an option premium. Hence, it is not surprising that the most frequently referenced derivation involving the Black-Scholes option pricing formula measures the sensitivity of the premium with respect to changing underlying prices.

This quantity is discussed in a prior section and is, of course, known as *delta*. To review, delta may be thought of as a measure of the expected change in the option premium given a small change in the underlying market price. Implicit in this definition is the assumption that all other variables are held constant.

Delta reflects the expected change in the option premium given a small change in the price of the underlying instrument, all other variables held constant.

Delta varies from 0 to 1.0 in the case of long calls or 0 to negative 1.0 (−1.0) in the case of long puts. This is intuitive in that if you buy a call and the market advances, the call premium is likewise expected to advance resulting in a positive delta.

If you own a put and the market advances, the put premium is expected to decline resulting in a negative delta. Likewise, the deltas associated with essentially bearish short calls and essentially bullish short puts are generally expressed as negative and positive numbers respectively.

Delta Orientation

	Call	Put
Long	(+)	(−)
Short	(−)	(+)

The formula for identifying deltas for call options on futures and for put options on futures was identified in an earlier chapter as follows:

$$\text{Call Delta} = e^{-rt} N(d_1)$$

$$\text{Put Delta} = e^{-rt} [N(d_1) - 1]$$

$$d_1 = [\ln(U/E) + 0.5tv^2]/v\sqrt{(t)}$$

Where:

r = Short-term interest rate.

t = Term until expiration, expressed in years, *e.g.*, 91 days/365 days in year equals 0.25 years.

U = Underlying price.

E = Exercise price.

N = Cumulative normal probability.

v = Volatility (standard deviation of expected percentage price changes).

Example: It is June 19, 1986. September deutsche mark futures are trading at 45.04 cents per mark. The call struck at 45 is trading at 1.21; the 45 put is at 1.17. These options have implied volatilities of 14.52 percent and 14.51 percent, respectively. There are 79 days until expiration (0.216 years) and short-term rates are at 6 percent. Calculate the call and put deltas.

Call

$$\text{Delta} = e^{-(.06)(.214)}\,(.5199)$$
$$= 0.51$$
$$d_1 = [\ln(45.04/45) + 0.5(.214)(.1452^2)]/(.1452)\sqrt{(.214)}$$
$$= 0.0468$$
$$N(d_1) = 0.5199$$

Put

$$\text{Delta} = e^{-(.06)(.214)}\,(.5199 - 1)$$
$$= -0.47$$
$$d_1 = [\ln(45.04/45) + 0.5(.214)(.1451)^2]/(.1451)\sqrt{(.214)}$$
$$= 0.0468$$
$$N(d_1) = 0.5199$$

These formulae were taken as the first derivative of the option pricing model with respect to the underlying price. From a conceptual standpoint, one may understand delta by envisioning the slope of a straight line drawn tangent at any particular point to the option premium curve (see Figures 5–1 and 5–2).

The farther an option is in-the-money, the steeper the slope of the tangent line and the greater the delta. The farther an option is out-of-the-money, the shallower the slope of the tangent line and the smaller the delta.

As expiration approaches, delta may move to an extreme. In other words, an in-the-money option delta will approach 1.0 (or -1.0 in the case of a bearish option position) as expiration draws near. An out-of-the-money delta will approach zero as expiration draws near.

As expiration approaches . . .

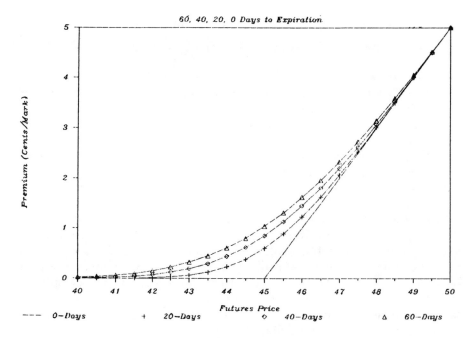

Figure 5-1   Deutsche mark 45 call premium.

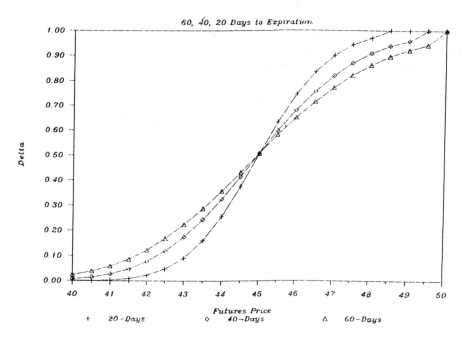

Figure 5-2   Deutsche mark 45 call delta.

In-the-money option   ⇒ delta approaches 1.0

Out-of-the-money option ⇒ delta approaches zero

A pivotal point is found when an option is at-the-money. An at-the-money delta will always remain at or near 0.5 (−0.5 in the case of a bearish position).

Because these deltas are calculated by taking the derivative of the option model with respect to price, they represent an "instantaneous" measure; they are only valid over a limited price movement over a limited period of time and a limited volatility range.

This is as opposed to the calculation of an "arc delta." An arc delta is calculated by comparing the current value of the premium with the theoretical value of the same given a somewhat higher or lower underlying value. By dividing the difference in the two premiums by the difference between the two underlying values, you calculate the arc delta.

The arc delta is sometimes preferred as a more realistic measure of the possible movement in the premium. Note, however, that the calculation requires you to identify the possible direction and magnitude of underlying price movement. Because this is a difficult proposition, most analysts settle for the instantaneous delta.

Gamma

If we can find the expected change in the option premium given a small change in the value of the underlying instrument, we can also find the expected change in the delta given a change in the value of the underlying instrument. This quantity is known as *gamma*.

> *Gamma* reflects the expected change in the delta given a small change in the value of the underlying instrument, all other variables held constant.

Gamma may be thought of as the "delta of the delta." From a conceptual point of view, if delta represents the velocity, gamma represents acceleration. Another way of thinking of gamma is that it represents the stability of the delta.

Gamma is calculated as the *second* derivative of the option premium with respect to price. It may be found graphically by drawing a straight line tangent to the delta graphic at any strike price. The slope of that tangent represents gamma. This may be expressed mathematically (for both puts and calls exercisable for futures contracts) as:

$$\text{Gamma} = [e^{-rt}/Uv \sqrt{(t)}] \, N'(d_1)$$

Where:

$$N'(x) = (1/\sqrt{(2\pi)})\ \exp(-x^2/2)$$
$$\pi = 3.1416$$

Example: Let us return to our example of June 19th illustrated earlier. Calculate the gamma for the put and call struck at 45 given a volatility of 14.51 percent:

$$\text{Gamma} = [e^{-(.06)(.214)}/(45.04)(.1451)\sqrt{(.214)}]\ (.3985)$$
$$= 0.1301$$

If

$$d_1 = .0468 \text{ (as calculated in the prior example)}$$

Then

$$N'(d_1) = (1/\sqrt{(2\pi)})\ \exp(-.0468^2/2) = .3985$$

This suggests that if the underlying price should fluctuate by one unit, the delta would fluctuate by approximately 0.1301 of one unit.

Because convexity (as measured by gamma) works to the benefit of the long and to the detriment of the short, long option gammas may be represented as a positive number while short option gammas may be represented as a negative number.

Figure 5–3 illustrates that, at any given point in time, gamma is highest for at- or near-the-money options. This is intuitive when you consider the magnitude of time premium associated with in-, at-, and out-of-the-money options.

In- and out-of-the-money options have little time value relative to at- or near-the-money options which have the greatest time value. *Deep* ins and outs have little or no time value—their premium is a pure function of the in-the-money value. The deltas are quite stable; deep in-the-money options have a delta of 1.0 which will not vary unless the option acquires some time value; deep out-of-the-money options have a delta near zero which is similarly stable.

At-the-money options whose time value is greatest tend to have the most unstable deltas and the highest gammas. The tendencies associated with in-, at-, and out-of-the-money options are exacerbated as expiration approaches; gammas rise for near-the-money options and fall for in- or out-of-the-money options.

Assume you want to buy a call in anticipation of rising prices. You may gauge the aggressiveness or conservativeness of various options by inspecting

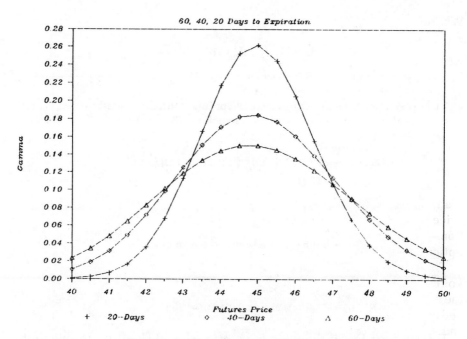

Figure 5–3   Deutsche mark 45 call gamma.

the gammas. Near-term, near-the-money options are more aggressive than are longer-term, away-from-the-money options. The stability of the delta as measured by gamma is the key to identifying aggressive and conservative options.

Stability of Delta

	Near-Term	Long-Term
At- or Near-the-Money	High and Rising Convexity	Moderate but Rising Convexity
In- or Out-of-the-Money	Low and Falling Convexity	Moderate but Falling Convexity

The aggressiveness or conservativeness of an option is sometimes referred to as "convexity." The term "convex" describes the shape of the option premium curve illustrated in Figure 5–3. An aggressive option with a high gamma has high convexity, that is, the premium curve is quite bowed in the area in which the option is trading. A conservative option with a low gamma has low convexity.

To illustrate this concept, consider the buyer of a call option. If the market rallies into-the-money, the delta starts to advance. Thus the call buyer is making money at an accelerating rate. If the market is falling, the call buyer is losing money, *but he is losing money at a decelerating rate*.

By contrast, the call seller is losing money at an accelerating rate when the market is rallying and making money at a decelerating rate as the market falls. Convexity thus works to the benefit of the option buyer and to the detriment of the option seller.

Theta

Many analysts concentrate their attention on the impact of underlying price movement on an option's premium. But the term until option expiration—the constant march of time—also has a significant impact on an option's premium.

The phenomenon of time value decay was discussed in a prior chapter. To review briefly, this term refers to the fact that as expiration draws near, the time value component of an option premium starts to decline. Such decay or erosion is most pronounced with at- or near-the-money options and accelerates as expiration nears. By contrast, time value decay may be quite linear for in- or out-of-the-money options. In fact, time value may reach a value of zero for deep in- and out-of-the-money options well before option expiration (see Figure 5–4).

Rates of Decay

	Near-Term	Long-Term
At- or Near-the-Money	Rapid Acceleration	Slight Acceleration
In- or Out-of-the-Money	Time Value May Bottom Out	Linear Decay

Theta may be used to measure the magnitude of time value decay. While delta represents the expected change in premium relative to a change in the underlying price, theta represents the expected change in the option premium relative to a change in term until expiration.

Theta reflects the expected change in the option premium given a small change in the option's term to expiration, all other variables held constant.

You can identify the theta by inspecting a diagram of premium over a range of dates. By drawing a straight line tangent to this diagram, you can get a feel for the magnitude of time value decay.

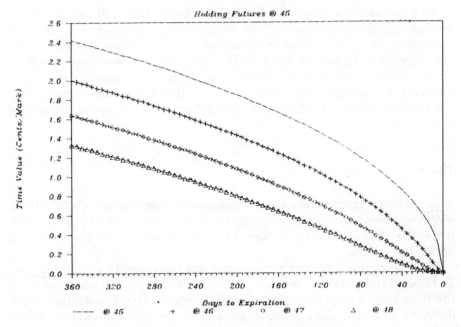

Figure 5–4   At- and out-money DM calls.

Mathematically, theta is calculated as the first derivative of the option pricing model with respect to time. Theta varies for put and call options exercisable for futures.

Call Theta $= e^{-rt}[(Uv/2 \sqrt{(t)})N'(d_1) + U(-r)N(d_1) + ErN(d_2)]$

Put Theta $= e^{-rt}[(Uv/2 \sqrt{(t)})N'(d_1) + U(-r)(N(d_1) - 1) + Er(N(d_2) - 1)]$

Where:

$$d_2 = d_1 - v \sqrt{(t)}$$

Example: Let us return to our example of June 19th illustrated earlier. Calculate the theta for the put and call struck at 45 given a volatility of 14.51 percent:

Call Theta $= e^{-(.06)(.214)}[((.4504)(.1451)/2\sqrt{.214})(.3985) + 45.04(-.06)(.5199)$
$+ 45(.06)(.4920)]$

$= 2.7033$ per year (.0074 per day)

Put Theta $= e^{-(.06)(.214)}[((.4504)(.1451)/2\sqrt{.214})(.3985) + 45.04(-.06)(.5199-1)$
$+ 45(.06)(.4920-1)]$

$= 2.7057$ per year $(.0074$ per day$)$

$d_2 = .0468 - (.1451)\sqrt{(.214)}$

$= -.0203$

$N(d_2) = .4920$

As calculated in the prior example:

$$N'(d_1) = .3485$$
$$N(d_1) = .5199$$

The thetas calculated above suggest time value decay at a rate of 2.7033 and 2.7057 cents per mark per unit of time (one year) for the call and put, respectively (see Figure 5–5). As such, the theta associated with a long position may be represented as a negative number; the theta associated with a short option is often identified as a positive number.

Typically, these values are expressed over the course of a much shorter period of time such as ten business days, five business days or even a single business day. For example, over the course of a single day, one might expect decay on the order of .0065 cents per mark.

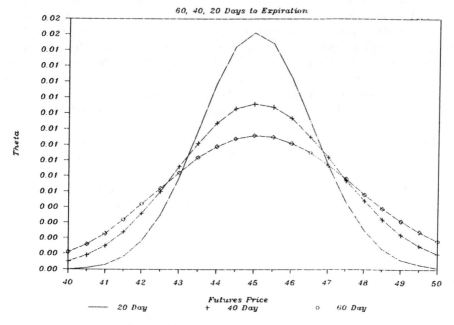

Figure 5–5   45 deutsche mark call theta.

Plotting theta over a range of underlying futures prices and at three different points in time prior to expiration confirms our earlier observation that time value decay is highest for near-the-money, near-term options. In- and out-of-the-money options display much less time value decay and actually decelerate in terms of time value decay as expiration approaches.

It is interesting to note that options which are highly affected by time value decay are also quite convex. This suggests that there are counteracting advantages and disadvantages to these options. If you sell options which experience rapidly accelerating time value decay, you are also selling options which will be most adversely affected by changing underlying price levels.

Vega

The third major variable which impacts an option premium is expected marketplace volatility. Although a prior chapter discusses ways of measuring volatility and the general impact on advancing or declining volatility on an option's price, we have not mentioned ways to measure the sensitivity of an option premium to a change in volatility.

Increasing (decreasing) volatility will generally induce an increase (decrease) in both put and call premiums regardless of the term to expiration or the in- or out-of-the-money amount. This is similar to the effect that term until expiration has on the option premium (the longer the term, the higher the volatility, the greater the premium). Thus volatility and term have "magnifying" or complementary effects. In support of this observation, it is interesting to note that whenever volatility (v) appears in the Black-Scholes pricing model, it is always multiplied by some function of term (t).

The magnitude of this advance or decline, however, will vary in accordance with general levels of volatility and the in- or out-of-the-money amount of the option. In general, at- or near-the-money options are proportional to shifting volatilities at any volatility level. Thus no matter if volatility is very low (for example, 0–6 percent) or relatively high (for example, 15 percent and beyond), near-the-money options will be uniformly sensitive to shifting volatilities.

This is not true for in- or out-of-the-money options. In- and out-of-the-money options are much less sensitive to shifting volatilities over low (0–6 percent) or moderate (7–14 percent) volatilities. In fact, at very low levels, in- and out-of-the-moneys are almost completely insensitive to shifting volatilities, although at relatively high levels, in-, at-, and out-of-the-moneys become almost equally sensitive (see Figures 5–6 and 5–7).

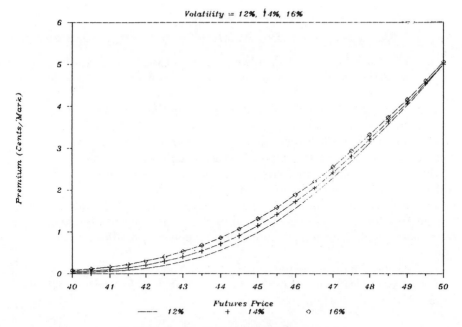

Figure 5-6   Deutsche mark 45 call premiums.

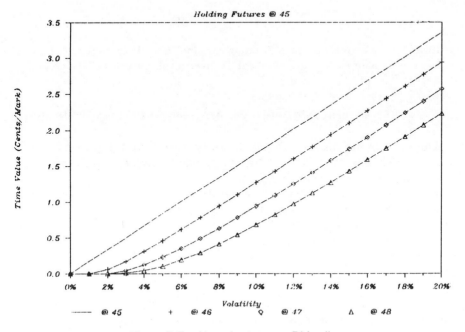

Figure 5-7   At- and out-money DM calls.

Sensitivity to Volatility

	Low-Volatility	High-Volatility
At- or Near-the-Money	Linear Sensitivity	Linear Sensitivity
In- or out-of-the-Money	Quite Insensitive	Sensitivity = Near-Moneys

This suggests that you should enter into near-the-money options to take advantage of shifting volatilities when volatilities are at low levels. When volatilities are at high levels, however, the absolute price movements of near- or away-from-the-money options are roughly equivalent.

Vega may be used to measure the sensitivity of the option premium to shifting volatility levels. Vega is calculated as the first derivative of the premium with respect to volatility. Again, you can inspect a diagram illustrating the premium over a range of volatilities, drawing tangent lines to identify the sensitivity of an option premium with respect to volatility (vega).

Vega measures the expected change in the option premium given a one percent (1%) change in the implied volatility of an option, all other variables held constant.

For either puts or calls exercisable for options on futures, the formula is as follows:

$$\text{Vega} = \sqrt{(t)}\, Ue^{-rt}N'(d_1)$$

Example: Let us return to our example of June 19th illustrated earlier. Calculate the vega for the options struck at 45 given a volatility of 14.51 percent:

Vega $= \sqrt{(.214)}\, 45.04e^{-(.06)(.214)}(.3985)$

  $= 8.1970$ per unit (100%) volatility or .0820 cents per 1% change in volatility

This calculation suggests that if volatility were to shift on the order of 1 percent, a change of .0820 cents per mark would be induced in the option premium (see Figures 5–8 and 5–9).

Vegas associated with long option positions are often assigned a positive value. Short option positions suffer from increasing volatility and, hence are depicted as a negative number.

Elasticity

A final statistic of interest is *price elasticity*. Price elasticity is quite similar to delta in that it measures the expected change in the premium given a change in the underlying price.

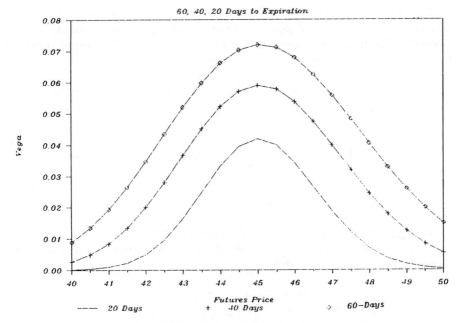

Figure 5-8   45 deutsche mark call vega.

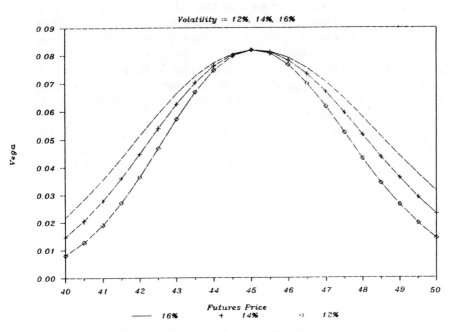

Figure 5-9   Deutsche mark 45 call vega.

This statistic differs from delta, however, in that it measures, not *absolute* price movement, but *percentage* or relative price movement, the expected percentage movement in the premium given a 1 percent move in the instrument for which the option may be exercised.

Price elasticity represents the expected percentage change in the option premium given a 1 percent movement in the underlying price.

Price elasticity is often regarded as a measure of the leverage associated with an option. Price elasticity may be calculated as delta multiplied by the underlying price divided by the premium:

$$\text{Price Elasticity} = \text{Delta (Underlying Price/Premium)}$$

Example: The deutsche mark call struck at 45 illustrated previously has a premium of 1.21 cents per mark, and a delta of 0.51 when the underlying price equals 45.04. Find its elasticity:

$$\text{Price Elasticity} = 0.51\ (45.04/1.21)$$
$$= 18.98\%$$

This figure suggests that the premium will change on the order of 18.98 percent given a 1 percent change in the value of the underlying instrument. This would lead one to believe that the option enjoys considerable leverage compared to the outright purchase of the underlying instrument.

Superficially, this appears to be true—indisputable in fact! Consider, however, that the buyer of an option exercisable for futures must pay the premium in full, in cash, and up front. By contrast, the trader who buys a deutsche mark futures contract generally puts up collateral (such as T-bills) to meet the initial margin.

There is therefore no initial opportunity cost associated with the purchase or sale of futures. Consequently, options on futures may be thought of as *negative* leverage investments! Still, this statistic is useful in that it allows you to measure the magnitude of this negative leverage.

Compare the elasticity of the near-the-money call struck at 45 with options with strikes ranging from 43 to 47:

Strike	Delta	×	(Price /	Premium)	=	Elasticity
43.00	0.75		45.04	2.45		13.8%
44.00	0.64		45.04	1.77		16.3%
45.00	0.51		45.04	1.21		19.0%
46.00	0.39		45.04	0.80		22.0%
47.00	0.27		45.04	0.50		24.3%

This result suggests out-of-the-money options are higher leveraged contracts and a more aggressive investment than comparable at- or in-the-money options! While in-the-moneys can be expected to exhibit greater absolute premium movement in response to movement in the value of the underlying instrument, out-of-the-moneys exhibit greater percentage response. In other words, you get "more bang for the buck" with out-of-the-money options!

VOLATILITY PLAYS

The intent of this section is to review a number of commonly used trading strategies and demonstrate how price, time, and volatility impact on the trade. Although it is obvious that all three of these factors have the potential to impact upon an option strategy, the strategies we are interested in are commonly referred to as *volatility plays*. This is due to the fact that all of these strategies outlined below—the *straddle, strangle, guts, butterfly,* and *condor*—are significantly affected by rising or falling volatilities.

As we will see, however, it is difficult as a practical matter to isolate the effect of volatility on an option strategy. It is obvious, for example, that price movement has a critical impact upon the market's assessment of volatility. It is also impossible to minimize the significance of time value decay. This is intuitive when we consider that price movement referenced by time *defines* volatility!

Short options may be thought of as vehicles which will permit you to capitalize on stable prices, the onset of time value decay, and falling volatility. Long options permit you to capitalize on heavily trending prices over short time periods and rising volatility.

Straddles

In the context of futures, the terms *straddle* and *spread* are used synonomously, but this is not true in the context of the option markets! A spread involves the purchase and sale of two puts or the purchase and sale of two calls. A straddle entails the purchase of a put and a call or the sale of a put and a call. These puts and calls share a common strike or exercise price and a common expiration date.

> A *straddle* entails the purchase of a put and a call or the sale of a put and a call. The two options which comprise the straddle share a common strike or exercise price and a common expiration date.

> A "long straddle" entails the purchase of a put and a call; a "short straddle" entails the sale of a put and a call.

Example: It is June 19th, 1986, and you buy a call exercisable for deutsche mark futures with a strike of 45 expiring in September for a 1.21 point premium ($1,512 per 125,000 mark contract). Simultaneously, you buy a 45 put for 1.17 points ($1,462 per contract).

Long 1 Sep. 45.00 Call(s)	@ 1.21	= – $1,512
Imp. Volatility = 14.52% Delta = 0.51		
Long 1 Sep. 45.00 Put(s)	@ 1.17	= – $1,462
Imp. Volatility = 14.51% Delta = – 0.48		
NET DEBIT		$2,975
NET DELTA		0.04

This trade entails an initial net debit of $2,975. What would happen if the strategy were held 78 days until expiration on September 5, 1986?
If the price falls to 41.00:

Abandon 1 Sep. 45.00 Call(s)	@ 0.00 =	$0
Exercise 1 Sep. 45.00 Put(s)	@ 4.00 =	$5,000
Original Net Debit/Credit	=	– $2,975
TOTAL PROFIT/LOSS		$2,025

If the price remains relatively stable at 45.00:

Abandon 1 Sep. 45.00 Call(s)	@ 0.00 =	$0
Abandon 1 Sep. 45.00 Put(s)	@ 0.00 =	$0
Original Net Debit/Credit	=	– $2,975
TOTAL PROFIT/LOSS		– $2,975

If the price rises to 49.00:

Exercise 1 Sep. 45.00 Call(s)	@ 4.00 =	$5,000
Abandon 1 Sep. 45.00 Put(s)	@ 0.00 =	$0
Original Net Debit/Credit	=	– $2,975
TOTAL PROFIT/LOSS		$2,025

The maximum loss associated with this trade equals the initial net debit. This occurs if the position is held to expiration, and the market trades to the common strike price. At this point, both options are at-the-money and, therefore, worthless. They are abandoned, and the trader is left with a loss equal to the initial debit.

The maximum possible profit is open ended. It is limited only by the extent to which the market may trend over the life of the options involved.

The strategy entails an upper and a lower breakeven equal to the common strike plus and minus the initial net debit. In this case, the net debit (expressed in cents per mark) equals 2.38, so the upper and lower breakeven may be calculated as 47.38 and 42.62, respectively.

Consider that at a price of 47.38, the put is out-of-the-money and worthless at expiration. The call is in-the-money and exercised for a gross profit on exercise of 2.38. This offsets the original net debit and results in a breakeven situation.

If the market falls to 42.62, the call is out-of-the-money and worthless. The put is exercised for 2.38, offsetting the original investment and, again, a breakeven situation occurs.

Long Straddle:

Maximum Loss = Initial Net Debit

Upper B/E = Strike + Net Debit

Lower B/E = Strike − Net Debit

You can earn a profit pursuing this strategy regardless of whether the market is trending upwards or downwards. The critical condition is that the market does indeed move significantly in either direction.

Thus this trade is nondirectional. Volatility, as defined in the context of option markets, is likewise nondirectional. An anticipation of high volatility implies no anticipation with respect to likely market direction. (The nondirectional nature of this trade is indicated by the initial net delta of 0.04—insignificantly different than zero!) The long straddle is the epitome of the volatility trade!

Unfortunately, time value decay takes its toll on the long straddle. This is particularly apparent when you place the straddle near-the-money and the market remains relatively stable. Not only does time value decay accelerate for near-the-moneys, but convexity is also most severe. This may be confirmed by following the value of the straddle as expiration draws near. The shorter the term to expiration, the more bowed the value curves become.

This means the value of a near-term long straddle can advance very sharply if the market should rise or fall by a relatively small amount, a situation which is particularly pronounced when you consider that fluctuating prices may well drive volatilities upward. Since vegas are relatively high for near-the-money options, this may have a dramatic effect upon the value of the straddle.

If you are slightly more bullish than bearish or bearish than bullish, you may wish to enter the straddle using options struck below the market (an in-the-money call and an out-of-the-money put) or struck above the market (an out-of-the-money call and an in-the-money put).

The bullish or bearish orientation of a long straddle is reflected in the net deltas and the relation of the upper and lower breakevens to the market. This is underscored by inspecting the probabilities that the market will run over or under the upper or lower breakeven by expiration, respectively.

Example: On June 19th, you could have entered into a variety of long straddles using options on September 1986 deutsche mark futures (see Figures 5–10 and 5–11). September futures were at 44.04 cents per mark. Calculate the net cost, net delta, breakevens, and probability of falling above the upper breakeven point, below the lower breakeven point, or between the two breakevens by expiration.

Long DM Straddles with Different Strikes

Strike	Cost	Net Delta	B/E Low	B/E High	Probability < Low BE	Probability Between	Probability > High BE
43.00	2.89	0.52	40.11	45.89	4.5%	56.3%	39.2%
44.00	2.51	0.29	41.49	46.51	11.2%	57.0%	31.7%
45.00	2.38	0.04	42.62	47.38	20.5%	57.0%	22.5%
46.00	2.55	−0.22	43.45	48.55	29.8%	56.7%	13.4%
47.00	2.93	−0.44	44.07	49.93	37.4%	56.1%	6.5%

(These probabilities were calculated based on the *average* implied volatility of the put and call.)

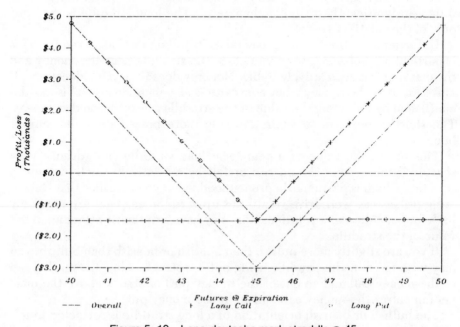

Figure 5–10   Long deutsche mark straddle @ 45.

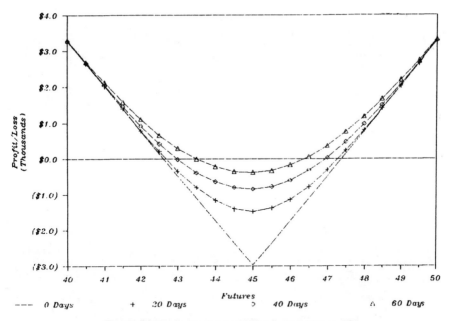

Figure 5–11   Long deutsche mark straddle @ 45.

Just as you can buy a put and a call to create a long straddle, you can sell a put and a call to create a short straddle. A short straddle allows you to take advantage of the possibility that the market will trade in a range between the breakeven points or that volatility will decline.

Just as the long straddle is a classic way to take advantage of volatility or heavily trending price movement (of an indeterminate direction), a short straddle is thought of as the classic way to take advantage of time value decay.

Example: It is June 19th, 1986, and you sell a call exercisable for deutsche mark futures with a strike of 45 expiring in September for a 1.21 premium ($1,512 per 125,000 mark contract) (see Figures 5–12 and 5–13). Simultaneously, you sell a 45 put for 1.17 ($1,462 per contract).

Short 1 Sep. 45.00 Call(s)	@ 1.21	=	$1,512
Imp. Volatility = 14.52% Delta = − 0.51			
Short 1 Sep. 45.00 Put(s)	@ 1.17	=	$1,462
Imp. Volatility = 14.51% Delta = 0.48			
NET CREDIT			$2,975
NET DELTA			− 0.04

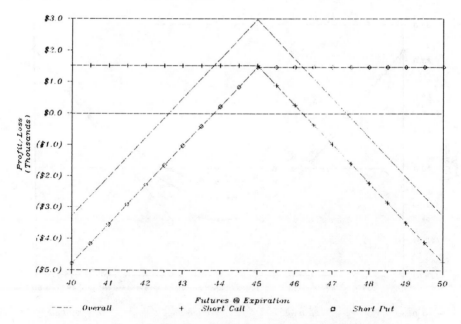

Figure 5–12   Short deutsche mark straddle @ 45.

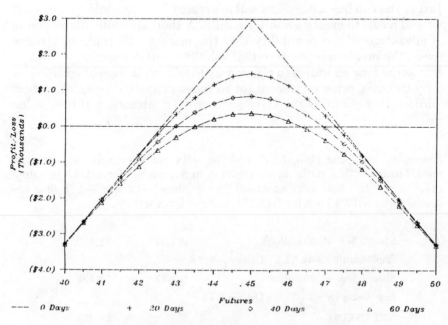

Figure 5–13   Short deutsche mark straddle @ 45.

130

This trade entails an initial net credit of $2,975. What would happen if the strategy were held 78 days until expiration on September 5, 1986?
    If the price falls to 41.00:

Abandon 1 Sep. 45.00 Call(s)	@ 0.00	=	$0
Exercise 1 Sep. 45.00 Put(s)	@ 4.00	=	– $5,000
Original Net Debit/Credit		=	$2,975
TOTAL PROFIT/LOSS			– $2,025

If the price remains relatively stable at 45.00:

Abandon 1 Sep. 45.00 Call(s)	@ 0.00	=	$0
Abandon 1 Sep. 45.00 Put(s)	@ 0.00	=	$0
Original Net Debit/Credit		=	$2,975
TOTAL PROFIT/LOSS			$2,975

If the price rises to 49.00:

Exercise 1 Sep. 45.00 Call(s)	@ 4.00	=	– $5,000
Abandon 1 Sep. 45.00 Put(s)	@ 0.00	=	$0
Original Net Debit/Credit		=	$2,975
TOTAL PROFIT/LOSS			– $2,025

The risk/reward parameters of the short straddle are the exact opposite of those of the long straddle. Rather than an initial net debit, the short straddle means you receive premium—an initial net credit. This credit (2.38 cents per mark or $2,975 in the case illustrated above) represents the maximum possible profit presuming that the market trades to the common strike price by expiration. Under these circumstances, both options are at-the-money and worthless at expiration, and you are left with the initial net credit.

If the market rallies, the call falls in-the-money. It will be exercised against the straddle seller. At some point, losses accruing from the exercise of the call will overcome the initial receipt of the net credit, resulting in a net loss. This occurs at a price equal to the common strike plus the net credit. In the preceding case, this occurs at 47.28 (the 45 strike price plus the credit of 2.38). This defines the upper breakeven point.

If the market falls, the put will be in-the-money. It too can be expected to be exercised. At some point losses accruing from the exercise of the put will overcome the initial receipt of the net credit, resulting in a net loss. This point occurs at the lower breakeven point or the common strike *less* the net credit. In this case, the lower breakeven may be calculated as 42.62 (45 less 2.38).

Short Straddle:

Maximum Profit = Initial Net Credit

Upper B/E = Strike + Net Credit

Lower B/E = Strike − Net Credit

Like the long straddle, the short straddle is generally placed at- or near-the-money. However, if you were just slightly bullish or bearish, you would sell straddles with strikes just above or below the market.

Do not get too far away from-the-money, however, or the straddle will backfire. The intent, after all, is to take advantage of time value decay. If you get too far away-from-the-money, you will be selling straddles with very little time value left to decay. Moreover, this decay will not accelerate. On the positive side, however, is the fact that convexity will not be as severe.

Strangles

A straddle involves the purchase of both a put and a call or the sale of a put and call. Likewise, a *strangle* involves either the purchase or sale of puts and calls. Unlike the straddle where both put and call share a common strike price, the strangle involves a low-struck put and a high-struck call.

A *strangle* entails the purchase of a put and a call or the sale of a put and a call. The two options which comprise the strangle share a common expiration date but differ with respect to strike price. In particular, the put has a low strike price, and the call has a higher strike price than the put.

A "long strangle" entails the purchase of a low-struck put and the purchase of a higher-struck call; a "short strangle" entails the sale of a low-struck put and the sale of a higher-struck call. Because strangles are generally placed when the market is trading between the two strike price levels, this implies that a strangle involves two out-of-the-money options.

Example: It is June 19th, 1986, and you buy a call exercisable for deutsche mark futures with a strike of 46 expiring in September for a 0.80 premium ($1,000 per 125,000 mark contract). Simultaneously, you buy a 44 put for .74 ($925 per contract).

Long 1 Sep. 46.00 Call(s)	@ 0.80	= − $1,000
Imp. Volatility = 14.67% Delta = 0.39		
Long 1 Sep. 44.00 Put(s)	@ 0.74	= − $925
Imp. Volatility = 14.60% Delta = − 0.35		
NET DEBIT		$1,925
NET DELTA		0.04

This trade entails an initial net debit of $1,925. What would happen if the strategy were held 78 days until expiration on September 5, 1986?

If the price falls to 41.00:

Abandon 1 Sep. 46.00 Call(s)	@ 0.00	=	$0
Exercise 1 Sep. 44.00 Put(s)	@ 3.00	=	$3,750
Original Net Debit/Credit		=	− $1,925
TOTAL PROFIT/LOSS			$1,825

If the price remains relatively stable at 45.00:

Abandon 1 Sep. 46.00 Call(s)	@ 0.00	=	$0
Abandon 1 Sep. 44.00 Put(s)	@ 0.00	=	$0
Original Net Debit/Credit		=	− $1,925
TOTAL PROFIT/LOSS			− $1,925

If the price rallies to 49.00:

Exercise 1 Sep. 46.00 Call(s)	@ 3.00	=	$3,750
Abandon 1 Sep. 44.00 Put(s)	@ 0.00	=	$0
Original Net Debit/Credit		=	− $1,925
TOTAL PROFIT/LOSS			$1,825

The long strangle is like the long straddle insofar as it permits you to take advantage of a market breaking sharply in either the upward or downward direction. But if the market should trade in an essentially neutral pattern between the two strikes, both options fall out-of-the-money at expiration and are worthless, and the strangle trader is left with the loss of the initial net debit. In the latter case this amounts to 1.54 points or $1,925.

If the market breaks over the upper strike, the call runs into-the-money. At some point, the profit on exercise of the call will overcome the initial net debit permitting the trader to earn a profit. If the market breaks under the lower strike, the put runs into-the-money. At some point, the profit on exercise of the put will overcome the initial net debit resulting in profit.

The upper and lower breakeven points may be defined as the call strike plus the net debit and the put strike less the net debit, respectively. In the latter case, these points may be calculated as 47.54 (46 + 1.54) and 42.46 (44 − 1.54).

Long Strangle:

Maximum Loss = Initial Net Debit

Upper B/E = Call Strike + Net Debit

Lower B/E = Put Strike − Net Debit

The trading characteristics of the long strangle are similar to those of the straddle, that is, it is a nondirectional volatility play which suffers from the phenomenon of time value decay. However, it is a "less cutting" strategy in a number of respects.

To illustrate this point, assume that you enter a strangle when the market is midway between the two strikes and a straddle which is struck at-the-money. At-the-money options are more responsive to time value decay and to shifting volatilities than are out-of-the-money options. As such, the strangle is often regarded as a more conservative strategy than the straddle.

This is apparent when you consider that the net debit (maximum risk) associated with the 44/46 strangle equals $1,925. The net debit (maximum risk) associated with the straddle illustrated earlier was much higher at $2,975. This is compensated, however, by the relatively wide breakevens on the strangle (42.46–47.54) as opposed to the straddle (42.62–47.38).

If you want to employ a more or less conservative strangle, you can vary the interval between strikes. In general, the greater the interval, the more conservative (less cost, wider range) is the strategy. Or you may want to apply a slightly bullish or bearish orientation to the strategy by using options with lower strikes as opposed to options with higher strikes.

Example: On June 19th, September 1986 deutsche mark options were available with a variety of strikes. Let us examine the cost, net delta, breakevens, and probability of running over or under the upper and lower breakeven by expiration.

Long DM Strangles with Different Strikes

Strikes	Cost	Net Delta	B/E Low	B/E High	Probability < Low BE	Probability > High BE
43/44	2.21	0.40	40.79	46.21	7.3%	35.3%
44/45	1.95	0.16	42.05	46.95	15.4%	26.9%
45/46	1.97	−0.09	43.03	47.97	24.9%	17.5%
46/47	2.25	−0.33	43.75	49.25	33.5%	9.4%
43/45	1.65	0.28	41.35	46.65	10.3%	30.2%
44/46	1.54	0.04	42.46	47.54	19.2%	21.2%
45/47	1.67	−0.20	43.33	48.67	28.3%	12.6%
43/46	1.24	0.15	41.76	47.24	13.3%	24.2%
44/47	1.24	−0.07	43.33	48.67	22.2%	15.6%
43/47	0.94	0.04	42.06	47.94	15.8%	18.0%

(These probabilities were calculated based on the *average* implied volatility of the put and call.)

Just as you can buy a put and a call to create a long strangle, you can sell a put and a call to create a short strangle. Like a short straddle, the short strangle allows you to take advantage of a neutral market or declining volatility, to capitalize on time value decay.

Example: It is June 19th, 1986, and you sell a call exercisable for deutsche mark futures with a strike of 46 expiring in September for a 0.80 premium ($1,000 per 125,000 mark contract). Simultaneously, you sell a 44 put for 0.74 ($925 per contract) (see Figures 5–14 and 5–15).

Short 1 Sep. 46.00 Call(s)	@ 0.80	=	$1,000
Imp. Volatility = 14.67% Delta = − 0.39			
Short 1 Sep. 44.00 Put(s)	@ 0.74	=	$925
Imp. Volatility = 14.60% Delta = 0.35			
NET CREDIT			$1,925
NET DELTA			− 0.04

This trade entails an initial net credit of $1,925. What would happen if the strategy were held 78 days until expiration on September 5, 1986?
   If the price falls to 41.00:

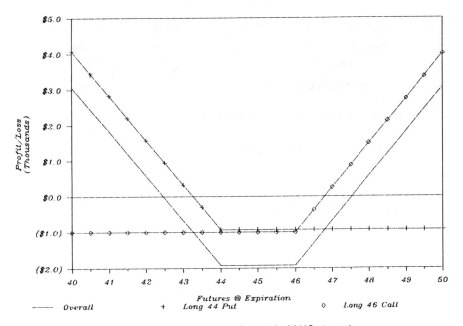

Figure 5–14   Long deutsche mark 44/46 strangle.

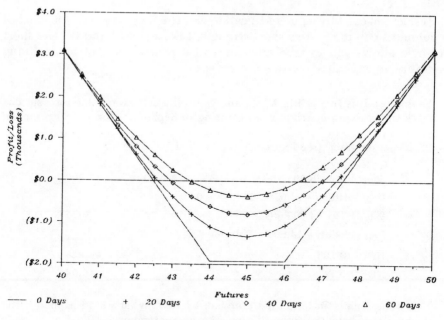

Figure 5–15   Long deutsche mark 44/46 strangle.

Abandon 1 Sep. 46.00 Call(s)	@ 0.00	=	$0
Exercise 1 Sep. 44.00 Put(s)	@ 3.00	=	– $3,750
Original Net Debit/Credit		=	$1,925
TOTAL PROFIT/LOSS			– $1,825

If the price remains relatively stable at 45.00:

Abandon 1 Sep. 46.00 Call(s)	@ 0.00	=	$0
Abandon 1 Sep. 44.00 Put(s)	@ 0.00	=	$0
Original net Debit/Credit		=	$1,925
TOTAL PROFIT/LOSS			$1,925

If the price rises to 49.00:

Exercise 1 Sep. 46.00 Call(s)	@ 3.00	=	– $3,750
Abandon 1 Sep. 44.00 Put(s)	@ 0.00	=	$0
Original Net Debit/Credit		=	$1,925
TOTAL PROFIT/LOSS			– $1,825

The risk/reward parameters of the short strangle are the exact opposite of those of the long strangle. Like a short straddle, the short strangle allows you to receive premium on balance—an initial net credit (see Figures 5–16 and 5–17).

This credit (1.54 cents per mark or $1,925 in the case illustrated previously) represents the maximum possible profit presuming that the market trades to the common strike price at expiration. Under these circumstances, both options fall out-of-the-money and worthless and you are left with the initial net credit.

If the market rallies beyond the upper strike, the call falls in-the-money. It will be exercised against the strangle seller. At some point, losses accruing from the exercise of the call will overcome the initial receipt of the net credit, resulting in a net loss. This occurs at a price equal to the call strike plus the net credit. In the preceding case, it falls at 47.54 (the 46 strike price plus the credit of 1.54), defining the upper breakeven point.

If the market declines, the put falls in-the-money. It too can be expected to be exercised. At some point losses accruing from the exercise of the put will overcome the initial receipt of the net credit, resulting in a net loss.

The lower breakeven point occurs at the common strike *less* the net credit. For this example, the lower breakeven may be calculated as 42.46 (44 less 1.54).

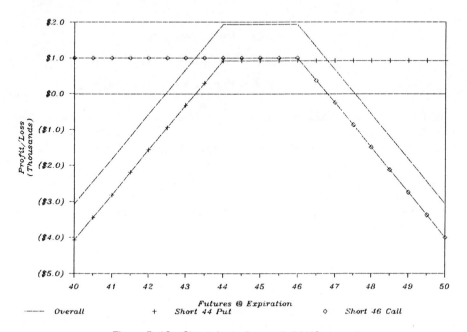

Figure 5–16   Short deutsche mark 44/46 strangle.

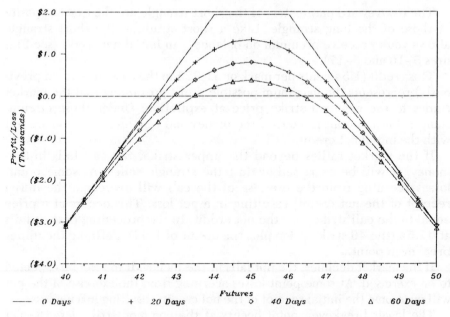

Figure 5–17   Short deutsche mark 44/46 strangle.

Short Strangle:

Maximum Profit = Initial Net Credit

Upper B/E = Call Strike + Net Credit

Lower B/E = Put Strike − Net Credit

Just as the long strangle is more conservative than the long straddle, the short strangle is also more conservative than the short straddle. The profitable range associated with a short strangle is somewhat wider than that of a short straddle, but the maximum profit is reduced.

Moreover, time value decay is not as strong for the out-of-the-money options that make up a strangle than the near-to-the-money options associated with a straddle. This is counterbalanced by the reduced convexity associated with strangles.

Guts

A *guts* trade is similar to a straddle or a strangle in that it involves the purchase of a put and a call or the sale of a put and a call. Straddles are often thought of as the purchase or sale of at-the-money puts and calls.

Strangles are thought of as the purchase or sale of out-of-the-money puts and calls.

Guts may be thought of as the purchase or sale of in-the-money options, that is, a guts trade involves a high-struck put and a low-struck call.

A *guts* entails the purchase of a put and a call or the sale of a put and a call. The two options which comprise the guts share a common expiration date but differ with respect to strike price. In particular, the put has a high strike price, and the call is put on at a relatively lower strike price.

A "long guts" is the purchase of a high-struck put and the purchase of a low-struck call; a "short guts" is the sale of a high-struck put and the sale of a low-struck call. Because guts are generally placed when the market is trading between the two strike prices, this implies that a guts involves two in-the-money options.

Example: It is June 19th, 1986, and you buy a call exercisable for deutsche mark futures with a strike of 44 expiring in September for a 1.77 cent premium ($2,212 per 125,000 mark contract). Simultaneously, you buy a 46 put for 1.75 cents ($2,187 per contract) (see Figures 5–18 and 5–19).

Long 1 Sep. 44.00 Call(s)	@ 1.77	=	– $2,212
Imp. Volatility = 14.64% Delta = 0.64			
Long 1 Sep. 46.00 Put(s)	@ 1.75	=	$2,187
Imp. Volatility = 14.70% Delta = – 0.60			
NET DEBIT			$4,400
NET DELTA			0.04

This trade entails an initial net debit of $4,400. What would happen if the strategy were held 78 days until expiration on September 5, 1986?

If the price falls to 41.00:

Abandon 1 Sep. 44.00 Call(s)	@ 0.00	=	$0
Exercise 1 Sep. 46.00 Put(s)	@ 5.00	=	$6,250
Original Net Debit/Credit		=	– $4,400
TOTAL PROFIT/LOSS			$1,850

If the price remains relatively stable at 45.00:

Exercise 1 Sep. 44.00 Call(s)	@ 1.00	=	$1,250
Exercise 1 Sep. 46.00 Put(s)	@ 1.00	=	$1,250
Original Net Debit/Credit		=	– $4,400
TOTAL PROFIT/LOSS			– $1,900

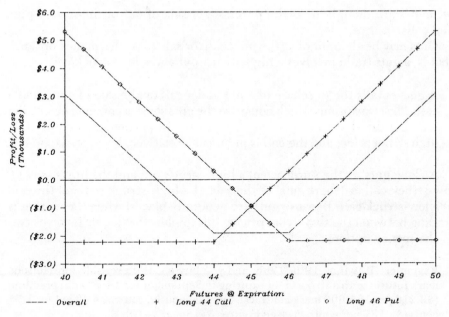

Figure 5-18   Long deutsche mark 44/46 guts.

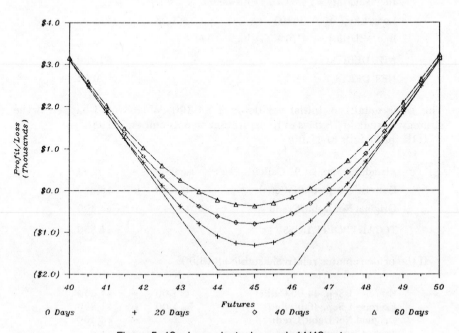

Figure 5-19   Long deutsche mark 44/46 guts.

If the price rallies to 49.00:

Exercise 1 Sep. 44.00 Call(s)	@ 5.00	=	$6,250
Abandon 1 Sep. 46.00 Put(s)	@ 0.00	=	$0
Original Net Debit/Credit		=	− $4,400
TOTAL PROFIT/LOSS			$1,850

The guts results in a relatively large initial debit. This 44/46 guts entails a net debit of $4,400; the 44/46 strangle debit is relatively low at $1,925. Yet the risk/reward profile of the long guts strongly resembles that of the long strangle. A fixed loss is realized between the two strikes, and profits may ensue if the market breaks in either direction. The magnitude of these profits and losses is similar.

To illustrate the similarity, if the market remains between the two strikes by expiration, both options fall in-the-money. Both are exercised. The profit on exercise will total to equal the difference in strikes. Thus the long guts generates a loss equal to the debit less the difference in strikes as long as the market trades within the two strike prices by expiration.

Assume that the market runs to 44.50. This means that the call is 0.50 in-the-money and the put 1.50 in-the-money for a total of 2.00 cents/ mark. The loss equals the 3.52 cent debit less 2.00 cents or 1.52 cents (or $1,900 per 125,000 mark contract). This is similar to the 1.54 cent loss on the long strangle.

If, however, the market breaks sharply in either direction, profits may result. The breakevens may be defined as the upper strike (the put strike) plus the maximum possible loss and the lower strike (the call strike) minus the maximum possible loss. This comes to 42.48 and 47.52—again quite similar to the range of 42.46 and 47.54 associated with the long strangle.

Long Guts:

Maximum Loss = Initial Net Debit − Difference in Strikes

Upper B/E = Put Strike + Maximum Loss

Lower B/E = Call Strike − Maximum Loss

The main difference between the long guts and long strangle is that the strangle results in a much reduced initial net debit. In other words, it takes less money to finance a strangle—a position with an analogous risk/reward structure.

Therefore, a strangle provides increased leverage! This follows from the observation that out-of-the-moneys have greater elasticity than do at- or in-the-money options. Note, however, that the market tends to compensate you in the sense that the maximum loss is slightly less and, therefore, the breakeven range is somewhat narrower with the long guts than with the long strangle.

A short guts is similar to a short strangle in terms of its risk/reward profile. The notable exception is that the short guts generates a much larger initial net credit—funds that presumably the trader will invest at some short-term interest rate.

Example: It is June 19th, 1986, and you sell a call exercisable for deutsche mark futures with a strike of 44 expiring in September for a 1.77 premium ($2,212 per 125,000 mark contract). Simultaneously, you sell a 46 put for 1.75 ($2,187 per contract) (see Figures 5–20 and 5–21).

Short 1 Sep. 44.00 Call(s) @ 1.77	=	$2,212
Imp. Volatility = 14.64% Delta = – 0.64		
Short 1 Sep. 46.00 Put(s) 1.75	=	$2,187
Imp. Volatility = 14.70% Delta = 0.60		
NET CREDIT		$4,400
NET DELTA		– 0.04

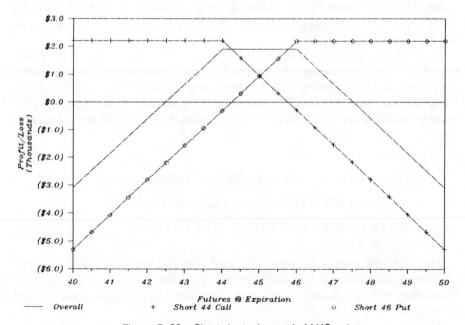

Figure 5–20   Short deutsche mark 44/46 guts.

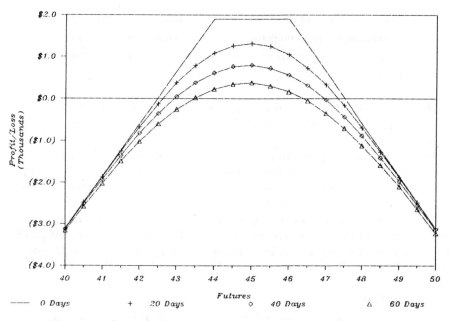

Figure 5–21   Short deutsche mark 44/46 guts.

This trade entails an initial net credit of $4,400. What would happen if the strategy were held 78 days until expiration on September 5, 1986?
    If the price falls to 41.00:

Abandon 1 Sep. 44.00 Call(s)	@ 0.00	=	$0
Exercise 1 Sep. 46.00 Put(s)	@ 5.00	=	– $6,250
Original Net Debit/Credit		=	$4,400
TOTAL PROFIT/LOSS			– $1,850

If the price remains relatively stable at 45.00:

Exercise 1 Sep. 44.00 Call(s)	@ 1.00	=	– $1,250
Exercise 1 Sep. 46.00 Put(s)	@ 1.00	=	– $1,250
Original Net Debit/Credit		=	$4,400
TOTAL PROFIT/LOSS			$1,900

If the price rises to 49.00:

Exercise 1 Sep. 44.00 Call(s)	@ 5.00	=	– $6,250
Abandon 1 Sep. 46.00 Put(s)	@ 0.00	=	$0
Original Net Debit/Credit		=	$4,400
TOTAL PROFIT/LOSS			– $1,850

Here the maximum return equals the net credit less the difference in strikes. In this case, that equals 3.52 less 2.00 or 1.52 ($1,900 per 125,000 mark contract).

Because the short guts entails a large initial net credit, the market may penalize the guts trader relative to the short strangle trader. Note that the maximum return associated with the short guts (1.52) is slightly less than the maximum return associated with the strangle (1.54).

The breakevens are at the upper strike (the put strike) plus the maximum profit and the lower strike (the call strike) less the maximum profit. This comes to 42.48 and 47.52, a range slightly narrower than the profit range (42.46 and 47.54) associated with the short strangle.

Short Guts:

Maximum Profit = Difference in Strikes – Initial Net Credit

Upper B/E = Put Strike + Maximum Profit

Lower B/E = Call Strike – Maximum Profit

Comparing Straddles, Strangles, and Guts

Compare the relative merits of entering the straddle, strangle, or guts trades illustrated in this chapter. We can do this by comparing the responsiveness of these trades to fluctuating prices, the onset of time, and shifting volatilities. This may be accomplished readily by examining the net deltas, gammas, vegas, and thetas associated with the three strategies.

	ImpVol	Elas.	Delta	Gamma	Vega	Theta
44 Call	14.64%	36.1%	0.64	0.120	0.076	0.007
45 Call	14.52%	42.3%	0.51	0.132	0.082	0.007
46 Call	14.67%	48.2%	0.39	0.124	0.079	0.007
44 Put	14.60%	47.0%	0.35	0.120	0.076	0.007
45 Put	14.51%	40.6%	0.47	0.130	0.082	0.007
46 Put	14.70%	34.4%	0.60	0.124	0.079	0.007

For now restrict this consideration to *long* strategies. While many of the statistics are quite similar (in some cases identical), the net vegas indicate

	Debit	Delta	Net Gamma	Vega	Theta
Long 45 Straddle	$2,975	0.04	0.002	0.164	−0.014
Long 44/46 Strangle	$1,925	0.04	0.004	0.155	−0.014
Long 44/46 Guts	$4,400	0.04	−0.004	0.155	−0.014

that the straddle is most sensitive to fluctuating volatility levels. This suggests that the greatest absolute profit may be found by using near-the-money straddles to take advantage of anticipated shifts in volatility.

Example: Let us illustrate what would happen if volatility rose by 2 percent over one day to 16.5 percent.
Long Straddle:

Sell 1 Sep. 45.00 Call(s)	@ 1.36	=	$1,700
Sell 1 Sep. 45.00 Put(s)	@ 1.32	=	$1,650
Original Net Debit/Credit		=	− $2,975
TOTAL PROFIT/LOSS			$375

Long Strangle:

Sell 1 Sep. 46.00 Call(s)	@ 0.94	=	$1,175
Sell 1 Sep. 44.00 Put(s)	@ 0.88	=	$1,100
Original Net Debit/Credit		=	− $1,925
TOTAL PROFIT/LOSS			$350

Long Guts:

Sell 1 Sep. 44.00 Call(s)	@ 1.90	=	$2,375
Sell 1 Sep. 46.00 Put(s)	@ 1.88	=	$2,350
Original Net Debit/Credit		=	− $4,400
TOTAL PROFIT/LOSS			$325

The straddle is marginally more responsive to the upward swing in volatility than are the strangle or guts. (Of course, the implied volatilities on the at-the-moneys which comprise the straddle were a little below the volatilities associated with the in- and out-of-the-moneys, so a jump to 16.5 percent can be expected to be slightly more significant.)

But compare the profit on the three strategies with the initial investment:

	Profit	Investment	Return
Straddle	$375	$2,975	12.6%
Strangle	$350	$1,925	18.2%
Guts	$325	$4,400	7.4%

While the straddle produces marginally superior absolute returns, the percentage profit associated with the strangle is by far the most attractive. This underscores the superior leverage associated with out-of-the-money options as opposed to in-the-money options.

Shorting Volatility with Limited Risk

Straddles and strangles are popular volatility plays. Many volatility traders, however, lament the fact that when you sell these strategies to capitalize on potentially declining volatility, you are subject to open-ended risks. As a result, many option traders turn to *anti-volatility plays* which entail strictly limited risk such as *butterflies* and *condors.*

In many respects, butterflies resemble straddles—returns are maximized or peaked at the strike price at which options are sold. Unlike the straddle, the butterfly is comprised of four, rather than two, options. Moreover, these options may be all calls, all puts, or a combination of puts and calls.

For example, a trader may buy two extreme-struck calls and sell two calls with an intermediate strike price or buy two-extreme-struck puts and sell two puts with an intermediate strike price. On the other hand, the strategy may be composed of a low-struck long call (put), an intermediate-struck short call (put), an intermediate-struck short put (call), and a high-struck long put (call).

This strategy is intended to capitalize on declining volatility or neutral markets. Nonetheless, the strategy generally results in an initial net debit and therefore, it is often referred to as a "long" butterfly.

A *long butterfly* represents a way to capitalize on stable prices, time value decay, or declining volatility. A long butterfly entails the purchase of extreme-struck options (with a high and a low strike price) and the sale of two options with an intermediate strike price. This strategy may be established with all calls, all puts, or a combination of puts and calls.

Example: On June 19th, you enter a long butterfly by buying one 44 deutsche mark call at 1.77, selling two 45 calls at 1.21 each piece, and buying one 46 call at 0.80 (see Figures 5–22 and 5–23). The market was at 44.05 at the time. This entails an initial net debit of $187.

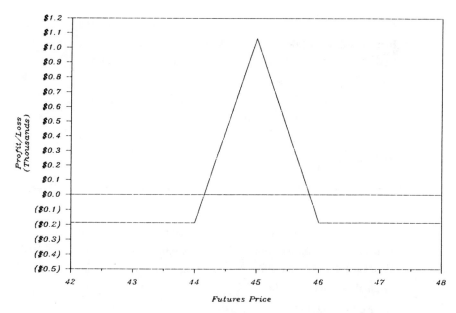

Figure 5–22   Long 44/45/46 deutsche mark butterfly.

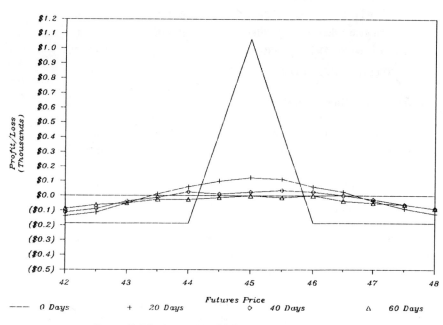

---- 0 Days   +   20 Days   ◇   40 Days   Δ   60 Days

Figure 5–23   Long 44/45/46 deutsche mark butterfly.

147

Long 1 Sep. 44.00 Call(s)	@ 1.77	=	−$2,212
Imp. Volatility = 14.64% Delta = 0.64			
Short 2 Sep. 45.00 Call(s)	@ 1.21	=	$3,025
Imp. Volatility = 14.52% Delta = − 0.51			
Long 1 Sep. 46.00 Call(s)	@ 0.80	=	−$1,000
Imp. Volatility = 14.67% Delta = 0.39			
NET DEBIT			$187
NET DELTA			0.00

What happens at expiration if the market rallies, remains stable, or declines?
If the price falls to 41.00:

Abandon 1 Sep. 44.00 Call(s)	@ 0.00	=	$0
Abandon 2 Sep. 45.00 Call(s)	@ 0.00	=	$0
Abandon 1 Sep. 46.00 Call(s)	@ 0.00	=	$0
Original Net Debit/Credit		=	$ − 187
TOTAL PROFIT/LOSS			$ − 187

If the price remains relatively stable at 45.00

Exercise 1 Sep. 44.00 Call(s)	@ 1.00	=	$1,250
Abandon 2 Sep. 45.00 Call(s)	@ 0.00	=	$0
Abandon 1 Sep. 46.00 Call(s)	@ 0.00	=	$0
Original Net Debit/Credit		=	$ − 187
TOTAL PROFIT/LOSS			$1,062

If the price rallies to 49.00:

Exercise 1 Sep. 44.00 Call(s)	@ 5.00	=	$6,250
Exercise 2 Sep. 45.00 Call(s)	@ 4.00	=	−$10,000
Exercise 1 Sep. 46.00 Call(s)	@ 3.00	=	$3,750
Original Net Debit/Credit		=	− $187
TOTAL PROFIT/LOSS			− $187

If the market remains at or under the lower of the three strikes by
expiration, all three options fall out-of-the-money and worthless, and the
butterfly buyer is left with a loss equal to the initial net debit of $187.

If the market trades to the intermediate strike price of 45 by expiration,
the 44 call is in-the-money by one point ($1,250) and exercised, the two
45 calls are at-the-money and worthless, while the single 46 call is out-of-
the-money and also worthless. Therefore the trade results in the maximum

profit equal to the in-the-money value of the low-struck long call less the initial net debit or $1,062 ($1,250 less $187).

If the market advances to the upper strike of 46 by expiration, the 44 call is exercised for its in-the-money value of $2,500. Unfortunately, the two 45 short calls are exercised against the trader for a loss of $1,250 each or $2,500 in total. The $2,500 profit is offset by the $2,500 loss, and the trader is left with a loss equal to the initial net debit of $187.

At all points over the higher of the two strikes, the higher-struck call is in-the-money and will be exercised along with the low-struck call. Unfortunately, profits accruing on the two long calls are offset by losses associated with the two short calls. The trader is left with a loss equal to the initial net debit.

An upper and a lower breakeven point may be identified as the intermediate strike price (45) plus and minus the maximum possible profit (0.85) or 44.15 and 45.85.

Long Butterfly:

Maximum Profit = Difference in Strikes − Initial Net Debit

Upper B/E = Intermediate Strike + Maximum Profit

Lower B/E = Intermediate Strike − Maximum Profit

Maximum Loss = Initial Net Debit

A butterfly resembles a straddle with the exception that risk is limited if the market rallies above or falls below the extreme strike prices. In its most basic terms, a butterfly may be thought of as the combination of a bullish vertical spread and a bearish vertical spread which share one common strike price.

A condor resembles a strangle with limited risk. It may be thought of as the combination of bullish and bearish vertical spreads except that the spreads do not share any common strikes. Again, the condor may be composed of all calls, all puts, or a combination of both calls and puts. Like a long butterfly, the long condor is intended to capitalize on time value decay or a neutral market.

The condor is generally more conservative than the butterfly. The strategy results in a constant return between the two intermediate strikes (like a strangle); this return is usually less than the maximum return associated with a butterfly. However, the profitable range is wider in compensation.

Example: On June 19th, you enter a long condor by buying a 44 deutsche mark call at 1.77, selling a 45 call at 1.21, selling a 46 call at 0.80 and buying a 47 call at 0.50 (see Figures 5–24 and 5–25). The market is at 44.05 at the time. This entails an initial net debit of $325.

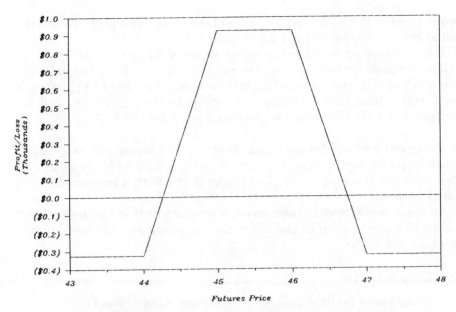

Figure 5-24   Long 44/45/46/47 deutsche mark condor.

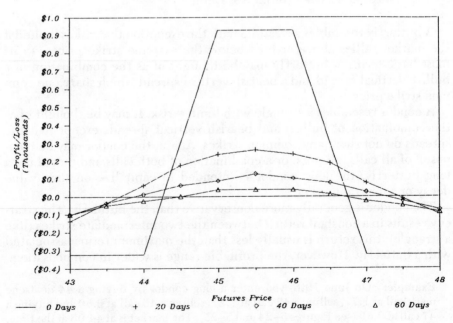

— 0 Days   + 20 Days   ◇ 40 Days   △ 60 Days

Figure 5-25   Long 44/45/46/47 deutsche mark condor.

150

Long 1 Sep. 44. Call(s)	@ 1.77	=	−$2,212
Imp. Volatility = 14.64% Delta = 0.64			
Short 1 Sep. 45.00 Call(s)	@ 1.21	=	$1,512
Imp. Volatility = 14.52% Delta = − 0.51			
Short 1 Sep. 46.00 Call(s)	@ 0.80	=	$1,000
Imp. Volatility = 14.67% Delta = − 0.39			
Long 1 Sep. 47.00 Call(s)	@ 0.50	=	− $625
Imp. Volatility = 14.73% Delta = 0.27			
NET DEBIT			$325.00
NET DELTA			0.01

What happens by expiration if the market rallies, remains stable, or declines? If the price falls to 41.00:

Abandon 1 Sep. 44.00 Call(s)	@ 0.00	=	$0
Abandon 1 Sep. 45.00 Call(s)	@ 0.00	=	$0
Abandon 1 Sep. 46.00 Call(s)	@ 0.00	=	$0
Abandon 1 Sep. 47.00 Call(s)	@ 0.00	=	$0
Original Net Debit/Credit		=	− $325
TOTAL PROFIT/LOSS			− $325

If the price remains relatively stable at 45.00:

Exercise 1 Sep. 44.00 Call(s)	@ 1.00	=	$1,250
Abandon 1 Sep. 45.00 Call(s)	@ 0.00	=	$0
Abandon 1 Sep. 46.00 Call(s)	@ 0.00	=	$0
Abandon 1 Sep. 47.00 Call(s)	@ 0.00	=	$0
Original Net Debit/Credit		=	− $325
TOTAL PROFIT/LOSS			$925

If the price rallies to 49.00:

Exercise 1 Sep. 44.00 Call(s)	@ 5.00	=	$6,250
Exercise 1 Sep. 45.00 Call(s)	@ 4.00	=	− $5,000
Exercise 1 Sep. 46.00 Call(s)	@ 3.00	=	− $3,750
Exercise 1 Sep. 47.00 Call(s)	@ 2.00	=	$2,500
Original Net Debit/Credit		=	− $325
TOTAL PROFIT/LOSS			− $325

As long as the market remains at or under the lower of the four strikes by expiration, all four options fall out-of-the-money and are worthless. The condor buyer is then left with a loss equal to the initial net debit of $325.

If the market trades to the lower intermediate strike price of 45 by expiration, the 44 call is in-the-money by one point or $1,250 and exercised. The 45 call is at–the-money and worthless, while the 46 and 47 calls are out-of-the-money and worthless. Therefore, the trade results in a maximum profit equal to the in-the-money value of the low-struck long call less the initial net debit or $925 ($1,250 less $325).

If the market advances to the upper intermediate strike of 46 by expiration, the 44 call is exercised for its in-the-money value of $2,500. Unfortunately, the short 45 is exercised against the trader for a loss of $1,250. The $2,500 profit is partially offset by the $1,250 loss as well as the initial forfeiture of the $325 debit, and the trader is left with a profit of $925.

At all points over the highest of the four strikes, all four options fall in-the-money and may be expected to be exercised. This results in a wash, and the trader is left with a loss equal to the original net debit.

Long condor:

Maximum Profit = Difference in Strikes – Initial Net Debit

Upper B/E = Upper Intermediate Strike + Maximum Profit

Lower B/E = Lower Intermediate Strike – Maximum Profit

Maximum Loss = Initial Net Debit

QUESTIONS

1. A straddle . . .
   (a) Is just like an option spread.
   (b) Means that you sell a put and a call.
   (c) Involves the purchase or sale of a put and a call at a common strike price.
   (d) Is executed at an initial net credit which represents your maximum profit potential.
   (e) All of the above.
2. A Eurodollar straddle is sold at a strike price of 93.00 for a net credit of 0.43. The upper breakeven point equals _____ and the lower breakeven point equals _____ (fill in the blanks).
3. Which statement is false? Time value decay . . .
   (a) Always accelerates as the option approaches expiration.
   (b) Is a positive factor for the seller of a straddle or a buyer of a butterfly.
   (c) May be explained by comparing an option to an insurance policy.
   (d) Works against the option buyer.
   (e) Tends to accelerate as expiration nears for at- or near-to-the-money options.

4. (a) A strangle is purchased by buying a 92 _____ (put or call) and a 92.50 _____ (put or call) on Eurodollar futures.

   (b) The put is purchased for 0.32 while the call is purchased for 0.12. The initial net _____ (debit or credit) equals _____. The upper and lower breakeven points equal _____ and _____.

5. The difference between a straddle and a strangle is . . .

   (a) A straddle involves two options of the same type with the same strike price.

   (b) A straddle involves a put and a call with the same strike; a strangle involves a low-struck put and high-struck call.

   (c) A strangle is a high-struck put and low-struck call; a straddle is a low-struck call and high-struck put.

   (d) A strangle is a low-struck put and high-struck call; a guts is a high-struck put and low-struck call.

   (e) All of the above.

6. Which statement is false?

   (a) You may either buy or sell a straddle, strangle, or guts.

   (b) When you sell a straddle, strangle, or guts, you position yourself to take advantage of time value decay.

   (c) A butterfly may be thought of as the combination of two vertical spreads.

   (d) A strangle always involves two out-of-the-money options.

   (e) A butterfly may be entered using puts, calls, or some combination of the two.

7. (a) A butterfly is put on in Eurodollar options by buying a 91.50 put at 0.04, selling two 92.00 puts at .14, and buying a 92.50 put at .39. You are _____ (long or short) the butterfly (fill in the blank).

   (b) What is the initial net _____ (debit or credit)?

   (c) What is the maximum possible profit? Where are the breakeven points?

8. Volatility . . .

   (a) Represents the possible upward price movement in the market.

   (b) Is a static concept.

   (c) May be measured using an "implied" or a "historic" volatility.

   (d) Can readily be quantified.

   (e) Increases with the market price.

9. Which statement is false?

   (a) Time value decay accelerates for at- or near-the-money options.

   (b) The time value associated with an in- or out-of-the-money option can "bottom out" prior to expiration.

   (c) It is better to sell a strangle or guts than a straddle to capitalize on time value decay when expiration is close at hand.

   (d) In- and out-of-the-money options react differently to time value decay than do at-the-moneys.

   (e) Changing volatility levels affect in-, at-, and out-of-the-moneys differently.

10. Vega represents _____ (fill in the blank).

11. Theta represents _____ (fill in the blank).

12. Gamma represents _____ (fill in the blank).

6
Hedging with Options

Options are extraordinarily versatile trading and risk-management instruments. This is particularly obvious when one compares the investment characteristics of options with those of futures.

It is often said that while futures may be used to offset or negate the risk associated with holding security or commodity positions, options may be used, not so much to *negate* risk, but to change the nature of the risks to which the hedger is subject! In other words, options allow one to closely tailor risks and rewards. In particular, a hedger can modify the range of potential outcomes to conform to one's price forecast and risk-management objectives.

This section will outline the mechanics and results associated with basic option hedge strategies. We discuss situations under which one strategy becomes more or less attractive relative to an alternate strategy. Finally, we consider more complex hedge strategies designed to capitalize on specific pricing scenarios and to achieve specific objectives.

OPTION HEDGING MECHANICS

The essential idea with a hedging program is to reduce the risks associated with cash market exposure. Consider, for example, a fixed income security investor holding long a cash bond. This is a bullish cash position. Unfortunately, this investor is exposed to the risk that interest rates will increase, diminishing the value of the investment.

The solution to this problem is to establish a bearish futures or options position which at least partially offsets the price risk associated with the long cash position. The three most basic bearish strategies using futures and options are to (1) sell futures, (2) buy puts, or (3) sell calls.

Although this chapter will focus on strategies which may be used to hedge long cash positions, options and futures may, of course, readily be used to hedge short cash positions as well. If one were to hold a short cash position, one would be exposed to the risk of falling interest rates. For example, a dealer may have committed to sell securities in quantities which exceed inventories on hand plus fixed commitments to buy. If rates fall (and prices rise), the dealer will be forced to cover those shorts at prices higher than those currently prevailing.

The solution to this problem is to take on a basically bullish position which at least partially reduces the risk inherent in the short position. Three basic *bullish* strategies are to (1) buy futures, (2) sell puts, and (3) buy calls. These strategies are analagous but opposite to the hedge of a long cash position.

Short Futures Hedge

In order to draw comparisons, let us review the possible results associated with a futures hedge.

Example: An institution buys $10 million face value of the 7 1/4 percent Treasury bond due in 2016 at a price of 101 percent of par on August 26, 1986. The basis point value weighted hedge ratio is equal to 1.25. To hedge this investment against the risk of a possible interest rate advance, the institution sells 125 December 1986 bond futures at 100–01 (See Figure 6–1).

Buy $10 MM 7 1/4% – 16 @ 101–00	=	$10,100,000
Accrued interest @ 8/26/86	=	$202,921
Sell 125 Bond futures @ 100–01	=	—
NET INVESTMENT	=	$10,302,921

Assume that cash/futures convergence occurs at an annual rate of 1.40 percent (that is, cost of carry equals 1.40 percent) and that the hedge is unwound on November 15, 1986. What might happen if the cash market fell 10 points, rose 10 points, or remained stable?

If 7 1/4s fall to 91–00:

Bond @ 11/15/86 @ 91–00	=	$9,100,000
Accrued interest rec'd	=	$0
Coupon income	=	$362,500
Reinvestment income @ 5.8%	=	$0
Long futures @ 92–11	=	$960,938
NET CREDITS	=	$10,423,438

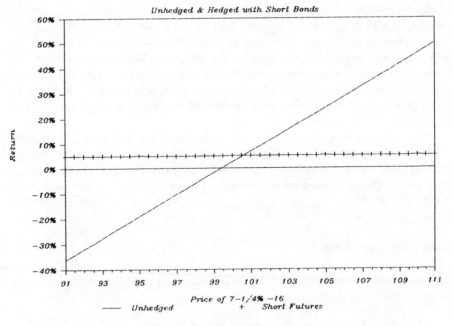

Figure 6–1   Returns on 7¼%–16.

If 7¼s remain stable at 101–00:

Bond @ 11/15/86 @ 101–00	=	$10,100,000
Accrued interest rec'd	=	$0
Coupon income	=	$362,500
Reinvestment income @ 5.8%	=	$0
Long futures @ 100–11	=	– $39,063
NET CREDITS	=	$10,423,437

If 7¼s rally to 111–00:

Bond @ 11/15/86 @ 111–00	=	$11,100,000
Accrued interest rec'd	=	$0
Coupon income	=	$362,500
Reinvestment income @ 5.8%	=	$0
Long futures @ 108–11	=	– $1,039,063
NET CREDITS	=	$10,423,437

The foregoing simulation is based on the assumption that the hedge ratio of 125 bonds per $10 million face value securities will, in fact, prove effective. In other words, basis risk is kept to a minimum.

Hedged and Unhedged Returns
(In Dollars and as a Percentage)

	Cash @ 91	@ 101	@ 111
Unhedged:	−$840,421	$159,579	$1,159,579
	−36.25%	6.88%	50.02%
Hedged	$120,516	$120,516	$120,516
w/futures:	5.20%	5.20%	5.20%

Note that this hedge ratio (1.25) is a little higher than is indicated by the conversion factor for delivery of the 7 1/4s into the December 1986 contract (0.9155). This ratio was calculated using the basis point value (BPV) weighted method.

The hedge ratio is higher than the conversion factor because the 7 1/4s were yielding approximately 60–70 basis points *less* than the cheapest to deliver bond. All other things being equal, low yielding bonds are more price sensitive to changing yields than high yielding bonds. Also, the modified duration of the low coupon/long maturity bond is much higher than the cheapest to deliver T-bond. Hence a higher hedge ratio. The futures price is simulated based on the assumption that it will essentially parallel the cash price in the ratio of the hedge ratio and that convergence will occur at the 1.4 percent annual rate.

Note that the futures hedge stabilized the returns no matter how low or how high the cash price fluctuated. But the hedged return at about 5.20 percent is somewhat lower than the current yield on the bond at 6.88 percent. This is due to cash/futures or basis convergence.

Consider that the hedger has committed, through the sale of futures, to deliver securities in the near term. This means the effective maturity or duration on the bond is synthetically shortened. As such, the hedger was successful in locking in (subject to some unpredictable basis risk) a *short-term* rate of return, rather than a long-term rate of return.

Long Put Hedge

The execution of a hedge using long puts is analogous to the purchase of "price insurance"; you guarantee the ability to sell fixed income instruments for at least a minimum price no matter how low the market declines. Assume, for example, that you own securities priced at par and buy an at-the-money par put against those securities for 2 points. If the market declines, you are at least partially compensated by your ability to exercise the option at a profit.

If the market declines to 95, you can exercise the puts by selling at par instruments worth 95. This implies a 5 point profit reduced by the forfeiture of the 2 point option premium for a net profit on the options of 3 points. This partially offsets the 5 point loss in the value of the securities for a net loss of 2 points. No matter how far the market declines, the worst case scenario is a loss of 2 points. Thus you lock in a "floor return." This constitutes price insurance.

This insurance, however, comes at a cost. The cost of option insurance is the option premium, so you may buy put options to hedge against the risk of price decline. If you do not need this insurance, you have nonetheless forfeited the option premium, but at least this cost is known in advance.

If the market either remains stable (at par) or rallies, you may realize portfolio appreciation because you are long securities. The cash outlay for the put offsets cash market appreciation. But the put represents a sunk cost. Once paid, it is irretrievable, so you are worse off by the option premium because you purchased the put as opposed to remaining unhedged.

When you are long puts and long the instrument for which the puts may be exercised, you have effectively created a synthetic long call. In other words, you have an essentially bullish position, but you enjoy limited risk in the event of a market decline. Participation in any possible price advance is limited only to the extent that you forfeit the option premium up front.

Example: An institution buys $10 million face value of the 7 1/4 percent Treasury bond due in 2016 at a price of 101 percent of par on August 26, 1986. To hedge this investment against the risk of a possible interest rate advance, the institution buys 125 December 1986 puts struck at 100 and exercisable for bond futures at 2 56/64ths (see Figure 6–2).

Buy $10 MM 7 1/4% – 16 @ 101–00	=	$10,100,000
Accrued interest@ 8/26/86	=	$202,921
Buy 125 100 puts @ 2–56	=	$359,375
NET INVESTMENT	=	$10,662,296

Assume that cash/futures convergence occurs at an annual rate of 1.4 percent and that the hedge is unwound on November 15, 1986. What might happen if the cash market fell 10 points, rose 10 points, or remained stable?

If 7 1/4s fall to 91–00:

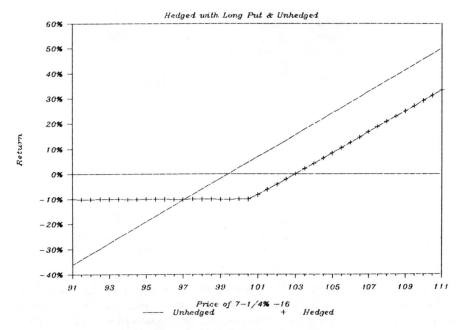

Figure 6-2   Returns on 7¼%-16.

Bond @ 11/15/86 @ 91-00	=	$9,100,000
Accrued interest rec'd	=	$0
Coupon income	=	$362,500
Reinvestment income @ 5.8%	=	$0
Exercise puts @ 7-42	=	$957,031
NET CREDITS	=	$10,419,531

If 7 ¼s remain stable at 101-00:

Bond @ 11/15/86 @ 101-00	=	$10,100,000
Accrued interest rec'd	=	$0
Coupon income	=	$362,500
Reinvestment income @ 5.8%	=	$0
Abandon puts @ 0-00	=	$0
NET CREDITS	=	$10,462,500

If 7 ¼s rally to 111-00:

Bond @ 11/15/86 @ 101–00	=	$11,100,000
Accrued interest rec'd	=	$0
Coupon income	=	$362,500
Reinvestment income @ 5.8%	=	$0
Abandon puts @ 0–00	=	$0
NET CREDITS	=	$11,462,500

Hedged and Unhedged Returns
(In Dollars and as a Percentage)

	Cash @ 91	@ 101	@ 111
Unhedged:	−$840,421	$159,579	$1,159,579
	−36.25%	6.88%	50.02%
Hedged	−$242,765	−$199,796	$800,204
w/puts:	−10.12%	−8.33%	33.36%

The foregoing example illustrates how a long put hedge may have worked under the same circumstances which were illustrated with respect to the short futures hedge. In this case, the hedge was placed utilizing the same ratio as was applicable for the futures hedge (the hedger purchases 125 put options). This is appropriate in the sense that, on exercise of the puts, the hedger would hold 125 short futures contracts. If, therefore, 125 futures are an appropriate quantity, a put hedge in this ratio is likewise appropriate.

In-, At-, Out-of-the-Money Puts

So far, we have considered the purchase of at- or near-the-money puts as a hedging device. Of course, one might readily use in- or out-of-the-money puts as an alternative.

Consider the pricing structure of in-, at-, and out-of-the-money puts exercisable for December 1986 T-bond futures as of August 26, 1986 (see Figure 6–3):

	Premium	Breakeven
Out-Money 98 Put:	2–00/64ths	96 00/32ds
At-Money 100 Put:	2–56	97–04
In-Money 102 Put:	4–03	97–31
Dec. bond futures: 100 01/32ds		

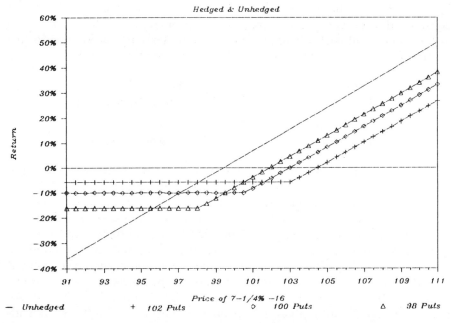

Figure 6-3   Returns on 7 1/4%-16.

The in-the-money put struck at 102 costs more (4–03) than the at- or out-of-the-money options (priced at 2–56 and 2–00, respectively). As such, the purchase of the in-the-money put as a hedge vehicle is a more costly proposition than the purchase of the out-of-the-money put. Therefore, you have more option premium risk by virtue of the higher premium. Note that the breakeven point associated with the in-the-money put (97–31) is closer to the underlying market price (100–01) than the breakeven points associated with the at- or out-of-the-money puts (97–04 and 96–00, respectively).

Thus an in-the-money put may be characterized as an *aggressive* investment. It entails a low probability of a large loss with a relatively high probability of a profit. An out-of-the-money put may be characterized as a *conservative* investment. It entails a high probability of a small loss with a relatively low probability of a profit.

In-the-money option ⇒ aggressive

Out-of-the-money option ⇒ conservative

When you combine a high-struck in-the-money put with a long position in the underlying market, you create a synthetic high-struck long call.

Because this synthetic call is struck over the market price, it may be considered to be out-of-the-money. The combination of a low-struck out-of-the-money put with a long position in the underlying market results in a synthetic low-struck long call, an in-the-money synthetic call!

$$\text{In-the-money long put} + \text{Long Cash} = \text{Out-of-the-money synthetic long call}$$

$$\text{Out-of-the-money long put} + \text{Long Cash} = \text{In-the-money synthetic long call}$$

You take an aggressive put and turn it into a conservative synthetic call. A conservative put may be turned into an aggressive synthetic call.

The implication is: You get what you pay for. The purchase of an in-the-money put entails a larger initial debit. That cost, however, is defrayed in the sense that an in-the-money put provides more protection in the event of a market downturn. By contrast, an out-of-the-money put entails a relatively small initial net debit, but you get less protection in the event of a market decline. However, an in-the-money put hedge generally limits your potential participation in a bull market by virtue of its high cost. An out-of-the-money put hedge provides much more opportunity to take advantage of a market advance.

How might the in-, at-, and out-of-the-money put purchase work in the context when you want to hedge that 7 1/4 percent bond of 2016 discussed in the previous example?

Example: Assume that you owned the 7 1/4s of 2016 and hedged by buying in-the-money 102 puts, at-the-money 100 puts, or out-of-the-money 98 puts?

	Cash @ 91	@ 101	@ 111
Unhedged:	− 36.25%	6.88%	50.02%
Hedged w/ puts:			
In-Money 102s:	− 5.73%	− 5.73%	26.88%
At-Money 100s:	− 10.12%	− 8.33%	33.36%
Out-Money 98s:	− 16.15%	− 3.81%	38.31%

The long put hedge provides a superior return in the event of a down market relative to the unhedged return. In an advancing market, the hedged returns are inferior to the unhedged returns. While the long put hedge limits your participation in an up market, you participate nonetheless. Finally, your returns are diminished in a neutral market because of the forfeiture of the option premium.

The hedge works in the sense that the range of returns is narrower with the in-, at-, or out-of-the-money hedge than it is on an unhedged basis.

Note, however, that the in-the-money returns have a much narrower range than the at- or out-of-the-money put hedge returns.

Price and Quantity Risk

Options are much better suited for many hedging situations relative to futures insofar as they can be used to hedge both price *and* quantity risk. This is quite helpful when a prospective hedger is uncertain about the value of the security in question and the amount which may be held. For example, a security dealer may place a bid on the purchase of security in an auction. By the time that bid is filled, the market may have fluctuated upwards or downwards; hence, price risk exists.

In addition, the dealer does not know how much, if any, of the bid will be filled. Consider the possibility that he hedges the risk of rising rates (falling prices) by selling futures. If prices rise and the bid is not filled, the dealer will be short futures in a rising market, so he is subject to a great deal of risk.

Mortgage bankers, savings and loan associations, and other entities engaged in originating mortgage loans are subject to a specific kind of exposure which entails both price and quantity risk. This is known as "mortgage pipeline risk."

Mortgage pipeline risk begins when a mortgage banker issues a commitment to make a mortgage loan. Assume that mortgage rates are at 10 percent. A prospective mortgagor (the borrower) applies and is approved at 10 percent. In many markets, this means that the mortgagee (the lender) grants a "commitment" guaranteeing that a 10 percent loan will be granted no matter where rates fluctuate as long as the loan is closed within the next 60 days.

The mortgage banker, therefore, essentially grants the borrower a put option. While normal practices may dictate a 2–4 percent loan origination fee (points), these points are normally not collected until the loan closes. Thus the mortgage banker is giving these put options away for free!

Because the mortgage banker is essentially short puts (at a zero premium), the solution is to buy put options. Unfortunately, these put options are not available for free. The costs of the put options are known in advance and are therefore manageable.

Mortgage bankers normally attempt to close loans and sell the resulting mortgage in the secondary market at prevailing prices. If rates decline and prices rise, the mortgage may be sold at a price greater than par for a profit. If rates rise and prices fall, the mortgage is sold less than par at a loss. This scenario illustrates price risk.

Quantity risk is also apparent in the sense that the mortgage banker is uncertain with respect to the number of mortgages which will close. A mortgage banker may expect that about 70 percent of mortgages in the pipeline will close. But this figure is highly contingent on interest rates.

For example, if rates advance from 10 percent to 11 percent, the mortgagor will normally find it desirable to close the loan; he will receive a below market rate mortgage. In other words, he exercises his in-the-money put option. But if rates decline from 10 percent to 9 percent, the mortgage may not close. Under these circumstances, the mortgagor may demand a rate concession or reapply with a different mortgage originator. In other words, the mortgagor will abandon the out-of-the-money put option.

Consider the possible results if rates advance or rates decline and if the mortgages close or fall through.

	Rates Advance	*Rates Decline*
Mortgages Close	Sell loans at loss; exercise puts.	Sell loans at profit; abandon puts.
Mortgages Fall Thru	No product; exercise puts.	No product; abandon puts.

Let us limit this discussion to extreme possibilities. For example, assume that 100 percent of all the mortgages close or 100 percent fall through, or that rates advance or decline by a large amount. Given these possibilities, one may also observe that only two of the four cells are very probable. If rates advance, it is more likely that the mortgages in the pipeline will be closed. If rates decline, it is more likely that the mortgages in the pipeline will fall though.

If rates advance and the mortgages close, the loans are sold below par at a loss in the secondary market. However, the puts may be exercised to at least partially offset the mortgage market loss. Still, the premium is a sunk cost and forfeited.

If rates decline and the mortgages fall through, there is no product to sell in the secondary market. The puts fall out-of-the-money and are abandoned. The mortgage banker is left with a loss equal to the option premium. While this is regrettable, this cost is at least known in advance and limited.

Consider the possibilities if the mortgage banker had hedged using either put options or futures under these two scenarios.

	Put Hedge	*Futures Hedge*
Rates Increase Mortgages Close	Lock-in floor return.	Lock-in short-term rate.
Rates Decline, Mortgages Fall Thru	Loss of Premium.	Short futures in rising market.

The results in the event that rates rise and the mortgages close are superior with the futures hedge. With the futures hedge, you lock in a specific return, perhaps represented by the implied repo rate, a short-term rate. The put hedge allows you to lock in a floor return.

If market interest rates decline and the mortgages fall through, your loss is limited to the option premium by hedging with puts. With a futures hedge, however, you will be caught short futures in a rising market. As such, losses may mount quickly.

Options are especially suitable for hedging mortgage pipeline price and quantity risks because of their contingent nature. The variance of returns with a put hedge is much smaller than with the futures hedge.

Although the loss of the option premium is regrettable, it is a necessary result of the strategy insofar as the mortgage banker essentially gives puts away for free. If this premium can be passed along to the mortgagor (perhaps by requiring part of the points to be paid upon commitment), the mortgagee can potentially offset price risk completely.

Short Call Hedge

The execution of a hedge using short calls is often referred to as "covered call writing," that is, you sell calls conveying the obligation to sell instruments (or a proxy for that instrument) which you already hold.

Assume that you own securities priced at par and sell an at-the-money par call against those securities for 2 points. If the market declines, you are at least partially compensated because you received the option premium on sale.

If the market declines to 95, you lose 5 points in terms of the declining market value of the cash securities. However, you still retain the 2 point premium, so the premium acts as a "cushion" against adversity. While losses mount up on the securities, you are nonetheless better off by the option premium having hedged (a 3 point loss) than not having hedged (a 5 point loss).

If the market rallies, the options may be exercised against you, forcing you to sell in a rising market. For example, if the market advances to 105, the option may be exercised against you for a 5 point loss. This loss offsets the 5 point advance in the value of the securities. Adding back the 2 point premium, you realize a profit of 2 points. This premium may effectively be thought of as a "ceiling" return. The fact that you lock in a ceiling return represents the cost of insurance. However, this cost may be thought of as an opportunity cost only and *not* an out-of-pocket expense.

The most attractive aspect of the covered call write is that you bring in the option premium up front. This represents income you would not otherwise realize. If the market is neutral or relatively stable, therefore, the covered call write strategy allows you to increase portfolio return.

Example: An institution buys $10 million face value of the 7 1/4 percent Treasury bond due in 2016 at a price of 101 percent of par on August 26, 1986. To hedge this investment against the risk of a possible interest rate increase, the institution sells 125 December 1986 T-bond futures calls struck at 100 for 2 58/64ths (see Figure 6–4).

Buy $10 MM 7 1/4% – 16 @ 101–00	=	$10,100,000
Accrued interest @ 8/26/86	=	$202,921
Sell 125 100 Calls @ 2–58	=	– $363,281
NET INVESTMENT	=	$9,939,640

Assume that cash/futures convergence occurs at an annual rate of 1.4 percent and that the hedge is unwound on November 15, 1986. What might happen if the cash market fell 10 points, rose 10 points, or remained stable?

If 7 1/4s fall to 91–00:

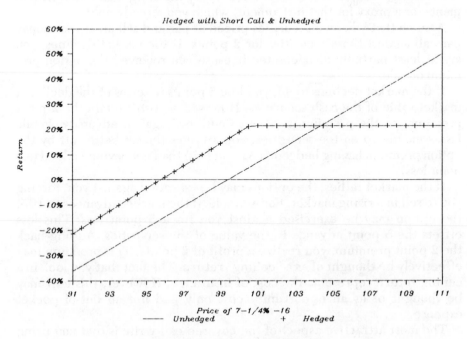

Figure 6–4   Returns on 7 1/4%–16.

Bond @ 11/15/86 @ 91–00	=	$9,100,000
Accrued interest rec'd	=	$0
Coupon income	=	$362,500
Reinvestment income @ 5.8%	=	$0
Abandon calls @ 0–00	=	$0
NET CREDITS	=	$9,462,500

If 7 1/4s remain stable at 101–00:

Bond @ 11/15/86 @ 101–00	=	$10,100,000
Accrued interest rec'd	=	$0
Coupon income	=	$362,500
Reinvestment income @ 5.8%	=	$0
Exercise calls @ 0–22	=	– $42,969
NET CREDITS	=	$10,419,531

If 7 1/4s rally to 111–00:

Bond @ 11/15/86 @ 111–00	=	$11,100,000
Accrued interest rec'd	=	$0
Coupon income	=	$362,500
Reinvestment income @ 5.8%	=	$0
Exercise calls @ 8–22	=	– $1,042,969
NET CREDITS	=	$10,419,531

Hedged and Unhedged Returns
(In Dollars and as a Percentage)

	Cash @ 91	@ 101	@ 111
Unhedged:	–$840,421	$159,579	$1,159,579
	–36.25%	6.88%	50.02%
Hedged	–$477,140	$479,891	$479,891
w/calls:	–21.33%	21.46%	21.46%

The foregoing example illustrates how a short call hedge may have worked under the same circumstances which were illustrated with respect to the short futures and long put hedges. We use the same ratio as was applicable for the futures hedge (the hedger sells 125 call options). This is appropriate in the sense that, upon exercise of the short calls (similar to long puts), the hedger would hold 125 short futures contracts.

In-, At-, Out-of-the-Money Calls

The foregoing examples have only considered the sale of at- or near-the-money calls as a hedging device. Of course, one might readily use in- or out-of-the-money calls as an alternative.

Consider the pricing structure of in-, at-, and out-of-the-money calls exercisable for December 1986 bond futures as of August 26, 1986 (see Figure 6–5).

In-Money 98 Call:	3 56/64ths	101 56/64ths
At-Money 100 Call:	2-58	102-58
Out-Money 102 Call:	2-01	104-01
Dec. bond futures:	100 01/32ds	

The in-the-money call struck at 98 costs more (3–56) than the at- or out-of-the-money options (priced at 2–58 and 2–01, respectively). The sale of the in-the-money call generates more cash up front than the sale of the out-of-the-money call—hence a larger maximum possible profit.

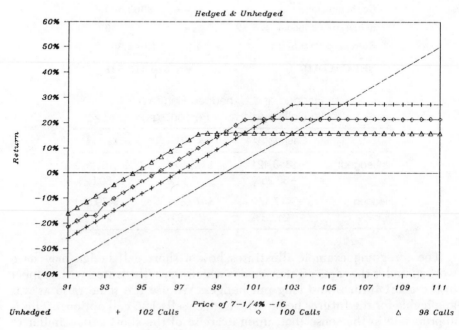

Figure 6–5   Returns on 7 1/4%–16.

Note, however, that the breakeven point associated with the in-the-money call (101–56) is lower and, therefore, closer to the currently prevailing underlying market price (100–01) than is the breakeven point associated with at- or out-of-the-money calls (at $102\,{}^{58}/_{64ths}$ and $104\,{}^{01}/_{64ths}$, respectively).

Thus an in-the-money call may be characterized as an *aggressive* strategy. It entails a low probability of a large profit along with a relatively high probability of a loss. An out-of-the-money call may be characterized as a *conservative* strategy. It entails a high probability of a small profit along with a relatively low probability of a loss.

In-the-money option $\Rightarrow$ aggressive

Out-of-the-money option $\Rightarrow$ conservative

When you combine a low-struck in-the-money call with a long position in the underlying market, you create a synthetic low-struck short put. Because this synthetic put is struck under the market price, it may be considered to be out-of-the-money.

The combination of a high-struck out-of-the-money call with a long position in the underlying market results in a synthetic high-struck short put, an in-the-money synthetic put!

In-the-money short call	+	Long Cash	=	Out-of-the-money synthetic short put
Out-of-the-money short call	+	Long Cash	=	In-the-money synthetic short put

You take an aggressive call and turn it into a conservative synthetic put. A conservative call may be turned into an aggressive synthetic put.

It is clear that the sale of an in-the-money call provides greater protection. The sale of an in-the-money call entails a larger initial credit. That credit provides larger insulation against the risk of a bear market. In contrast, an out-of-the-money call entails a relatively small initial net credit; thus you get less protection in the event of a market decline.

While an in-the-money call hedge generally limits your potential portfolio appreciation in a bull market. An out-of-the-money call hedge provides much more opportunity to take advantage of a market advance.

How might the in-, at-, and out-of-the-money call writing program work when you want to hedge that $7\,{}^{1}\!/_{4}$ percent bond of 2016 discussed in the previous example?

Example: Assume that you hedge the $7\,{}^{1}\!/_{4}$s of 2016 by selling in-the-money 98 calls, at-the-money 100 calls, or out-of-the-money 102 calls?

	Cash @ 91	@ 101	@ 111
Unhedged:	− 36.25%	6.88%	50.02%
Hedged w/ calls:			
In-Money 98s:	− 16.12%	15.89%	15.89%
At-Money 100s:	− 21.33%	21.46%	21.46%
Out-Money 102s:	− 26.02%	18.20%	27.35%

All of the hedged positions provide insulation in the event of a market decline but limit returns in the event of a market advance. If the market remains neutral, returns are enhanced by the initial receipt of the premium.

Note that the range of possible returns is narrowest when hedging with in-the-money calls. It is widest when hedging with out-of-the-money calls. In all cases, however, the hedged returns using in-, at-, or out-of-the-money calls has a narrower variance than the unhedged returns.

Managing the Hedge

The covered call writing strategy is designed to take advantage of time value decay. Therefore, it makes sense to sell at- or near-the-money options to take advantage of maximum time value decay. There are some very real risks associated with this strategy but there are ways to minimize those risks.

Having sold at- or near-the-money options, if the market moves up or down, the original at-the-money calls will move in- or out-of-the-money, respectively. In order to maintain a short call position which is always at- or near-the-money, one may attempt to "roll" the hedge to the next higher or next lower strike price as appropriate. That is, you may wish to buy back the original call and sell the next higher- or next lower-struck call, depending upon whether the market is moving up or down. Thus you "roll up" or "roll down."

By rolling down to what was formerly an in-the-money call, you extend your protection downwards. This is because a low-struck synthetic short put has a lower breakeven point relative to a high-struck synthetic short put. By rolling up to what was formerly an out-of-the-money call, you augment your ability to participate in price advances. This is because the maximum profit or ceiling return on a high-struck synthetic short put is greater than that associated with a low-struck synthetic short put.

What criterion should be used to determine whether to roll up or roll down? The simplest method is to roll up or down when the underlying market price has penetrated the midpoint between the original strike and the next higher or lower strike.

This, however, is a rather crude method. A more subtle and potentially effective method is to roll up or down contingent upon the option delta penetrating some level. We know than an at-the-money option delta will center around 0.50. We may define an at-the-money option as an option whose delta is within the range of 0.40 to 0.60, for example.

If the market rallies such that the delta of the original at-the-money call penetrates 0.60, then roll up to the next higher-struck call whose delta will (presumably) fall within the 0.40–0.60 range. If the market declines such that the delta of the original at-the-money call penetrates 0.40, then roll down to the next lower-struck call.

The risk is that the market will be very volatile and create a series of whipsaws. You roll up in a bull market by buying back calls at a loss; the market reverses and you roll down to the original call. All the while, commission costs and the possibility of execution skids and errors mount.

In order to reduce that possibility, you may wish to expand or reduce the delta range. If market volatility (as measured by an implied volatility) is very high, the range may be expanded to 0.38–0.62, for example. If volatility is low, contract the range to 0.42–0.58.

Rolling up and rolling down will permit you to maintain a short call position in an at- or near-the-money option. Of course, those are precisely the options which are most subject to convexity.

Convexity (high sensitivity to small price movements) works against the covered call writer. Think of it this way: When there is a short term until expiration, there is relatively small time value left to capture, and the time value decay promises to be very swift. Still, if the market breaks sharply upwards, the call delta will quickly run upwards to 1.0. Thus it is as if the covered call writer is short futures in a rising market!

Convexity may be measured by an option gamma—a statistic which measures the stability of the delta. One may reference gamma in order to avoid holding short options which suffer from high convexity.

The recommended technique is to "roll over" by liquidating the original call (presumably sold in the nearby month) and reestablishing the position by selling calls in the first deferred month. This transaction may be triggered by gamma. When convexity becomes "too high" as measured by gamma, roll the option over. Longer term options display less convexity (and less severe time value decay) than do near-term options.

Managing the Hedge

When delta is too high ⇒ Roll up.

When delta is too low ⇒ Roll down.

When gamma is too high ⇒ Roll over.

For example, gamma may be considered high when it reaches 0.10, 0.12, or 0.15. The specific level should be determined in accordance with the degree of convexity with which the hedger is willing to live.

This technique of rolling up, rolling down, and rolling over is sometimes known as "dynamic covered call writing." The intention is to capture time value decay while minimizing the potential ill effects of convexity.

Basis Risk

Basis risk is the risk that the relationship between the cash item to be hedged and the futures contract with which the hedge is constructed will deteriorate. This is a continual question in a futures hedge, but basis risk is often ignored in the context of an option hedge. Basis risk, however, may affect an option hedge just as dramatically as a futures hedge—under one special condition.

Let us return to the analogy between futures and options and double- and single-edged blades. Futures cut both two ways. If you are right about the market, your return may be great. If you are wrong, losses of an equally significant magnitude may result.

Long options have a limited risk feature. If you buy puts, for example, your loss is limited if the market rallies over the strike price. Your profits may mount up quickly if the option trends into-the-money as the market declines below the strike price.

Short options have a limited return feature. By selling calls, you have limited return possibilities if the market declines below the strike price. On the other hand, if the market rallies into-the-money, losses may accrue very quickly.

Thus options only cut when they are in-the-money! Likewise, basis risk is only relevant in the context of an option hedge when the options run into-the-money (as when the market declines when using a long put hedge or when the market rallies when using a short call hedge).

When an option is out-of-the-money, either the loss (long option) or profit (short option) is limited and fixed at the original premium. Thus basis risk becomes irrelevant!

HEDGING ALTERNATIVES

We have already considered three alternate hedge strategies for a long cash security: (1) short futures, (2) long puts, and (3) short calls. However, we have not considered the relative merits of these three strategies. This section discusses this issue and attempts to provide an answer by examining the hedge effectiveness of the three strategies in a bullish, a bearish, and a neutral market environment.

Market Performance

It is clear from the foregoing analysis that the return distribution on a hedged basis exhibits much less variance than the return distribution on an unhedged basis. But can we rank those returns in the event of a bull, bear, or neutral market?

The following table summarizes the returns potentially associated with the hedge of the 7 1/4 percent bond of 2016 in the event of a 10 point decline, a 10 point advance, or a perfectly stable market.

Hedged and Unhedged Returns

	Cash @ 91	@ 101	@ 111
Unhedged:	−36.25%	6.88%	50.02%
Hedged w/futures:	5.20%	5.20%	5.20%
Hedged w/puts:			
In-Money 102s:	−5.7%	−5.73%	26.88%
At-Money 100s:	−10.12%	−8.33%	33.36%
Out-Money 98s:	−16.15%	−3.81%	38.31%
Hedged w/calls:			
In-Money 98s:	−16.12%	15.89%	15.89%
At-Money 100s:	−21.33%	21.46%	21.46%
Out-Money 102s:	−26.02%	18.20%	27.35%

Limiting our focus to the at-the-money option hedge, let us see if we can prioritize these strategies pursuant to the three market scenarios outlined.

Clearly, the short futures position is the superior hedge vehicle in the event of a bear market. Its return at 5.20 percent is much better than the returns of −10.12 percent and −21.33 percent associated with the long put and short call hedge, respectively. Thus we may rank short futures, long puts, and short calls as one, two, three in a decidedly bear market.

In a bull market, our returns indicate that long puts, short calls, and short futures are the best *hedge* positions with returns of 33.36 percent, 21.46 percent, and 5.20 percent, respectively. Note, however, that there is really no substitute for an unhedged position in an advancing market!

Finally, our ranking in a neutral market is short calls, short futures, and long puts with returns of 21.46 percent, 5.20 percent, and negative 8.33 percent, respectively.

Preferred Hedges

Bear	Neutral	Bull
(1) Short Futures	Short Calls	Long Puts
(2) Long Puts	Short Futures	Short Calls
(3) Short Calls	Long Puts	Short Futures

This ranking is interesting in that no single strategy dominates. Each of the strategies holds a number one, number two, and number three ranking in one of the three market scenarios. It *is* clear that one's market scenario makes a sizable difference when it comes to determining which hedge strategy you will pursue (see Figure 6–6).

These are "simple" market forecasts. We may identify "complex" market forecasts as well. For example, one may adopt a bearish to neutral forecast or a bullish to neutral forecast. Finally, a strongly bullish or strongly bearish forecast may be adopted.

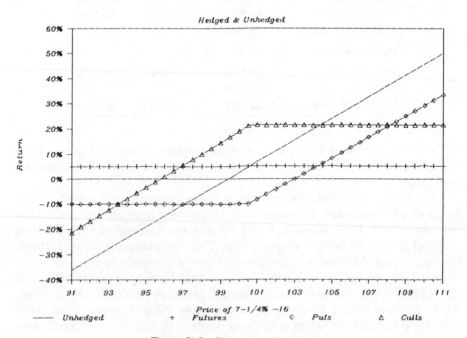

Figure 6–6   Returns on 7 1/4%–16.

Let us rank each of the three strategies pursuant to our three more subtle market forecasts. To do this, we will adopt a rating systen. in which we sum the ranking of the particular strategy over the two relevant simple market forecasts.

In a bearish market scenario, the short futures position is ranked number one. In a neutral market, the short futures hedge is ranked number two. One plus two equals three. This represents the short futures hedge's ranking in a neutral to bearish market. By the same token, the short call hedge represents the number four ranking (one in a neutral market plus three in a bear market). A long put hedge represents the number five ranking (two in a bear market, three in a neutral market).

We may rank the short futures hedge, short call hedge, and long put hedge number one, two, and three in a neutral to bearish market. Using the same logic, we can identify the preferred hedging strategies under the other two complex forecasts as follows:

Preferred Hedges

Bearish to Neutral	Bullish to Neutral	Bearish or Bullish
(1) Short Futures	Short Calls	Long Puts
(2) Short Calls	Long Puts	Short Futures
(3) Long Puts	Short Futures	Short Calls

This does not even take into consideration the possibility of using in- or out-of-the-money puts or calls. The possibilities become almost endless!

What Is Hedging?

For many years, futures brokers have told their clients that they need not develop an interest rate, equity price, foreign exchange, or commodity price forecast to hedge with options. Rather, they tried to convince their clients that they could simply negate risk with the use of futures.

The emergence of options as viable trading vehicles has signaled an end to this way of thinking. It is clear that price behavior has an important impact upon the outcome of a hedging program. If one can anticipate, even with only marginal success, future market movements, it is natural and completely appropriate to use that information to help guide hedging activities.

A second point relates to the hedger's risk-management objectives. Many prospective hedgers have already adopted long-term investment objectives which imply fundamental beliefs about market performance or investment constraints, either self-imposed or imposed by regulation.

For example, many pension funds adopt policies to the effect that they will invest largely in long-term fixed income securities. This implies a fundamental belief that those instruments most closely conform to the fund's investment objectives in the long term.

In other words, these funds are largely content to accept the risks and rewards inherent in fixed income investment vehicles. In many or even most situations, they will not want to negate these risks, for to do so suggests that they will negate potential rewards as well. Sometimes, however, they may feel that it is worthwhile to partially offset risks or to change the nature of the basic risk/reward structure. In other words, the fund manager may want to take advantage of anticipated market performance within the constraints imposed by investment policies.

But is this hedging? Traditionally, hedging has been thought of as a means to offset or negate risks. The existence of options underscores the necessity of adopting a more liberal definition of hedging. In this context, hedging may be thought of as any strategy which reduces the variability of possible outcomes regardless of whether it skews the risk/rewards "profile" one way or the other.

This introduces expanded flexibility—a creative slant—to one's risk-management activities. This is a role that options are well suited to play.

DELTA HEDGING

Delta is a very useful concept for an option hedger. As the term implies, delta refers to changes. Because delta summarizes the risk of an option position relative to that of the underlying instrument, it may be used to define a reasonable hedge strategy.

The idea is to offset losses and gains in the cash market with gains and losses, respectively, in the option market. While a delta hedging program may be quite effective, one has to be cognizant of the properties of delta insofar as a delta hedge may deteriorate as prices fluctuate and as time moves forward.

Properties of Delta

Delta is a *dynamic* concept. Delta fluctuates as the underlying instrument price changes and as the option approaches expiration.

Deltas range between zero and 1.0. At-the-money option deltas will be about 0.50. Deep in-the-money option deltas approach 1.0. Deep out-of-the-money option deltas approach zero.

Delta is understood when one considers the interaction between an option's intrinsic and time value. As an option trends in-the-money, its intrinsic value advances while its time value declines. This occurs because advancing intrinsic values compromise option leverage. As the option goes into-the-money, its premium becomes pure intrinsic value and runs one-for-one with movements in the underlying commodity.

As an option trends out-of-the-money, the probability that it will ever run into-the-money to permit a profitable exercise diminishes. At some point, it will have no time value. When the premium bottoms out, small fluctuations in the underlying commodity will have little or no effect on the premium, hence, a delta equal to zero.

Delta

In-the-money $\Rightarrow 1.00$

At-the-money $\Rightarrow 0.50$

Out-of-the-money $\Rightarrow 0.00$

Long call deltas are often denoted by a positive number because you profit if the market advances. By the same token an essentially bullish short put delta will also be denoted by a positive number. Deltas associated with essentially bearish long put and short call positions are expressed with a negative number.

Deltas are also sensitive to time as well as price. As time marches on, the delta associated with an out-of-the-money option will begin to decline to zero. In-the-money call and put deltas will inch towards 1.0 (or −1.0). At-the-money deltas remain stable near 0.50.

Neutral Hedge Ratio

The objective with a delta hedge is to use an appropriate number of options such that the fluctuating value of the option premium perfectly offsets any fluctuation in the value of the hedged instrument.

A long bond is essentially bullish; therefore, you can offset the risk associated with this position with an essentially bearish short call or long put position. (Note that long put and short call options have negative deltas.) The ratio of options to units held in the underlying instrument is known as the *neutral ratio*.

Change (Cash) = Change (Premium) × Neutral Ratio

Or:

Neutral Ratio = Change(Cash)/Change(Premium)

But we know that the change in the option premium given a change in the underlying instrument may be represented by delta. Thus taking the reciprocal of delta gives us the neutral ratio.

$$\text{Neutral Ratio} = 1/\text{Delta}$$

If delta equals 0.30, this implies that approximately three options $(3.33 = 1/0.30)$ must be used, that is, a ratio of ten options for every three units held in the underlying instrument. If delta equals 0.80, this implies that 1.25 options $(1/0.80)$ are needed, that is, a ratio of five options for every four units held in the underlying instrument.

But we have assumed that the options in question may be exercised directly for the instrument to be hedged. In most cases, a cross-hedge of sorts is indicated. For example, you may attempt to hedge a cash Treasury item with options on T-bond futures.

The neutral ratio reconciles the expected change in the value of the options to the change in value of the T-bond futures contract for which the options may be exercised. The next step is to reconcile the expected change in the value of the futures for which the options may be exercised to the change in the value of the cash instrument to be hedged.

This may be done by employing the appropriate futures hedge ratio. Many techniques for developing hedge ratios may be appropriate—from a simple "conversion factor weighted hedge," a "basis point value weighted hedge" or other more exotic techniques. These techniques are discussed in detail in another chapter. Suffice it to say that the neutral ratio must be multiplied by the appropriate futures hedge ratio in order to construct an effective delta hedge.

$$\text{Ratio} = \text{Futures Hedge Ratio} \times \text{Neutral Ratio}$$

Forget about the futures hedge ratio for the moment and concentrate on the neutral ratio. Because deltas are unstable over price and time, a delta hedge is likewise unstable over price and time. In other words, delta hedges are effective only over a relatively narrow price range and over a relatively short period of time.

This means that a delta hedge must be managed continually to remain effective. The hedge must be adjusted by putting on more options or taking off options as appropriate to remain *delta neutral*. A delta neutral position is one in which a cash position is perfectly balanced by an offsetting option position.

	Long Cash/Short Calls	*Long Cash/Long Puts*
Market Advances	Liquidate° Calls	Buy More Puts
Market Declines	Sell More Calls	Liquidate° Puts

°"Liquidate" means that you offset a previously established position.

Long Delta Hedge

As just indicated, the first question that faces a hedger when implementing a delta hedge is simply: What is the appropriate hedge ratio?

In our prior examples, we worked with the assumption that you held $10 million face value of the 7¼ percent bond of 2016 and wished to hedge with options on T-bond futures. What is the appropriate number of put options which will allow the institution to become delta neutral? The delta associated with the near-the-money puts struck at 100 (when futures were trading at 100–01) equals 0.4837 (or, more appropriately, −0.4837).

This delta measures the expected change in the option premium given a small change in the value of the futures contract for which the option may be exercised, *not* the cash bond to be hedged. This implies that the futures contract is assigned a delta of 1.0 in the case of a long position and −1.0 in the case of a short position. If the appropriate futures hedge ratio equals 1.25, or 125 of the $100,000 face value unit contracts per $10 million face value in cash, this implies that the delta of the cash bond equals 1.25 per $100,000 face value unit.

Use this information to find the appropriate hedge ratio:

$$\text{Ratio} = \text{Futures Hedge Ratio} \times \text{Neutral Ratio}$$

$$= 1.25 \times (1/.4837)$$

$$= 2.58 \text{ options per } \$100,000 \text{ face value unit}$$
$$\textit{or } 258 \text{ options per } \$10 \text{ million face value.}$$

Example: A delta hedge is implemented by buying 258 at-the-money 100 puts to hedge $10 million face value of the 7¼s on August 26th (see Figure 6–7). This means that you hold a cash portfolio with an effective delta of 125. You buy puts with a delta of −.4837 or −124.81 for 258 options. Thus your initial net delta equals 0.19.

		Delta
Buy $10 MM 7¼% – 16 @ 101–00 =	$10,100,000	125.00
Buy 258 100 puts @ 2–56 =	$741,750	− 124.81
	NET DELTA	0.19

What might happen to the principal value of the investment if over the next day the cash market rises, falls, or remains stable?

If 7¼s rise to 104–00:

	Bond Price	*Option Premium*
8/26	Buy @ 101–00 = $10,100,000	Buy @ 2–56 = $741,750
8/27	Sell @ 104–00 = $10,400,000	Sell @ 1–54 = $475,688
	NET = $300,000	NET = ($266,062)

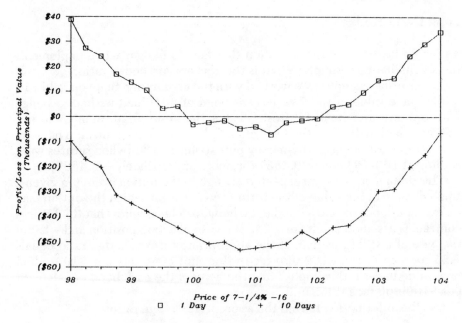

Figure 6–7   Long delta put hedge over time.

If 7 1/4s rise to 102–16:

	Bond Price	**Option Premium**
8/26	Buy @ 101–00 = $10,100,000	Buy @ 2–56 = $741,750
8/27	Sell @ 102–16 = $10,250,000	Sell @ 2–20 = $596,625
	NET = $150,000	NET = ($145,125)

If 7 1/4s remain stable at 101–00:

	Bond Price	**Option Premium**
8/26	Buy @ 101–00 = $10,100,000	Buy @ 2–56 = $741,750
8/27	Sell @ 101–00 = $10,100,000	Sell @ 2–55 = $737,719
	NET = $0	NET = ($4,031)

If 7 1/4s fall to 99–16:

	Bond Price	**Option Premium**
8/26	Buy @ 101–00 = $10,100,000	Buy @ 2–56 = $741,750
8/27	Sell @ 99–16 = $9,500,000	Sell @ 3–30 = $894,938
	NET = ($150,000)	NET = $153,188

If 7 1/4s fall to 98–00:

	Bond Price		Option Premium	
8/26	Buy @ 101–00 = $10,100,000		Buy @ 2–56 =	$741,750
8/27	Sell @ 98–00 = $9,800,000		Sell @ 4–12 =	$1,080,375
	NET =	($300,000)	NET =	$338,625

Change in Principal Value
(Over 1 Day)

Price	Bonds	Options	Net
104–00	$300,000	($266,062)	$33,938
102–16	$150,000	($145,125)	$4,875
101–00	$0	($4,031)	($4,031)
99–16	($150,000)	$153,188	$3,188
98–00	($300,000)	$338,625	$38,625

Let us define "hedge effectiveness" as the ability of a hedger to *perfectly* offset advances or declines in the value of the cash instrument with declines or advances in the value of the option position, respectively (no losses, no profits).

One may infer from these results and the accompanying graphic that a delta hedge can be reasonably effective over a limited price movement. (Although it is also clear that if the market falls or rallies significantly, the long put hedge can result in an attractive positive return!)

Note, however, these results presuppose that the hedge remains completely unadjusted over time. In other words, as the market declines or advances, you remain long $10 million face value bonds and long 258 puts. But if the market fluctuates, the delta fluctuates as well. As the market declines, the put delta advances and the neutral ratio falls. As the market advances, the put delta declines, implying an increasing neutral ratio.

For example, if the cash market falls to 98–00, the delta might be expected to advance to 0.6090. This implies that the hedger should have only 205 puts instead of 258. If the market advances to 104–00, the delta declines to 0.3509. This implies that the hedger should hold 356 puts.

Adjusted Hedge Ratios
(Over 1 Day)

Price	Put Delta	# Options
104–00	0.3509	356
102–16	0.4120	303
101–00	0.4776	262
99–16	0.5428	230
98–00	0.6090	205

These results illustrate the effects of price volatility on the long delta hedge. In particular, a delta hedger with long options will generally benefit from volatility or convexity.

As the market declines, the long put delta becomes higher (or more negative if you associate the long put with a negative delta). Thus you make money on the puts at an accelerating pace relative to the mounting losses on the cash side. Fewer options are required to preserve a perfectly offsetting position.

As the market advances, the long put delta gets closer to zero, so you are losing money on the puts at a decelerating pace relative to the mounting profits on the cash side. More options are required to preserve a perfectly offsetting position.

Volatility or convexity has a positive impact on an unadjusted long delta hedge! What happens as expiration draws near?

Example: What results may be expected if you place the long delta put hedge and hold it unadjusted over the next 10 days until September 5th?

Change in Principal Value
(Over 10 Days)

Price	Bonds	Options	Net
104–00	$300,000	($306,375)	($6,375)
102–16	$150,000	($193,500)	($43,500)
101–00	$0	($52,406)	($52,506)
99–16	($150,000)	$108,844	($41,156)
98–00	($300,000)	$290,250	($9,750)

While volatility or convexity has a positive impact from the standpoint of the long delta hedger, time value decay has an adverse on the long delta hedge.

Unfortunately, there is nothing that may be done to prevent or offset the ill effects of time decay short of employing an alternative strategy. This is intuitive if you consider the fact that delta simply reflects the change in the premium given a change in the underlying market price. It makes no statement whatsoever with respect to time. This underscores the idea that delta hedging is most applicable over both short periods of time and over limited price movements.

Short Delta Hedge

If an unadjusted long hedge is positively affected by convexity and adversely affected by time value decay, what can we conclude with respect to an unadjusted short delta hedge?

Examine the idea of selling calls against long bonds in order to achieve delta neutrality. At the time that the near-the-money 100 put had a delta of 0.4736, the call struck at 100 had a delta of 0.5161 (more appropriately expressed as −0.5161).

$$\text{Ratio} = \text{Futures Hedge Ratio} \times \text{Neutral Ratio}$$
$$= 1.25 \times (1/.5161)$$
$$= 2.42 \text{ options per } \$100,000 \text{ face value unit}$$
$$or \; 242 \text{ options per } \$10 \text{ million face value.}$$

What results can be expected if you implement a delta hedge using short calls in the ratio indicated above over a 1 day and a 10 day period?

Example: A delta hedge is implemented by selling 242 at-the-money 100 calls to hedge $10 million face value of the 7 1/4s on August 26th. This means that you hold a cash item with an effective delta of 125. You sell calls with a delta of −0.5161 or −124.90 for all 242 of the options. Thus your initial net delta equals 0.10.

		Delta
Buy $10 MM 7 1/4% − 16 @ 101–00 =	$10,100,000	125.00
Sell 242 100 calls @ 2–58 =	$703,313	− 124.90
	NET DELTA	0.10

Change in Principal Value
(Over 1 Day)

Price	Bonds	Options	Net
104–00	$300,000	($332,749)	($32,749)
102–16	$150,000	($158,812)	($8,812)
101–00	$0	$3,782	$3,782
99–16	($150,000)	$143,688	($6,312)
98–00	($300,000)	$264,688	($35,312)

Change in Principal Value
(Over 10 Days)

Price	Bonds	Options	Net
104–00	$300,000	($298,718)	$1,282
102–16	$150,000	($121,000)	$29,000
101–00	$0	$41,594	$41,594
99–16	($150,000)	$177,719	$27,719
98–00	($300,000)	$302,500	$2,500

It is apparent that the short delta hedge deteriorates in the event that the market rallies or declines significantly; volatility or convexity works against the short delta hedger. But time value decay works for the short delta hedger (see Figure 6–8).

An at- or near-the-money option experiences accelerated time value decay and is most sensitive to the effects of convexity. Thus the short delta hedger is subject to the greatest risk as a result of convexity and the greatest potential profit as a result of time value decay if the options stay near-the-money.

This is just the opposite of the long delta hedge which deteriorates over time but is positively affected by volatility or convexity.

	Convexity or Volatility	*Time Value Decay*
Long Delta Hedge	(+)	(–)
Short Delta Hedge	(–)	(+)

Of course, a delta hedge requires continual adjustments in order to remain delta neutral. For example, if the cash market rallies to 104, the call delta runs up to 0.6361. This implies the use of only 197 options. If the market declines to 98, the delta falls to 0.3779 which implies the use of 331 options.

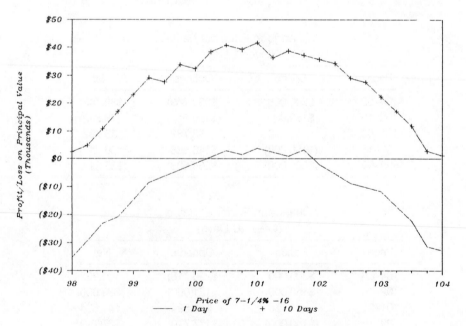

Figure 6–8   Short delta call hedge over time.

Adjusted Hedge Ratios
(Over 1 Day)

Price	Call Delta	# Options
104–00	0.6361	197
102–16	0.5750	217
101–00	0.5093	245
99–16	0.4442	281
98–00	0.3779	331

By liquidating or putting on additional options as appropriate, a delta hedger can protect against the ill effects of price volatility. There is, of course, no way to compensate for the effects of time value decay—and no reason for the short delta hedger to be concerned either!

The short delta hedge is often regarded as superior to the long delta hedge in that you can, in fact, offset some of the effects of convexity. Since time marches on continually, no adjustments are indicated or necessary to offset the effects of time value decay! But the short delta hedge must be adjusted to fight convexity.

Portfolio Insurance versus Dynamic Covered Call Writing

Earlier, we discussed the concept of dynamic covered call writing. This is the technique whereby one rolls up or rolls down to the next higher- or lower-struck call by reference to delta or rolls over to the next month by reference to gamma. The intent is to take advantage of the natural time value decay associated with a short call while limiting the potential ill effects of convexity.

This dynamic method is similar to the more traditional method of looking at delta hedging discussed immediately above. Traditional delta hedging techniques would have the hedger alter the *number of calls* held short at a *fixed strike*. Dynamic covered call writing means that you roll a *fixed number of calls* at a *variable strike*. In either case, the results may be similar: effectively to execute a synthetic short futures hedge or to "flatten out" one's returns while at the same time capitalizing on time value decay.

Portfolio insurance is a technique which has attracted a great deal of attention in recent years, particularly in the context of the stock markets. This may be thought of as a means of using short futures to simulate a long put hedge, to simulate the convexity properties of a long put without being subject to the disadvantages associated with time value decay.

This technique requires one to sell futures in the ratio of the delta associated with a put whose performance one wishes to simulate. Assume, for example, that one wishes to simulate a hedge with the use of an at- or near-the-money long put. We know that the delta associated with this long put may be represented as near −0.50. If the futures hedge ratio suggests that you use 100 contracts, use 50 instead (see Figure 6–9).

Over the short term, over a small price movement, your portfolio consisting of a long position in the cash market coupled with a short futures position will simulate that of a long put hedge *without* the ill effects of time value decay.

If the market falls, the delta on the put will get closer to −1.00. Assume that the market declines such that delta associated with the long put equals −0.60. Sell an additional 10 futures to bring the total up to 60.

If the market advances, the delta on the put will get closer to zero. Assume that the market declines such that the delta associated with the long put moves from −0.50 to −0.40. Cover 10 of the short futures contracts to bring the total to 40.

By selling additional futures in a downward trending market and buying back the shorts in an upward trending market, by reference to delta, your performance will tend to simulate that of a long put. (Actually, this technique is quite intuitive in that many hedgers may sell more futures in a downward trending market and cover those shorts in an upward trending market as a matter of course without reference to delta!)

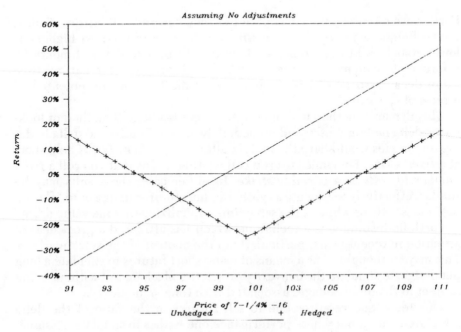

Figure 6–9   Long delta put hedge at expiration.

Portfolio insurance allows you to simulate the most attractive feature associated with a long put hedge—convexity! At the same time, we know that a short futures position will not suffer from time value decay.

Unfortunately, you do suffer from whipsaws and potentially high transaction costs in a neutral or nontrending market. The possibility of whipsaws and high transaction costs also detracts from our dynamic covered call writing program. But dynamic covered call writing and portfolio insurance offer other interesting contrasts.

Dynamic call writing attempts to capitalize on time value decay while avoiding the ill effects of convexity, to simulate a short futures hedge while still taking advantage of time value decay by virtue of the use of short calls (see Figure 6–10). Portfolio insurance attempts to capitalize on convexity while avoiding the ill effects of time value decay, to simulate a long put hedge, taking advantage of convexity, but using short futures positions in an attempt to avoid time value decay.

Which approach is best? The answer is: Neither method is universally superior. The best method is the one which conforms to the demands of the situation! In a strongly volatile, sharply trending market, portfolio insurance may provide a better hedge. In a neutral market characterized by falling volatilities, dynamic covered call writing will tend to provide superior results.

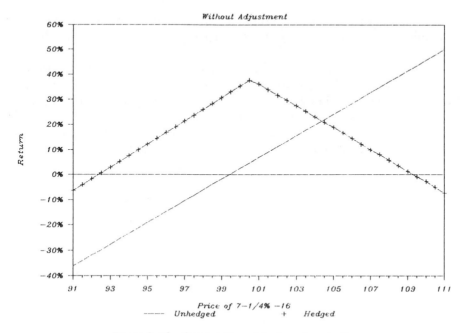

Figure 6-10   Short delta call hedge at expiration.

Weighted Option Hedges

Our discussion about delta hedging with options has largely centered on the ways in which the hedge deteriorates as prices fluctuate and as time marches on, that is, the use of unadjusted delta hedges. But these unadjusted hedges represent legitimate hedging techniques in themselves!

Our previous examples illustrated how one might use roughly twice as many long puts or short calls than would otherwise be indicated by the futures hedge ratio. These hedges are sometimes referred to as "overbuy" or "overwrite" strategies, respectively. In practice, these strategies tend to resemble long or short straddles if they are held unadjusted to expiration.

To understand this point, consider the possibility of holding one futures contract and buying puts to hedge the risk of a price decline. Assume that these puts are at-the-money with a delta equal to 0.50. Thus you can create a delta neutral position of buying two puts.

The combination of one long put with one long futures contract creates a synthetic long call. The combination of that synthetic long call with the remaining long put resembles a long straddle, or an overbuy.

Long Futures + Long Put = Synthetic Long Call

Synthetic Long Call + Long Put = Synthetic Long Straddle

Thus a hedger can actually create a risk/reward profile which strongly resembles that of a straddle—a trade normally thought of as a speculative strategy.

By the same token, a hedger can use short calls to create a position which resembles a short straddle. Consider the possibility of buying one futures contract and hedging the futures position by selling two at-the-money calls with a delta close to 0.50.

The combination of one short call with one long futures contract creates a synthetic short put. The combination of that synthetic short put with the remaining short call resembles a short straddle, or an overwrite.

Long Futures + Short Call = Synthetic Short Put

Synthetic Short Put + Short Call = Synthetic Short Straddle

The overbuy strategy conforms to a market expectation which is bullish or bearish. The overwrite strategy conforms to a neutral market expectation. It is clear that there is a certain speculative element associated with an option hedge.

What would happen if a hedger were to use fewer puts or calls than are indicated by the futures hedge ratio? In that case, he would create an "underbuy" or an "underwrite" situation. For example, assume that the hedger buys one half the number of puts indicated by the futures hedge ratio? In that case, the hedger would maintain a moderately bullish position as indicated by a relatively high net delta.

Example: You buy 63 puts (one half of the futures hedge ratio of 125 futures contracts) against $10 million face value of the 7 1/4s (see Figure 6–11). The net delta equals 94.52.

			Delta
Buy $10 MM 7 1/4% − 16 @ 101–00	=	$10,100,000	125.00
Buy 63 100 puts @ 2–56	=	$181,125	− 30.48
		NET DELTA	94.52

Example: You sell 63 calls (one half of the futures hedge ratio of 125 futures contracts) against $10 million face value of the 7 1/4s (see Figure 6–12). The net delta equals 92.49.

			Delta
Buy $10 MM 7 1/4% − 16 @ 101–00	=	$10,100,000	125.00
Sell 63 100 calls @ 2–58	=	$183,094	− 32.51
		NET DELTA	92.49

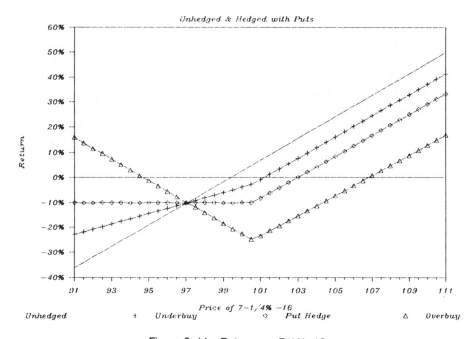

Figure 6–11   Returns on 7 1/4%–16.

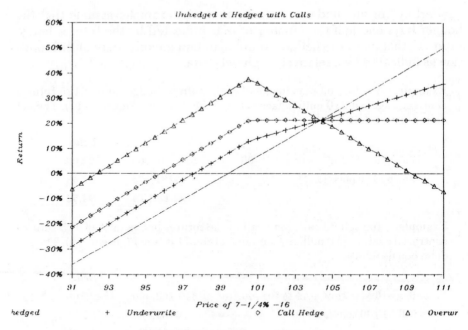

Figure 6–12   Returns on 7 ¼%–16.

The underbuy and underwrite strategies represent legitimate hedges insofar as they reduce the variance of possible outcomes associated with the cash instrument. In other words, your returns are increased in the event of a market decline, but they are reduced relative to an unhedged position in a market advance.

Nonetheless, the variance of returns is much wider with the underbuy or underwrite than it is in a fully hedged position or an overbuy or overwrite. This is reflected in the initial net deltas associated with the total position.

Net Delta

	Put Hedge	Call Hedge
Under-hedge	94.52	92.49
Fully-hedged	64.53	60.49
Over-hedge	0.19	0.10

These deltas suggest that the underbuy and undersell hedges resemble a situation where you are long 94.52 or 92.49 futures. The full hedges resemble long futures positions of 64.53 and 60.49 for the put and call hedges, respectively. Finally, the overbuy and overwrite situations have net deltas which are insignificantly different than zero—equivalent to zero futures contracts.

Thus the underbuy and underwrite strategies are quite bullish in character. The overbuy and oversell situations are initially much more neutral. But remember that delta is a dynamic concept. Deltas are only valid over limited time intervals and over limited price fluctuations. These six option hedges behave differently at expiration as illustrated in Figures 6–11 and 6–12.

FENCES AND REVERSE FENCES

As previously indicated, the covered call writing strategy is very attractive in the sense that it allows an institution to augment its current income. Unfortunately, it does not fully insulate an institution from the risk of an interest rate advance and the resulting price decline. Buying put options allows the institution to establish a firm floor return, but this comes at the risk of forfeiting the option premium.

As a result, many institutions have begun to use a strategy which permits one to enjoy some of the benefits of selling calls *and* some of the benefits of buying puts. These strategies are known as *fences*.

Synthetic Short Futures

A fence represents the simultaneous sale of a call and the purchase of a put, in combination with a long security or futures position. Generally, the put and call are struck at different levels. As a precursor to our discussion of the fence, however, let us examine the idea of selling calls and buying puts with the same strike.

Assume that bond futures are at 100–01 and you sell a 100 struck call for $2\,^{58}/_{64ths}$ and buy a 100 put for $2\,^{56}/_{64ths}$. This is equivalent to simply selling a futures contract at the 100 strike price plus the $^2/_{64ths}$ net credit—or selling futures at $100\,^{02}/_{64ths}$. This translates to $100\,^{01}/_{32ds}$ or the same as the prevailing futures price.

If the market falls to 95 by expiration, the put is exercised for its 5 point in-the-money value. The position was initially established at a $^1/_{32ds}$ credit, so you make 5–01 net—the same as if you had sold futures at 100–01. If the market rallies to 105, you lose 5 points, the in-the-money amount of your short call less the 1/32d credit for a net loss of $4\,^{31}/_{32ds}$. This results in the same loss as selling futures at 100–01.

What would happen if you entered this synthetic futures contract 125 times in order to hedge $10 million face value of the $7\,^1/_4$s of 2016?

Example: You own $10 million face value of the $7\,^1/_4$ percent bond of 2016 and hedge by selling 125 calls struck at 100 and priced at 2–58; and buy 125 puts struck at 100 and priced at 2–56 (see Figure 6–13).

Buy $10 MM 7¼% − 16 @ 101−00	=	$10,100,000
Accrued interest @ 8/26/86	=	$202,921
Sell 125 100 calls @ 2−58	=	− $363,281
Buy 125 100 puts @ 2−56	=	$359,375
NET INVESTMENT	=	$10,299,015

Assume that cash/futures convergence occurs at an annual rate of 1.4 percent and that the hedge is unwound on November 15, 1986. What might happen if the cash market fell 10 points, rose 10 points, or remained stable?

If 7¼s fall to 91−00:

Bond @ 11/15/86 @ 91−00	=	$9,100,000
Accrued interest rec'd	=	$0
Coupon income	=	$362,500
Reinvestment income @ 5.8%	=	$0
Exercise puts @ 7−42	=	$957,031
Abandon calls @ 0−00	=	$0
NET CREDITS	=	$10,419,531

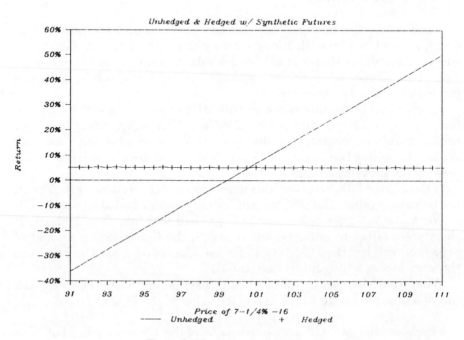

Figure 6–13   Returns on 7¼%–16.

If 7 1/4s remain stable at 101–00:

Bond @ 11/15/86 @ 101–00	=	$10,100,000
Accrued interest rec'd	=	$0
Coupon income	=	$362,500
Reinvestment income @ 5.8%	=	$0
Abandon puts @ 0–00	=	$0
Exercise calls @ 0–22	=	– $42,969
NET CREDITS	=	$10,419,531

If 7 1/4s rally to 111–00:

Bond @ 11/15/86 @ 101–00	=	$11,100,000
Accrued interest rec'd	=	$0
Coupon income	=	$362,500
Reinvestment income @ 5.8%	=	$0
Abandon puts @ 0–00	=	$0
Exercise calls @ 8–22	=	– $1,042,969
NET CREDITS	=	$10,419,531

Hedged and Unhedged Returns
(In Dollars and as a Percentage)

	Cash @ 91	@ 101	@ 111
Unhedged:	–$840,421	$159,579	$1,159,579
	–36.25%	6.88%	50.02%
Hedged:	$120,516	$120,516	$120,516
	5.20%	5.20%	5.20%

This strategy allows you to lock in a stable return no matter whether the market goes up, down, or sideways. This return, however, more closely resembles a short-term rate of return rather than a long-term rate of return.

Because this strategy performs like a short futures hedge, it is labeled a "synthetic short futures." (Similarly, if you buy calls and sell puts at the same strike, this represents a "synthetic long futures" strategy.)

Again, the analogy between futures and options and double- and single-edged blades comes to mind. The combination of two single-edged blades (a long put and a short call option) resembles one double-edged blade (a short futures contract).

Fence

When you combine a synthetic short futures contract with a long futures contract, you achieve a flat rate of return. Profits or losses associated with one option contract offset losses or profits associated with the other option contract. Fences are more interesting because they involve options struck at different levels. This means that you can establish two fixed returns—one above the upper strike and another below the lower strike.

Normally, a fence entails selling an at- or near-the-money call, bringing in a fair amount of premium. Ideally, you would like to "ride down" the time value component in a neutral market.

If the market advances, you establish a ceiling return, limiting your participation in possible windfall profits. But perhaps more distressing is the idea that, if the market declines, you are still subject to loss. This loss is cushioned by the initial receipt of the premium but is by no means limited.

A fence entails buying a cheap out-of-the-money put in addition to selling a near-the-money call. By buying the put, you establish not only a ceiling return (as in a covered call strategy), but you also establish a floor return. Thus if the market declines sharply, the profits accruing from the put, which is being driven farther and farther in-the-money, tend to offset the loss on the cash position.

> **Example:** You own $10 million face value of the 7¼ percent bond of 2016 and hedge by selling 125 calls struck at 100 and priced at 2–58; buy 125 puts struck at 96 and priced at 1–21 (see Figure 6–14).

Buy $10 MM 7¼% – 16 @ 101–00	=	$10,100,000
Accrued interest @ 8/26/86	=	$202,921
Sell 125 100 calls @ 2–58	=	– $363,281
Buy 125 96 puts @ 1–21	=	$166,016
NET INVESTMENT	=	$10,105,656

Assume that cash/futures convergence occurs at an annual rate of 1.4 percent and that the hedge is unwound on November 15, 1986. What might happen if the cash market fell 10 points, rose 10 points, or remained stable?

If 7¼s fall to 91–00:

Bond @ 11/15/86 @ 91–00	=	$9,100,000
Accrued interest rec'd	=	$0
Coupon income	=	$362,500
Reinvestment income @ 5.8%	=	$0
Exercise puts @ 3–42	=	$457,031
Abandon calls @ 0–00	=	$0
NET CREDITS	=	$9,919,531

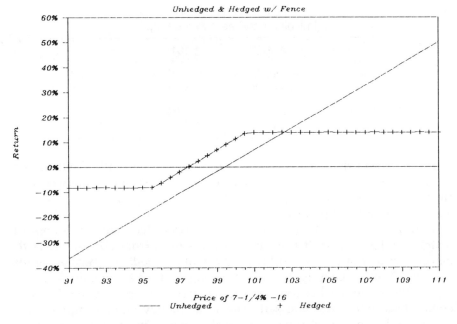

Figure 6–14   Returns on 7 1/4%–16.

If 7 1/4s remain stable at 101–00:

Bond @ 11/15/86 @ 101–00	=	$10,100,000
Accrued interest rec'd	=	$0
Coupon income	=	$362,500
Reinvestment income @ 5.8%	=	$0
Abandon puts @ 0–00	=	$0
Exercise calls @ 0–22	=	– $42,969
NET CREDITS	=	$10,419,531

If 7 1/4s rally to 111–00:

Bond @ 11/15/86 @ 101–00	=	$11,100,000
Accrued interest rec'd	=	$0
Coupon income	=	$362,500
Reinvestment income @ 5.8%	=	$0
Abandon puts @ 0–00	=	$0
Exercise calls @ 8–22	=	– $1,042,969
NET CREDITS	=	$10,419,531

Hedged and Unhedged Returns
(In Dollars and as a Percentage)

	Cash @ 91	@ 101	@ 111
Unhedged:	−$840,421	$159,579	$1,159,579
	−36.25%	6.88%	50.02%
Hedged:	−$186,124	$313,876	$313,876
	−8.19%	13.80%	13.80%

If the market declines, profits accruing on the put will offset much of the loss on the hedged security. (Often the put may be purchased sometime subsequent to the initial sale of the call as a defensive strategy in anticipation of a falling market.)

With the short call hedge our results indicate that your loss is approximately −8.19 percent if the cash bond declines from 101 to 91. If the market advances from 101 to 111, you establish a ceiling return of approximately 13.80 percent, giving up potential profits in a rising market.

Finally, if the market remains relatively stable, you augment your income. This is because you sell a near-the-money call, bringing in net premium. If the market remains near-the-money, you will enjoy accelerated time value decay with the near-the-money call. The out-of-the-money put will tend to display a more linear time value decay pattern.

The risk/reward profile of this strategy strongly resembles that of a bull put spread. This is intuitive in that the combination of a near-the-money short call and the long security creates a synthetic short put. Combining this near-the-money synthetic short put with an out-of-the-money long put creates something that resembles a *vertical bull put spread*.

Long Futures	+	High-Struck Short Call	=	Synthetic High-Struck Short Put
Synthetic High-Struck Short Put	+	Low-Struck Long Put	=	Vertical Bull Put Spread

Reverse Fence

If a fence entails the sale of a near-the-money call and the purchase of an *out-of-the-money* put, a *reverse fence* entails the sale of a near-the-money call and the purchase of an *in-the-money* put.

Example: You own $10 million face value of the 7¼ percent bond of 2016 and hedge by selling 125 calls struck at 100 and priced at 2–58. You buy 125 puts struck at 102 and priced at 4–03 (see Figure 6–15).

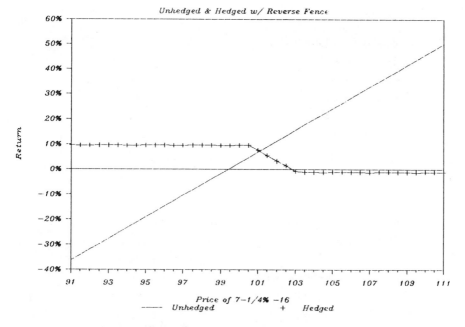

Figure 6-15   Returns on 7 1/4%-16.

Buy $10 MM 7 1/4% – 16 @ 101–00	=	$10,100,000
Accrued interest @ 8/26/86	=	$202,921
Sell 125 100 calls @ 2–58	=	– $363,281
Buy 125 102 puts @ 4–03	=	$505,859
NET INVESTMENT	=	$10,445,499

Assume that cash/futures convergence occurs at an annual rate of 1.4 percent and that the hedge is unwound on November 15, 1986. What might happen if the cash market fell 10 points, rose 10 points, or remained stable?

If 7 1/4s fall to 91–00:

Bond @ 11/15/86 @ 91–00	=	$9,100,000
Accrued interest rec'd	=	$0
Coupon income	=	$362,500
Reinvestment income @ 5.8%	=	$0
Exercise puts @ 9–42	=	$1,207,031
Abandon calls @ 0–00	=	$0
NET CREDITS	=	$10,669,531

If 7 1/4s remain stable at 101–00:

Bond @ 11/15/86 @ 101–00	=	$10,100,000
Accrued interest rec'd	=	$0
Coupon income	=	$362,500
Reinvestment income @ 5.8%	=	$0
Abandon puts @ 1–42	=	$207,031
Exercise calls @ 0–22	=	– $42,969
NET CREDITS	=	$10,626,563

If 7 1/4s rally to 111–00:

Bond @ 11/15/86 @ 101–00	=	$11,100,000
Accrued interest rec'd	=	$0
Coupon income	=	$362,500
Reinvestment income @ 5.8%	=	$0
Abandon puts @ 0–00	=	$0
Exercise calls @ 8–22	=	– $1,042,969
NET CREDITS	=	$10,419,531

Hedged and Unhedged Returns
(In Dollars and as a Percentage)

	Cash @ 91	@ 101	@ 111
Unhedged:	–$840,421	$159,579	$1,159,579
	–36.25%	6.88%	50.02%
Hedged:	$224,032	$181,063	–$25,968
	9.53%	7.70%	–1.10%

Again, you can think of the combination of the short near-the-money call with the long security as a synthetic short put. Combined with the long in-the-money put, it resembles a *vertical bear put spread.*

Long Futures	+	Low-Struck Short Call	=	Synthetic Low-Struck Short Put
Synthetic Low-Struck Short Put	+	High-Struck Long Put	=	Vertical Bear Put Spread

In other words, you have a ceiling return in the event of a down market—a floor return in the event of an up market.

QUESTIONS

1. To hedge a short position in the cash market, you may . . .
   (a) Take a bearish position in the futures, put, or call markets.
   (b) Buy futures, buy calls, or sell puts.
   (c) Take a synthetic futures position by buying puts and selling calls.
   (d) Buy futures, buy puts, or sell calls.
   (e) None of the above.
2. The combination of a short call and long cash or futures position . . .
   (a) Will allow you to hedge against the risk of falling interest rates.
   (b) Will allow you to lock in a floor return for the sale of your cash or futures instrument(s).
   (c) May be thought of as a synthetic long put.
   (d) May be thought of as a synthetic short put.
   (e) Augments your current income at the risk of giving up the initial net debit.
3. You may want to sell call options against a long cash bond portfolio . . .
   (a) To augment current income at the risk of forfeiting the opportunity to participate in windfall profits.
   (b) To capitalize on a neutral trading range.
   (c) To negate the risk of sharply rising rates.
   (d) All of the above.
   (e) (a) and (b) above.
   (f) (a) and (c) above.
4. Which statement is true?
   (a) Buying a put option will allow you to lock in an implied repo rate at worst.
   (b) The out-of-the-money option is a more conservative hedge instrument compared to an in- or at-the-money option.
   (c) The combination of an in-the-money long put and a long futures position resembles an out-of-the-money short call.
   (d) Buying a put option against a cash instrument allows you to retain much of the upside profit potential.
   (e) The combination of a short futures position with a long put represents a synthetic long call.
5. (a) You buy a bond futures contract at 86 and sell an 84 call for $2\,^{32}/_{64}$ths. What is your return if the market remains stable at 86 until option expiration?
   (b) What is your return if the market goes to 84 by expiration?
   (c) What is your return if the market goes to 81 by expiration?
6. (a) You buy 125,000 DMs at 0.4350 ($/mark) and buy a Chicago Mercantile Exchange DM put option struck at 0.4400 at the "Merc" for 0.0140. What is your return if the option is held to term and the market trades to 0.4000, 0.4400 or 0.4600?
   (b) Rather than using the in-the-money 0.4400 put, you buy a 0.4300 put for 0.0090. What is your return if the option is held to term and the market trades to 0.4000, 0.4300 or 0.4600?

7. Which statement is false?
   (a) If rates advance sharply, it is more likely that mortgages in the pipeline will fall through rather than close.
   (b) Long puts can be used to hedge price and quantity risk because of the contingent nature of an option.
   (c) A mortgage banker may suffer large losses if he hedges his pipeline with short futures and rates fall.
   (d) (a) and (b) above.
   (e) (b) and (c) above.

8. You have hedged Eurodollar holdings by selling at-the-money calls. How could the hedged position be adjusted in the event that the market declines?
   (a) Roll up into the next higher strike or buy an in-the-money put.
   (b) Liquidate the original at-the-money call.
   (c) Put on a fence by selling more calls at the strike price.
   (d) Put on a fence by buying an in-the-money put and rolling down into the next lower strike.
   (e) Put on a fence by buying an out-of-the-money put or rolling down into the next lower strike.

9. Rank the performance of these hedging strategies in a bear market:
   (a) Short futures, short calls, long puts.
   (b) Short calls, short futures, long puts.
   (c) Short futures, long calls, short puts.
   (d) Short futures, long puts, short calls.
   (e) Unhedged, short futures, short calls, long puts.

10. Which statement is false?
    (a) The sale of a call against a fixed income security portfolio effectively reduces your investment.
    (b) Short futures is a superior hedging strategy in a neutral or sideways trading market.
    (c) The purchase of a put against a fixed income security portfolio effectively increases your investment.
    (d) The Treasury futures basis is defined as the cash price less the adjusted futures price.
    (e) Cash/futures convergence works against a hedger using a short call or long put strategy in a positive yield curve environment.

11. You own DMs and exchange them for dollars, investing the cash in Treasury bonds. What would you do to guarantee a minimum return in terms of DMs?

12. Track the effectiveness of a hedge of a financial instrument of your choice using short futures, nearest-to-the-money long puts, and nearest-to-the-money short calls over the next week using daily closing prices. Ratio the hedge if necessary. Which strategy performed best? Why?

13. Delta . . .
    (a) Is the expected change in the underlying price given a particular change in the value of a security.
    (b) Is most stable for near-to-the-money options.

    (c) Changes constantly as the market price fluctuates and as the option approaches expiration.

    (d) Is most stable for at-the-money options.

    (e) All of the above.

14. Which statement is true?

    (a) Over time, delta will approach zero for in-the-money options and one for out-of-the moneys.

    (b) An at-the-money delta will grow more stable as it approaches expiration.

    (c) A short call and a short put delta may be represented as a negative number.

    (d) Delta may be referenced directly to find the neutral ratio.

    (e) The neutral ratio for options on futures may be multiplied by the futures hedge ratio to define a delta neutral hedge strategy.

15. You put on a delta neutral strategy by buying an at-the-money call with a delta of 0.51 against a short futures position. What happens if the market declines sharply within the same day?

    (a) The delta may be expected to rise.

    (b) Losses will start to accrue as the market falls.

    (c) You will need fewer calls to hedge the risk.

    (d) You will start to make money in the futures market faster than you lose money in the call market.

    (e) (c) and (d) above.

16. (a) You delta hedge $50 million face value of Eurodollars by selling CME call options on Eurodollar futures with a delta of 0.45. How many calls do you need to become delta neutral?

    (b) The market falls and the delta falls to 0.38. What do you do to adjust the position?

17. (a) You delta hedge $20 million face value of the cheapest-to-deliver notes with long puts exercisable for note futures. Your conversion factor equals 1.2300. The puts have a delta of 0.56. How many puts do you need?

    (b) The market falls and delta rises to 0.64. What do you do to adjust the position?.

18. Which statement is false?

    (a) Volatility works for, and time value decay works against, a long delta hedger.

    (b) Choppy markets and frequent adjustments can diminish the effectiveness of the delta hedge.

    (c) An unadjusted long delta hedge will start to resemble a long strangle over time.

    (d) Volatility works against, and time value decay works for, a short delta hedger.

    (e) An unadjusted delta hedge using short options will begin to resemble a short straddle over time.

19. Gamma . . .

    (a) May be thought of as the derivative of the premium with respect to time.

(b) Is the derivative of the premium with respect to time.
(c) Is the expected change in the neutral hedge ratio given a fluctuation in the underlying price.
(d) Represents the stability of the delta.
(e) Is always lower for at-the-money options than in- or out-of-the-moneys.

7

Floating Rate Risk Management

Commercial borrowers face a greater challenge than ever before. Because interest rates have been extremely volatile, a loan or project, financed on a floating rate basis, may quickly turn from a profitable to an unprofitable venture. As a result, many commercial borrowers have sought insurance over-the-counter options. These products are intended to provide cap rate protection for floating rate loans.

The price of this insurance protection is market determined and quoted as an option premium. Premiums may be determined either through the open outcry auction system at a recognized futures exchange or through direct dealer/customer negotiation in the over-the-counter market.

> **Example:** Assume that a real estate developer wants to borrow $50 million from a commercial bank for a period of one year. No matter whether the loan rate floats daily as a function of the prime rate or is reset periodically based on some other rate, for example, the London Interbank Offered Rate (LIBOR), the borrower is exposed to the risk of rising rates.

Both borrower and lender will benefit if interest rate uncertainty is eliminated. By putting a cap on the interest rate, the borrower is free to concentrate on the development project. The lender gains from the increased probability of timely performance on the part of the borrower (and may as a result offer a reduced loan rate).

The transactions which create the cap may be executed directly by the borrower or by the lender. In the latter case, the costs of establishing the cap may be passed on to the borrower, presumably in the form of a somewhat higher interest rate.

PRIME RATE LOAN

Many commercial loans are tied to the prime rate and float daily. Over-the-counter (OTC) caps are available and may be purchased from a variety of financial institutions to guard against the risk of an increasing prime rate.

These caps are priced against an average of the prime rates of 10 money center banks as published by the Federal Reserve Bank of New York. Interest payable in excess of the cap rate generally accrues daily and is payable to the cap purchaser on a quarterly basis. The premium is payable at the initiation of the cap rate agreement. The purchase of the prime rate cap effectively transforms a floating rate loan into a loan with a ceiling rate somewhat higher than the initial rate.

LIBOR-BASED LOAN

Assume that the loan rate is reset every 90 days based on LIBOR plus 175 basis points. Interest is paid quarterly. To hedge an increase in Eurodollar rates, one may buy put options (the right to sell a $1 million face value 90-day Eurodollar futures contract). To protect against an interest rate increase, a "strip" of Eurodollar puts could be purchased. For example, fifty 90-day, fifty 180-day and fifty 270-day puts could be purchased in a strip.

Assume that the initial Eurodollar rate is 6¾ percent and the initial annual rate is 8½ percent. A strip of Eurodollar put options struck at-the-money (at the 93.25 strike price reflecting a yield of 6.75 percent) are available at 24, 36, and 45 basis points, respectively. This translates to $600, $900, and $1,125 per $1 million face value contract, for a total premium of $131,250 for the $50 million loan. (One basis point on a $1 million 90-day instrument equates to $25.)

The initial quarterly interest payment is equal to $1,062,500 based on the 8½ percent annual rate. If the 90-day Eurodollar rate increases to 8½ percent at the time of the first reset and remains at that level, the borrower's effective annual interest rate increases to 10¼ percent. Quarterly interest payments increase to $1,281,250. This results in additional interest expense of $218,750 per quarter or $656,250 for the three remaining periods.

At the same time, each of the three options in the strip would be valued at 175 basis points at expiration. This is equivalent to $4,375 per $1 million face value contract, $218,750 per 50 contracts, or $656,250 for all 150 contracts. Thus the hedger would have limited his additional interest expense from $656,250 over the three quarters to the option premium of $131,250—a savings of $525,000. Of course, if rates had remained stable, the hedger's costs would have been increased by the amount of the option premium.

THE MARKET PRICE OF INSURANCE

The market price of an interest rate cap will depend upon the following factors:

1. The strike price(s) chosen. The borrower may select the desired amount of insurance protection. At-the-money strike prices are available effectively to provide "zero deductible" insurance protection while various levels of out-of-the-money strike prices are available to provide a lesser degree of protection. Synthetic strike prices may be created using a mix of exchange listed strike prices.
2. The level of spot and implied forward Eurodollar rates.
3. The time frame of the interest rate cap program. Longer-term cap programs are more costly than shorter-term programs. Note, however, that longer-term options tend to retain their value better than do shorter-term options.
4. The level of anticipated market volatility. The cost of a cap program will be directly related to the market's assessment of future interest rate volatility. Higher implied volatilities increase the cost of an option based cap rate program.

A COMPLEX EXAMPLE

Eurodollar put options may be used in much the same way as described above to hedge the floating rate financing associated with a commercial building project. Let us discuss a scenario in which a development company is planning to construct a major multipurpose structure.

For purposes of this discussion, make some key assumptions:

1. Our hypothetical project will be financed at a rate equal to the 90-day LIBOR rate (as published in the financial press) plus 120 basis points.
2. The total financing required for the project equals approximately $142 million. Such funds are to be drawn as required over the course of four and one-half years from June 1986 through 1990, the cumulative loan balance to be repaid fully at the conclusion of 1990.
3. Funds are to be drawn in accordance with the schedule as set forth in Table 7–1.
4. Assume that the quarterly draws shown in Table 7–1 are taken at the commencement of each quarterly period. The loan rate will be reset

Table 7-1   Project ABC Quarterly Draw Schedule
in 000s

	Draw Schedule	Cumulative Balance
1986:		
Thru 6/31	18,073	18,073
7/1–09/30	10,321	28,393
1. 10/1–12/31	10,493	38,887
1987:		
2. 1/1–03/31	20,962	59,848
3. 4/1–06/31	17,212	77,060
4. 7/1–09/30	17,380	94,440
5. 10/1–12/31	10,313	104,753
1988:		
6. 1/1–03/31	5,758	110,511
7. 4/1–06/31	5,758	116,269
8. 7/1–09/30	5,758	122,027
9. 10/1–12/31	5,757	127,784
1/1–12/31	23,031	127,784
1989:		
10. 1/1–03/31	2,801	130,585
11. 4/1–06/31	2,800	133,385
12. 7/1–09/30	2,801	136,186
13. 10/1–12/31	2,800	138,986
1/1–12/31	11,202	138,986
1990 (prorated scheduled):		
14. 1/1–03/31	700	139,686
15. 4/1–06/31	699	140,385
16. 7/1–09/30	699	141,084
17. 10/1–12/31	699	141,783
1/1–12/31	2,797	141,783

every 90 days. Thus the $20.9 million taken from January 1 through March 31, 1987, is reset near the end of March 1987, near the end of June 1987, September 1987, December 1987, March 1988, etc. These reset dates roughly correspond to the expiration of the Eurodollar futures contract (near the middle of the month on the March "quarterly cycle.")

5. The developers are interested in putting a cap of either 9 percent or 9 ½ percent on their effective borrowing costs.

The questions which arise are: How many Eurodollar puts should be purchased, in what months, and how much will it cost?

One would prefer to construct a strip of puts with expirations ranging from September 1986 to September 1990. Unfortunately, this is not possible because options are only available as of this date with expirations running out to June 1987. Moreover, it is generally not recommended to trade Eurodollar options with expirations which extend more than two quarterly expiration months in the future. This is because the more deferred options tend to suffer from poor liquidity.

The recommended procedure is a "strip/stack." This entails buying put options (in numbers corresponding to the cumulative draw) "stripped out" as far as possible given reasonable liquidity, and then "stacking" additional options in the most deferred month to cover risk in subsequent quarters.

Once initially constructed, these stacked options are to be "rolled forward" out into deferred months, that is, some stacked options are to be liquidated and the position reestablished in a more deferred month. Thus the strip/stack requires management subsequent to the initial placement. Consequently, the up-front cost and additional management costs must be considered.

A cap of 9 percent implies the use of options with a strike or exercise price of 92.20. A cap of $9\frac{1}{2}$ percent implies the use of options with a strike or exercise price of 91.70. These figures are calculated as: $100 - (\text{effective cap rate} - 120 \text{ basis points})$.

For example

$$\text{Strike} = 100.00 \text{ points less } (9.00 \text{ points} - 1.20 \text{ points})$$

$$= 100.00 \text{ less } 7.80$$

$$= 92.20$$

$$\text{Strike} = 100.00 \text{ points less } (9.50 \text{ points} - 1.20 \text{ points})$$

$$= 100.00 \text{ less } 8.30$$

$$= 91.70$$

Unfortunately, options are only available with strike prices set at 50 basis point intervals under 92.00 and at 25 basis point intervals over 92.00. (Options are available with strikes at 90.50, 91.00, 91.50, 92.00, 92.25, 92.50, 92.75, 93.00, etc.) So rather than examining caps of 9 percent and $9\frac{1}{2}$ percent, let us examine strategies which will allow one to put on a cap of approximately 9.20 percent (92.00 strike price) and 8.70 percent (92.50 strike price).

Bear in mind that caps with effective rates of 8.95 (92.25 strike price), 8.45 (92.75 strike price), 8.20 percent (93.00 strike price), 7.95 percent (93.25 strike price), 7.70 percent (93.50 strike price), and so on may also be constructed. In general, the higher the strike price (the lower the cap rate), the more the program costs.

9.20 PERCENT CAP

In order to cap one's maximum borrowing costs at about 9.20 percent, the initial recommended transaction is as follows. This example was constructed using data available at 10:00 A.M. Friday, July 18, 1986. (Each basis point or .01 equals $25 per $1 million 90-day contract.)

		Qty.	Mo.	Strike		Price Per Contract		Total
	Strip:							
1.	Buy	39	Sep '86	92.00	@	0.01	=	$975
2.	Buy	60	Dec '86	92.00	@	0.04	=	$6,000
	SUBTOTAL:					Long 99 Puts for $6,975		
	Stack:							
3.	Buy	77	Dec '86	92.00	@	0.04	=	$7,700
4.	Buy	94	Dec '86	92.00	@	0.04	=	$9,400
5.	Buy	105	Dec '86	92.00	@	0.04	=	$10,500
6.	Buy	111	Dec '86	92.00	@	0.04	=	$11,100
7.	Buy	116	Dec '86	92.00	@	0.04	=	$11,600
8.	Buy	122	Dec '86	92.00	@	0.04	=	$12,200
9.	Buy	128	Dec '86	92.00	@	0.04	=	$12,800
10.	Buy	131	Dec '86	92.00	@	0.04	=	$13,100
11.	Buy	133	Dec '86	92.00	@	0.04	=	$13,300
12.	Buy	136	Dec '86	92.00	@	0.04	=	$13,600
13.	Buy	139	Dec '86	92.00	@	0.04	=	$13,900
14.	Buy	140	Dec '86	92.00	@	0.04	=	$14,000
15.	Buy	140	Dec '86	92.00	@	0.04	=	$14,000
16.	Buy	141	Dec '86	92.00	@	0.04	=	$14,100
17.	Buy	142	Dec '86	92.00	@	0.04	=	$14,200
	SUBTOTAL:					Long 1,855 Puts for $185,500		
	TOTAL:					Long 1,954 Puts for $192,475		

The number of contracts in each of the 17 transactions in the strip and stack correspond to the number of million dollar units to be repriced at each successive (assumed) reset date. Thus the first transaction (long 39 92.00 September 1986 puts) allows one to hedge the initial $18.1 million draw, the subsequent $10.3 million draw (assumed to commence at the beginning of the third quarter 1986) and the following $10.5 million draw (assumed to commence at the beginning of the fourth quarter 1986).

The second transaction (long 60 December 1986 puts) allows one to hedge the $39 million loan balance already outstanding as of December 1986 *plus* the $21.0 million draw assumed to commence as of the beginning of the first quarter 1987. This completes the strip. The 15 transactions which comprise the stack correspond to the 15 different "reset dates" from the beginning of the second quarter 1987 to the beginning of the fourth quarter 1990.

For example, the third transaction (long 77 December 1986 puts) allows one to hedge the $60 million loan balance already outstanding as of March 1987 plus the additional draw of $17.2 million assumed to commence as of the beginning of the second quarter 1987. Thus we are reducing the overall loan to a series of 90-day loans.

Subsequent to the initial placement of the hedge, it must be managed. September 1986:

- 39 Sep '86 puts 92.00 expire.
- Roll over 1,855 puts in stack by buying 1,855 Mar '87 92.00 puts. (Sell the Dec '86 puts and buy the Mar '87 puts.)

December 1986:

- 60 Dec '86 puts 92.00 expire.
- Roll over 1,778 Mar '87 92.00 puts into 1,778 Jun '87 92.00 puts.

[This leaves 77 (1,855 − 1,778) long puts in Mar '87 to cover the third reset date.]
March 1987:

- 77 Mar '87 92.00 puts expire.
- Roll over 1,684 Jun '87 92.00 puts into 1,684 Sep '87 92.00 puts.

[This leaves 94 (1,778 − 1,684) long puts in Jun '87 to cover the fourth reset date. This pattern continues as the stack is "unwound."]
June 1987:

- 94 Jun '87 92.00 puts expire.
- Roll over 1,579 Sep '87 92.00 puts into 1,579 Dec '87 92.00 puts.

September 1987:

- 105 Sep '87 92.00 puts expire.
- Roll over 1,468 Dec '87 92.00 puts into 1,468 Mar '88 92.00 puts.

December 1987:

- 111 Dec '87 92.00 puts expire.
- Roll over 1,352 Mar '88 92.00 puts into 1,352 Jun '88 92.00 puts.

March 1988:

- 116 Mar '88 92.00 puts expire.
- Roll over 1,230 Jun '88 92.00 puts into 1,230 Sep '88 puts.

June 1988:

- 122 Jun '88 puts expire.
- Roll over 1,102 Sep '88 92.00 puts into 1,102 Dec '88 92.00 puts.

September 1988:

- 128 Sep '88 92.00 puts expire.
- Roll over 971 Dec '88 92.00 puts into 971 Mar '89 92.00 puts.

December 1988:

- 131 Dec '88 92.00 puts expire.
- Roll over 838 Mar '89 92.00 puts into 838 Jun '89 92.00 puts.

March 1989:

- 133 Mar '89 92.00 puts expire.
- Roll over 702 Jun '89 92.00 puts into 702 Sep '89 92.00 puts.

June 1989:

- 136 Jun '89 92.00 puts expire.
- Roll over 563 Sep '89 92.00 puts into 563 Dec '89 92.00 puts.

September 1989:

- 139 Sep '89 92.00 puts expire.
- Roll over 423 Dec '89 92.00 puts into 423 Mar '90 92.00 puts.

December 1989:

- 140 Dec '89 92.00 expire.
- Roll over 283 Mar '90 92.00 puts into 283 Jun '90 92.00 puts.

March 1990:

- 140 Mar '90 92.00 puts expire.
- Roll over 142 Jun '90 92.00 puts into 142 Sep '90 92.00 puts.

June 1990:

- 141 Jun '90 92.00 puts expire.

September 1990:

- 142 Sep '90 92.00 puts expire.

The question becomes: How much will it cost to execute each of these roll overs? The answer may be found by examining the time value decay patterns associated with options under different market conditions.

As of Friday, July 18, 1986, market offers conformed to the following structure:

	Eurodollar Futures	*92.00 Put Options*
Sep. '86	93.60	0.01
Dec. '86	93.58	0.04
Mar. '87	93.40	0.11

Bids were generally two basis points lower. If the market stands still over the life of the hedge, one may expect to roll over by buying deferred options worth roughly 4 basis points and liquidating options which are basically worthless. This implies a loss of 4 basis points per contract ($100). A total of 15,970 contracts are rolled over. This implies an approximate cost of $1,597,000.

Of course, the market may move up or down. If the market moves up, the puts will become less costly. If the market moves down, the puts become more costly. If, however, the puts become more costly, this implies that rates are advancing. Existing puts will increase in value and perhaps be exercised; they will serve to protect possible advances in the loan price.

Estimated Value of 9.20% Cap
(Without Transaction Costs)

Initial Transactions	$ 192,475
Subsequent Transactions	$1,597,000
TOTAL	$1,789,475

This appears to be a great deal of money; however, consider that a 1 percent increase in the loan rate of a $142 million balance over four and one-half years equals approximately $6.39 million.

8.70 PERCENT CAP

In order to cap one's maximum borrowing costs at about 8.70 percent, the initial recommended transaction is as follows. This example was constructed using data available at 10:00 A.M. Friday, July 18, 1986. (Each basis point or .01 equals $25 per $1 million 90-day contract.)

		Qty.	Mo.	Strike		Price Per Contract		Total
	Strip:							
1.	Buy	39	Sep '86	92.50	@	0.01	=	$975
2.	Buy	60	Dec '86	92.50	@	0.07	=	$10,500
	SUBTOTAL:					Long 99 Puts for $11,475		
	Stack:							
3.	Buy	77	Dec '86	92.50	@	0.07	=	$13,475
4.	Buy	94	Dec '86	92.50	@	0.07	=	$16,450
5.	Buy	105	Dec '86	92.50	@	0.07	=	$18,375
6.	Buy	111	Dec '86	92.50	@	0.07	=	$19,425
7.	Buy	116	Dec '86	92.50	@	0.07	=	$20,300
8.	Buy	122	Dec '86	92.50	@	0.07	=	$21,350
9.	Buy	128	Dec '86	92.50	@	0.07	=	$22,400
10.	Buy	131	Dec '86	92.50	@	0.07	=	$22,925
11.	Buy	133	Dec '86	92.50	@	0.07	=	$23,275
12.	Buy	136	Dec '86	92.50	@	0.07	=	$23,800
13.	Buy	139	Dec '86	92.50	@	0.07	=	$24,325
14.	Buy	140	Dec '86	92.50	@	0.07	=	$24,500
15.	Buy	140	Dec '86	92.50	@	0.07	=	$24,500
16.	Buy	141	Dec '86	92.50	@	0.07	=	$24,675
17.	Buy	142	Dec '86	92.50	@	0.07	=	$24,850
	SUBTOTAL:					Long 1,855 Puts for $324,625		
	TOTAL:					Long 1,954 Puts for $336,100		

How much will the roll overs cost? The roll-over schedule conforms to the schedule as outlined above except that you use a 92.50 strike rather than a 92.00 strike.

As of Friday, July 18, 1986, the market offers conformed to the following structure:

	Eurodollar Futures	*92.50 Put Options*
Sep. '86	93.60	0.01
Dec. '86	93.58	0.07
Mar. '87	93.40	0.18

Bids were generally 2 basis points lower. If the market stands still over the life of the hedge, one may expect to roll over by buying deferred options worth roughly 7 basis points and selling options which were basically worthless. This implies a loss of 7 basis points per contract ($175).

A total of 15,970 contracts are rolled over. This implies an approximate cost of $2,794,750. Again, it must be emphasized that this is a stand-still estimate only.

Estimated Value of 8.70% Cap
(Without Transaction Costs)

Initial Transactions	$ 336,100
Subsequent Transactions	$2,794,750
TOTAL	$3,130,850

QUESTIONS

1. Which of the following is true?
   (a) A cap is a guarantee that the interest rate paid on a loan will not fall below a specified amount.
   (b) It is easy to hedge prime rate risk using exchange traded products.
   (c) Eurodollar options may be stripped out into the future indefinitely.
   (d) A cap may be thought of as a form of an option contract.
   (e) None of the above.
2. LIBOR-based loans . . .
   (a) May be hedged with an over-the-counter product or with an exchange traded product.
   (b) Mean that the interest rate on the loan is directly reflected in the T-bill rate.
   (c) Are the most common type of loan granted real estate developers by commercial banks.
   (d) Are only available to European companies.
   (e) (A) and (C) above.
3. (a) Describe how one might buy a strip of Eurodollar put options.
   (b) Describe how a strip differs from a stack; a strip/stack.

8
Option Arbitrage

Someone once remarked that the only certain things in life are death and taxes. While we do not wish to dispute this observation, we can point out that there are a number of option strategies which, while not completely riskless, nonetheless allow traders to lock in specific returns with a high degree of certainty.

These strategies are known as *arbitrage* transactions, and the traders who practice these techniques are known as *arbitrageurs*. The strategies that option arbitrageurs pursue are known as *conversions, reverse conversions* (or simply reversals), and *boxes*.

These trades allow one to take advantage of temporary discrepancies in the option pricing structure, that is, where premiums trade "out-of-line" with the price of the instrument for which the option may be exercised or with the price of other options. Because these plays entail low risk, they also imply small returns.

These opportunities, when they exist, may not be accessible to all option traders. In fact, it is likely that only professional floor traders standing in the trading pit who place their trades at very low transaction costs can successfully execute option arbitrage. Still, every option trader should be cognizant of these opportunities when they exist and understand that these trades are critical to maintaining equilibrium or fair-market option pricing.

CONVERSIONS AND REVERSALS

Conversions and reversals represent the combination of a futures position with a put and a call position. These are the most fundamental and most frequently practiced option arbitrage opportunities.

Once executed, the conversion and reversal imply a flat or constant return no matter where the market trades. Further, the conversion and reversal are "self-liquidating" in the sense that the combinations of positions are mutually offsetting. Provided that one can successfully place a conversion or reversal at prices that imply a profit, the arbitrageur can be fairly confident of realizing that profit.

Conversion

A conversion represents (1) the sale of a call option, (2) the purchase of a put option at the same strike price and with the same expiration date, and (3) the purchase of the underlying instrument for which those options may be exercised.

> A *conversion* represents the sale of a call, the purchase of a put which shares a common strike and expiration date with the call, and the purchase of the instrument for which those options may be exercised. Once executed, this arbitrage implies a constant return to expiration.

Once executed, this trade implies a flat return at any market level which may subsequently be realized. This strategy is completely self-liquidating in the sense that by holding it until expiration, all three legs of the strategy are offsetting.

For example, assume that S&P 500 futures are trading at 250 and that the 250 call on S&P futures is trading at 6 points. Given this information, we know that the fair value of the 250 put equals 6 points as well. (At-the-money puts and calls exercisable for futures should trade at the same level.)

But what if you can buy the put at 5.85 points? This pricing discrepancy would imply a conversion opportunity. Specifically, one might buy the put at 5.85, sell the call at 6.00, and buy futures at 250. This entails an initial net credit of 0.15 points or $75 ($500 per full point).

If the market declines to 245, you can exercise the put by selling futures at 250. This liquidates the original long futures contract at a wash. The call falls out-of-the-money and is abandoned. Thus you are left with a profit equal to the initial net credit of $75.

If the market advances to 255, the call is exercised against the conversion holder. You are forced to sell futures at 250, offsetting the original long futures contract at a wash. The put falls out-of-the-money and is abandoned, and you are left with the initial net credit of $75.

This is an extremely straightforward conversion. The options are struck at-the-money and the strategy results in an initial net credit. You lock in the 0.15 points or $75—the initial net credit—no matter whether the market rallies, declines, or remains stable. If this conversion were to result in an initial net debit, you would lock in a *loss* equal to that amount.

Most conversions are not quite as simple. These transactions usually involve options which are struck either above or below the market. As such, these conversions may result in an initial net credit or an initial net debit, but no matter whether a debit or a credit results, these transactions may be profitable or unprofitable.

The problem arises in identifying the possible magnitude of profit or loss. Fortunately, you *can* identify the prospective profit or loss associated with a conversion. This is accomplished by studying the actual level of option premium relative to the theoretical premium levels. These theoretical levels may be generated by an option pricing model as shown in Table 8–1.

Assume that S&P 500 futures are trading at 250.45. Our table suggests that the 250 call should be trading at 9.20, the 250 put at 8.75. But what if the call is underpriced relative to the call at 8.65? This suggests that a conversion may be profitable.

Example: A conversion is established by buying the December 1986 S&Ps at 250.45, buying a December put struck at 250 for 8.65 ($4,325), and selling a 250 call for 9.20 ($4,600). This entails an initial net credit of $275.

Long	1 Dec. Futures	@ 250.45		
Long	1 Dec. 250.00 Put(s)	@ 8.65	=	– $4,325
Short	1 Dec. 250.00 Call(s)	@ 9.20	=	$4,600
NET CREDIT				$275

What would happen if the market declines, advances, or remains stable by the time expiration rolls around in December?

If the market falls to 245.00:

Sell	1 Dec. Futures	@ 245.00	=	– $2,725
Exercise	1 Dec. 250.00 Put(s)	@ 5.00	=	$2,500
Abandon	1 Dec. 250.00 Call(s)	@ 0.00	=	$0
Original Net Debit/Credit			=	$275
TOTAL PROFIT/LOSS				$50

If the market remains stable at 250.00:

Sell	1 Dec. Futures	@ 250.00	=	– $225
Abandon	1 Dec. 250.00 Put(s)	@ 0.00	=	$0
Abandon	1 Dec. 250.00 Call(s)	@ 0.00	=	$0
Original Net Debit/Credit			=	$275
TOTAL PROFIT/LOSS				$50

Table 8–1   Theoretical Premium/Delta Matrix

Options on Dec. '86 S&P Futures

| Today's Date: 9/08/86 | | | | | Volatility: 17.25% | |
| Expiration Date: 12/20/86 | | | | | Short-term Rate: 6.00% | |

| | | | | Exercise Price | | |
Underlying/		240	245	250	255	260
250.30	Call	14.80	11.75	9.15	6.95	5.20
	Delta	0.68	0.60	0.51	0.43	0.35
	Put	4.65	6.55	8.85	11.55	14.70
	Delta	0.30	0.38	0.47	0.55	0.63
250.35	Call	14.80	11.80	9.15	7.00	5.20
	Delta	0.30	0.38	0.47	0.55	0.63
	Put	4.65	6.50	8.80	11.55	14.70
	Delta	0.30	0.38	0.47	0.55	0.63
250.40	Call	14.85	11.80	9.20	7.00	5.20
	Delta	0.68	0.60	0.52	0.43	0.35
	Put	4.60	6.50	8.75	11.50	14.65
	Delta	0.30	0.38	0.47	0.55	0.63
250.45	Call	14.90	11.85	9.20	7.00	5.25
	Delta	0.68	0.60	0.52	0.43	0.35
	Put	4.60	6.50	8.75	11.50	14.60
	Delta	0.30	0.38	0.47	0.55	0.63
250.50	Call	14.90	11.85	9.25	7.05	5.25
	Delta	0.68	0.60	0.52	0.43	0.35
	Put	4.60	6.45	8.75	11.45	14.60
	Delta	0.30	0.38	0.46	0.55	0.63
250.55	Call	14.95	11.90	9.25	7.05	5.25
	Delta	0.69	0.60	0.52	0.43	0.35
	Put	4.60	6.45	8.70	11.45	14.55
	Delta	0.30	0.38	0.46	0.55	0.63
250.60	Call	15.00	11.95	9.30	7.10	5.30
	Delta	0.69	0.60	0.52	0.44	0.35
	Put	4.55	6.40	8.70	11.40	14.50
	Delta	0.30	0.38	0.46	0.55	0.63

If the market rallies to 255.00:

Sell	1 Dec. Futures	@ 255.00	=	$2,275
Abandon	1 Dec. 250.00 Put(s)	@ 0.00	=	$0
Exercise	1 Dec. 250.00 Call(s)	@ 5.00	=	– $2,500
Original Net Debit/Credit			=	$275
TOTAL PROFIT/LOSS				$50

Despite the fact that this strategy results in a rather large initial net credit of $275, it only allows you to lock in a net profit of $50. This $50 or 0.10 points equals the amount by which the put was initially underpriced.

Conversions may result in an initial net debit or an initial net credit. When the market is trading higher than the common strike price, the conversion results in an initial net credit. When the market is trading lower than the common strike, the conversion results in an initial net debit.

$$\text{Conversions} \ldots$$

$$\text{Market} > \text{Strike} \Rightarrow \text{Credit}$$

$$\text{Market} < \text{Strike} \Rightarrow \text{Debit}$$

Whether a debit or a credit results has no impact on the profitability of the strategy. There is a convenient formula which may be used to identify whether a conversion held to expiration will result in a profit or loss.

$$\text{Conversion Return} = (\text{Call Premium} - \text{Put Premium})$$
$$\text{Less}$$
$$(\text{Market Price} - \text{Strike Price})$$

In the foregoing example:

$$\text{Conversion Return} = (9.20 - 8.65) - (250.45 - 250.00)$$

$$= 0.55 - 0.45$$

$$= 0.10 \text{ or } \$50.$$

Reverse Conversion

A reverse conversion or reversal is, as its name implies, just the opposite of a conversion. A reversal entails (1) the purchase of a call option, (2) the sale of a put option at the same strike price and with the same expiration date, and (3) the sale of the underlying instrument for which those options may be exercised.

A *reverse conversion* or *reversal* represents the purchase of a call, the sale of a put which shares a common strike and expiration date with the call, and the sale of the instrument for which those options may be exercised. Once executed, this arbitrage implies a constant return to expiration.

Like the conversion, the reversal implies a flat return at any subsequent market level. This strategy is completely self-liquidating in the sense that by holding it until expiration, all three legs of the strategy are offsetting.

For example, assume that S&P 500 futures are trading at 250 and that the 250 call on S&P futures is trading at 6 points. Given this information, we know that the fair value of the 250 put equals 6 points as well. (At-the-money puts and calls exercisable for futures should trade at the same level.)

But what if you can sell the put at 6.20 points? This pricing discrepancy implies a reverse conversion opportunity. Specifically, one might sell the put at 6.20, buy the call at 6.00, and sell futures at 250. This entails an initial net credit of 0.20 points or $100 ($500 per full point).

If the market advances to 255, you can exercise the call by buying futures at 250. This offsets the original short futures contract at a wash. The put falls out-of-the-money and is abandoned; you are left with a profit equal to the initial net credit of $100.

If the market declines to 245, the put is exercised against the reversal holder. Thus the trader is required to go long futures at 250. This offsets the original short futures contract at a wash. The call falls out-of-the-money and is abandoned; you are left with a profit equal to the initial net credit of $100.

Of course, this is a very simple reversal. You lock in 0.20 points or $100—the initial net credit—whether the market rallies, declines, or remains stable. If this reversal were to result in an initial net debit, you would lock in a *loss* equal to that amount.

Most reversals, however, are not placed at-the-money. They are usually placed when the market is above or below the strike price in question. You can identify the prospective profit or loss by examining the relationship between actual market premiums and theoretical premiums as indicated by Table 8–1.

Assume that the market is trading at 250.45. Our table suggests that the 250 call should be trading at 9.20 and the 250 put at 8.75. But what if the put is overpriced relative to the call at 8.90? This implies the use of a reversal.

Example: A reversal is put on by selling the December 1986 S&Ps at 250.45, selling a December put struck at 250 for 8.90 ($4,450), and buying a 250 call for 9.20 ($4,600). This entails an initial net debit of $150.

Short	1 Dec. Futures	@ 250.45		
Short	1 Dec. 250.00 Put(s)	@ 8.90	=	$4,450
Long	1 Dec. 250.00 Call(s)	@ 9.20	=	$4,600
NET DEBIT				$150

What would happen if the market declines, advances, or remains stable by the time expiration rolls around in December?

If the market falls to 245.00:

Buy	1 Dec. Futures	@ 245.00	=	$2,725
Exercise	1 Dec. 250.00 Put(s)	@ 5.00	=	– $2,500
Abandon	1 Dec. 250.00 Call(s)	@ 0.00	=	$0
Original Net Debit/Credit			=	– $150
TOTAL PROFIT/LOSS				$75

If the market remains stable at 250.00:

Buy	1 Dec. Futures	@ 250.00	=	$225
Abandon	1 Dec. 250.00 Put(s)	@ 0.00	=	$0
Abandon	1 Dec. 250.00 Call(s)	@ 0.00	=	$0
Original Net Debit/Credit			=	– $150
TOTAL PROFIT/LOSS				$75

If the market rallies to 255.00:

Buy	1 Dec. Futures	@ 255.00	=	– $2,275
Abandon	1 Dec. 250.00 Put(s)	@ 0.00	=	$0
Exercise	1 Dec. 250.00 Call(s)	@ 5.00	=	$2,500
Original Net Debit/Credit			=	– $150
TOTAL PROFIT/LOSS				$75

Even though this strategy results in an initial net debit of $150, it actually allows you to lock in a profit equal to the amount by which the put was underpriced—0.15 points or $75.

Reversals may result in an initial net debit or an initial net credit. When the market is greater than the common strike price, the reversal results in an initial net debit. When the market is trading lower than the common strike, the reversal results in an initial net credit.

Reversals . . .

Market > Strike ⇒ Debit

Market < Strike ⇒ Credit

Whether a debit or a credit results has no impact on the profitability of the strategy. The reversal return may be calculated in just the opposite manner that the conversion return is calculated.

$$\text{Reversal Return} = (\text{Put Premium} - \text{Call Premium})$$
$$\text{Less}$$
$$(\text{Strike Price} - \text{Market Price})$$

In the foregoing example:

$$\text{Reversal Return} = (8.90 - 9.20) - (250.00 - 250.45)$$
$$= (-0.30) - (-0.45)$$
$$= 0.15 \text{ or } \$75.$$

Synthetic Futures

Like many option strategies, conversions and reversals break down into simpler strategies. Many times it is easier to think of these arbitrage strategies as combinations of simpler strategies.

For example, the combination of a long put and a short call, as found in a conversion, represents a synthetic short futures contract. Combine a synthetic short futures with an actual long futures contract and the positions offset. Thus you are able to lock in a fixed rate of return.

Long Put + Short Call = Synthetic Short Futures

Synthetic Short Futures + Long Futures = Fixed Return

Example: Our previous conversion example had the trader buy a 250 put at 8.65 and sell a 250 call at 9.20 for a 0.55 initial net credit. This is equivalent to selling futures at the 250 strike plus the .55 credit or 250.55. If you short futures at 250.55 and go long at 250.45, this implies a profit of 0.10 points or $50.

Synthetic Short @	250.55
Long @	− 250.45
RETURN =	0.10

If a conversion represents the combination of a synthetic short with an actual long, a reversal represents the combination of a synthetic long with an actual short. The long call and short put components of the reversal represent a synthetic long futures contract. Combine a synthetic long futures with an actual short futures contract, and the positions offset. Thus you are able to lock in a fixed rate of return.

Long Call + Short Put = Synthetic Long Futures

Synthetic Long Futures + Short Futures = Fixed Return

Example: The reversal illustrated previously had the trader buy a 250 call at 9.20 and sell a 250 put at 8.90 for a 0.30 initial net debit. This is equivalent to buying futures at the 250 strike plus the .30 credit or 250.30. If you buy futures at 250.30 and go short at 250.45, this implies a profit of 0.15 points or $75.

Synthetic Long @   – 250.30
Short @   250.45
RETURN =   0.15

Synthetic Options

A conversion or reversal may be thought of as the combination of synthetic and actual futures. Likewise, it may be thought of as the combination of synthetic and actual options.

For example, the combination of a long put and a long futures contract, as found in a conversion, represents a synthetic long call. Combine a synthetic long call with an actual short call, and the positions offset. Thus you are able to lock in a fixed rate of return.

Long Put + Long Futures = Synthetic Long Call

Synthetic Long Call + Short Call = Fixed Return

Example: Our previous conversion example had the trader buy a 250 put at 8.65 and buy a futures contract at 250.45. This is equivalent to buying a 250 call for the put premium of 8.65 plus its out-of-the-money amount of 0.45 points or 9.10. If you buy a call at 9.10 and sell a call at 9.20, this implies a profit of 0.10 points or $50.

Synthetic Long Call @   – 9.10
Short Call @   9.20
RETURN =   0.10

Likewise, the combination of a short call and a long futures contract represents a synthetic short put. Combine a synthetic short put with an actual long put, and the positions offset. Thus you are able to lock in a fixed rate of return.

Short Call + Long Futures = Synthetic Short Put

Synthetic Short Put + Long Put = Fixed Return

Example: The conversion illustrated above had the trader selling a 250 call at 9.20 and buying an S&P 500 futures contract at 250.45. This is equivalent to selling a 250 put for the call premium of 9.20 less its in-the-money amount of 0.45 points or 8.75. If you sell a put at 8.75 and buy a put at 8.65, this implies a profit of 0.10 points or $50.

Synthetic Short Put @	8.75
Long Put @	− 8.65
RETURN =	0.10

The conversion may be thought of as a combination of a synthetic short futures plus an actual long futures, a synthetic long call plus an actual short call, or a synthetic short put plus an actual long put.

Conversion =

Synthetic Short Futures + Long Futures or

Synthetic Long Call + Short Call or

Synthetic Short Put + Long Put.

A reverse conversion also represents a combination of synthetic and actual positions: a synthetic long futures plus an actual short futures, a synthetic short call plus an actual long call, or a synthetic long put plus an actual short put.

Reversal =

Synthetic Long Futures + Short Futures or

Synthetic Short Call + Long Call or

Synthetic Long Put + Short Put.

Example: Our previous reversal example had the trader selling a 250 put at 8.90 and selling a futures contract at 250.45. This is equivalent to selling a 250 call for the put premium of 8.90 plus its out-of-the-money amount of 0.45 points or 9.35. If you sell a call at 9.35 and buy a call at 9.20, this implies a profit of 0.15 points or $75.

Synthetic Short Call @	9.35
Long Call @	− 9.20
RETURN =	0.15

Example: This reversal also means that the trader buys a 250 call at 9.20 and sells futures at 250.45. This is equivalent to buying a 250 put for the call premium of 9.20 less its in-the-money amount of 0.45 points or 8.75. If you buy a put at 8.75 and sell a put at 8.90, this implies a profit of 0.15 points or $75.

$$\text{Synthetic Long Put @} \quad -8.75$$
$$\text{Short Put @} \quad \quad 8.90$$
$$\text{RETURN =} \quad \quad 0.15$$

Conversions and reversals are probably the most common option arbitrage strategies. However, they are not *exclusively* option strategies in that they combine futures and options.

BOX SPREADS

Box spreads (boxes) also represent common arbitrage strategies. These trades involve options exclusively. Therefore, they may be easier to execute on the part of arbitrageurs who do not have ready access to the underlying market or where that underlying market is slightly thin.

Bear in mind that any arbitrage strategy implies marginal profits at best. You must compare the magnitude of the transaction costs (commissions, transaction fees, possible execution skids, errors, etc.) to the possible profit before executing the arbitrage. Because boxes entail *four* positions rather than just three, as found in the conversion and reversal, these arbitrages entail higher transaction costs.

Debit Box

A box involves the purchase and sale of a put and call at one strike price coupled with the purchase and sale of a call and a put at a different strike price. All four legs of the box share a common expiration date.

The idea is to capture a fixed return resulting from the temporary mispricing of one or more options. This means that you sell overpriced and buy underpriced options in combination with the other components of the strategy. For example, you can buy a low-struck call and a high-struck put and sell a high-struck call and a low-struck put. This creates a *debit box*.

A *debit box* entails the combination of four options—two puts and two calls strung out over 2 strike prices. In particular, this entails the purchase of a low-struck call and a high-struck put and the sale of a high-struck call and a low-struck put. These options share a common expiration date. Once executed, this arbitrage implies a constant return at expiration.

Example: A debit box is established by buying a 245 call and a 250 put and selling a 250 call and a 245 put. This strategy is motivated by the opportunity to capitalize on the relatively low price associated with the 250 put at 8.60. This strategy entails an initial net debit of \$2,425.

Long	1 Dec. 245.00 Call(s)	@ 11.90	=	– \$5,950
Short	1 Dec. 250.00 Call(s)	@ 9.20	=	\$4,600
Short	1 Dec. 245.00 Put(s)	@ 6.45	=	\$3,225
Long	1 Dec. 250.00 Put(s)	@ 8.60	=	– \$4,300
NET DEBIT				\$2,425

What would happen if the market declines, advances, or remains stable by the time expiration rolls around in December?
    If the market falls to 245.00:

Abandon	1 Dec. 245.00 Call(s)	@ 0.00	=	\$0
Abandon	1 Dec. 250.00 Call(s)	@ 0.00	=	\$0
Abandon	1 Dec. 245.00 Put(s)	@ 0.00	=	\$0
Exercise	1 Dec. 250.00 Put(s)	@ 5.00	=	\$2,500
Original Net Debit/Credit			=	– \$2,425
TOTAL PROFIT/LOSS				\$75

If the market remains relatively stable at 250.00:

Exercise	1 Dec. 245.00 Call(s)	@ 5.00	=	\$2,500
Abandon	1 Dec. 250.00 Call(s)	@ 0.00	=	\$0
Abandon	1 Dec. 245.00 Put(s)	@ 0.00	=	\$0
Abandon	1 Dec. 250.00 Put(s)	@ 0.00	=	\$0
Original Net Debit/Credit			=	– \$2,425
TOTAL PROFIT/LOSS				\$75

If the market rises to 255.00:

Exercise	1 Dec. 245.00 Call(s)	@ 10.00	=	\$5,000
Exercise	1 Dec. 250.00 Call(s)	@ 5.00	=	– \$2,500
Abandon	1 Dec. 245.00 Put(s)	@ 0.00	=	\$0
Abandon	1 Dec. 250.00 Put(s)	@ 0.00	=	\$0
Original Net Debit/Credit			=	– \$2,425
TOTAL PROFIT/LOSS				\$75

This strategy appears to be quite complicated. Fortunately, there is an easy way to identify the potential return associated with the box strategy.

Debit Box Return = Difference in Strikes − Net Debit

The 0.15 point or $75 return illustrated in the previous example may be confirmed with the use of this formula:

Return = $2,500 (5 points) − $2,425

= $75

Like the conversion or reversal, this strategy is also self-liquidating.

If the market falls below the lower of the two strikes, the puts are in-the-money and exercised. The short futures established as a result of the exercise of the long put is offset by the long futures established as a result of the exercise of the short put. The calls fall out-of-the-money and are abandoned.

If the market trades between the two strikes, the long call and long put are exercised. The long and short futures which are acquired offset each other. The short call and short put are out-of-the-money and are abandoned.

Finally, if the market advances above the upper of the two strikes, the calls are in-the-money. The long futures established as a result of the exercise of the long call is offset by the short futures established as a result of the exercise of the short call. The puts are out-of-the-money and abandoned.

Credit Box

A *credit box* may be created by selling a low-struck call and a high-struck put and buying a high-struck call and a low-struck put.

A *credit box* entails the combination of four options—two puts and two calls strung out over two strike prices. In particular, this entails the sale of a low-struck call and a high-struck put and the purchase of a high-struck call and a low-struck put. These options share a common expiration date. Once executed, this arbitrage implies a constant return at expiration.

Example: A credit box is established by selling a 245 call and a 250 put and buying a 250 call and a 245 put. This strategy is motivated by the opportunity to capitalize on the relatively high price associated with the 250 put at 8.90. This strategy entails an initial net credit of $2,575.

Short	1 Dec. 245.00 Call(s)	@ 11.90	=	$5,950
Long	1 Dec. 250.00 Call(s)	@ 9.20	=	− $4,600
Long	1 Dec. 245.00 Put(s)	@ 6.45	=	− $3,225
Short	1 Dec. 250.00 Put(s)	@ 8.90	=	$4,450
NET DEBIT/CREDIT				$2,575

What would happen if the market declines, advances, or remains stable by the time expiration rolls around in December?

If the market falls to 245.00:

Abandon	1 Dec. 245.00 Call(s)	@ 0.00	=	$0
Abandon	1 Dec. 250.00 Call(s)	@ 0.00	=	$0
Abandon	1 Dec. 245.00 Put(s)	@ 0.00	=	$0
Exercise	1 Dec. 250.00 Put(s)	@ 5.00	=	– $2,500
Original Net Debit/Credit			=	$2,575
TOTAL PROFIT/LOSS				$75

If the market remains relatively stable at 250.00:

Exercise	1 Dec. 245.00 Call(s)	@ 5.00	=	– $2,500
Abandon	1 Dec. 250.00 Call(s)	@ 0.00	=	$0
Abandon	1 Dec. 245.00 Put(s)	@ 0.00	=	$0
Abandon	1 Dec. 250.00 Put(s)	@ 0.00	=	$0
Original Net Debit/Credit			=	$2,575
TOTAL PROFIT/LOSS				$75

If the market rises to 255.00:

Exercise	1 Dec. 245.00 Call(s)	@ 10.00	=	– $5,000
Exercise	1 Dec. 250.00 Call(s)	@ 5.00	=	$2,500
Abandon	1 Dec. 245.00 Put(s)	@ 0.00	=	$0
Abandon	1 Dec. 250.00 Put(s)	@ 0.00	=	$0
Original Net Debit/Credit			=	$2,575
TOTAL PROFIT/LOSS				$75

This strategy appears to be quite complicated. Fortunately, there is an easy way to identify the potential return associated with the strategy.

Credit Box Return = Net Credit – Difference in Strikes

The 0.15 point or $75 return illustrated in the previous example may be confirmed with the use of this formula:

Return = $2,575 – $2,500 (5 points)
= $75

Like the debit box, the credit box is self-liquidating. If the market falls below the lower of the two strikes, the long and short puts are in-the-money and exercised, resulting in an offset. The calls fall out-of-the-money and are abandoned.

If the market trades between the two strikes, the short call and short put are exercised. The short and long futures which are acquired offset each other. The long call and long put are out-of-the-money and are abandoned.

Finally, if the market advances above the upper of the two strikes, the calls are in-the-money and exercised, resulting in an offset. The puts are out-of-the-money and abandoned.

Combining Vertical Spreads

Another way of looking at the box trade is to break it down into simpler option strategies. In particular, the debit box illustrated previously may be broken down into two vertical debit spreads: a bullish 245/250 call spread and a bearish 245/250 put spread. The trick with a box is to identify a situation where the maximum risk associated with one spread (represented by the net debit) is less than the maximum reward (represented by the difference in strikes less the net debit) on the other spread.

Remember: A bull (bear) spread achieves the maximum gain (loss) when futures are at or over the upper strike at expiration. Likewise, a bull (bear) spread achieves the maximum loss (gain) at or under the lower strike.

Example: The debit box just illustrated is comprised of a 245/250 bull call and 245/250 bear put spread. Compare the maximum risk and the maximum rewards associated with these spreads above and below the upper and lower strike prices.

	< 245	> 250
245/250 Bull Call Spread	− 2.70 pts	2.30 pts
245/250 Bear Put Spread	2.85 pts	− 2.15 pts
	0.15 pts	0.15 pts

The debit or maximum risk on the bull call spread equals 2.70 points or $1,350; the debit on the bear put spread equals 2.15 points or $1,075. The maximum potential profit equals the difference in strikes less the net debit or 2.30 ($1,150) and 2.85 ($1,425) for the bull and bear spread, respectively.

The maximum return on the bull spread of 2.30 points ($1,150) realized at prices over the upper 250 strike is $75 more than the bear spread debit of 2.15 ($1,075). And the maximum return on the bear spread of 2.85 points ($1,425) realized at prices under the lower 245 strike is $75 more than the debit on the bull spread of 2.70 points $1,350.

Long Low- Struck Call	+	Short High- Struck Call	= Bull Vertical Call Spread
Long High- Struck Put	+	Short Low- Struck Put	= Bear Vertical Put Spread

Bull Call Spread + Bear Put Spread = Debit Box

If a debit box represents the combination of two debit vertical spreads, a credit box represents the combination of two *credit* vertical spreads.

Example: The credit box just illustrated is comprised of a 245/250 bear call and 245/250 bull put spread. Compare the maximum risk and the maximum rewards associated with these spreads above and below the upper and lower strike prices.

	< 245	> 250
245/250 Bear Call Spread	2.70 pts	− 2.30 pts
245/250 Bull Put Spread	− 2.55 pts	2.45 pts
	0.15 pts	0.15 pts

The credit on the bear call spread equals 2.70 points or $1,350; the credit on the bull put spread equals 2.45 points or $1,225. The maximum risk associated with credit spreads equals the difference in strikes less the net credits 2.30 points ($1,150) and 2.55 ($1,275) for the bear and bull spreads, respectively.

Thus the maximum loss on the bear spread of 2.30 points ($1,150) realized at prices above the upper 250 strike is $75 less than the bull spread credit of 2.45 ($1,225). And the maximum return on the bear spread of 2.70 points ($1,350) realized at prices under the lower 245 strike is $75 more than the maximum risk on the bull spread of 2.55 points $1,275.

Short Low- Struck Call	+	Long High- Struck Call	= Bear Vertical Call Spread
Short High- Struck Put	+	Long Low- Struck Put	= Bull Vertical Put Spread

Bear Call Spread + Bull Put Spread = Credit Box

Combining Synthetic Futures

Many traders view a box as the combination of two vertical spreads. Others point out that a box also represents the combination of two synthetic futures contracts.

Consider the debit box. By combining a long low-struck call with the short low-struck put, you create a synthetic long futures contract. By combining the short high-struck call with the long high-struck put, you create a synthetic short futures contract. In order for a debit box to be profitable, the effective purchase price of the synthetic long must be lower than the effective sale price of the synthetic short.

Example: The debit box illustrated above was comprised of a long 245 call and a short 245 put. This synthetic long was put on at a debit of 5.45. Thus the effective purchase price of the synthetic futures contract equals the 245 strike plus the 5.45 debit or 250.45—the prevailing futures price at the time.

The box also comprised a long 250 put with a short 250 call for a 0.60 credit. This is like selling futures at the 250 strike plus the 0.60 credit or 250.60. You buy synthetic futures at 250.45 and sell synthetic futures at 250.60 for a 0.15 or $75 profit!

$$
\begin{array}{ll}
\text{Synthetic Long @} & -250.45 \text{ pts} \\
\text{Synthetic Short @} & \underline{250.60 \text{ pts}} \\
& 0.15 \text{ pts}
\end{array}
$$

Long Low-Struck Call	+	Short Low-Struck Put	= Synthetic Long Futures
Long High-Struck Put	+	Short High-Struck Call	= Synthetic Short Futures
Synthetic Long Futures	+	Synthetic Short Futures	= Debit Box Spread

Consider the credit box. By combining a long high-struck call with the short high-struck put, you create a synthetic long futures contract. By combining the short low-struck call with the long low-struck put, you create a synthetic short futures contract.

Example: The credit box illustrated previously was comprised of a long 250 call and a short 250 put. This synthetic long was put on at a debit of 0.30. Thus the effective purchase price of the synthetic futures contract equals the 250 strike plus the 0.30 debit or 250.30.

The box also comprised a long 245 put with a short 245 call for a 5.45 credit. This is like selling futures at the 245 strike plus the 5.45 credit or 250.45—the prevailing futures price at the time. You buy synthetic futures at 250.30 and sell synthetic futures at 250.45 for a 0.15 or $75 profit!

$$
\begin{array}{ll}
\text{Synthetic Long @} & -250.30 \text{ pts} \\
\text{Synthetic Short @} & \underline{250.45 \text{ pts}} \\
& 0.15 \text{ pts}
\end{array}
$$

Long High-Struck Call	+	Short High-Struck Put	= Synthetic Long Futures
Long Low-Struck Put	+	Short Low-Struck Call	= Synthetic Short Futures
Synthetic Long Futures	+	Synthetic Short Futures	= Credit Box Spread

A final way of looking at box spreads is as the combination of strangles and guts. The debit box may be thought of as the combination of a short strangle and a long guts. A short high-struck call combined with a short low-struck put represents a short strangle. The combination of a long low-struck call and a long high-struck put represents a long guts. The credit box, on the other hand, may be thought of as the combination of a long strangle and a short guts. A long high-struck call combined with a long low-struck put represents a long strangle. The combination of a short low-struck call and a short high-struck put represents a short guts.

PUT-CALL PARITY AND OTHER NASTY DETAILS

Lest we paint too bright a picture regarding the potential benefits of conversions, reversals, and boxes, let us review a number of complications which perennially plague option arbitrageurs. These complications fall into several categories: (1) put-call parity, (2) cashflow mismatches, and (3) early exercise.

Put-Call Parity

Put-call parity refers to the equilibrium relationship between put and call premiums when both options share a common strike price. This relationship may be quite helpful in identifying option arbitrage opportunities.

Let P and C be the put and call premiums, E and F the exercise price and futures price, and r and t the short-term interest rate and term to expiration, respectively. The put-call parity relationship for options on futures can be expressed as:

$$C - P = (F - E) \times e^{-rt}$$

The term e^{-rt} is simply the present value of \$1 received t years in the future, discounted at rate r. If t = 0.50 or one-half year and r = 0.06 or 6 percent, then $e^{-rt} = 0.9704$.

This factor is important because a trader who enters a debit conversion or a debit box loses the opportunity to earn interest on the net premium over the life of the strategy. A credit conversion or credit box trader takes advantage of this opportunity.

When you discuss put-call parity in the context of a box, you are really discussing *two* put-call parity relationships because there are two sets of puts and calls. Since a box entails options with two different strike prices, we must distinguish these last three variables. Two equilibrium relationships may be defined:

$$C(1) - P(1) = [F - E(1)] \times e^{-rt}$$
$$C(2) - P(2) = [F - E(2)] \times e^{-rt}$$

In order for both of these relationships to hold at the same time, the following must hold true:

$$[C(1) - P(1)] - [C(2) - P(2)] = [E(2) - E(1)] \times e^{-rt}$$

In other words, the value of the box is the *discounted* difference in strike prices. This is because the debit box entails lost interest income, and the credit box earns interest.

The put-call parity relationship is interesting because it underscores a point often ignored: You must consider whether an arbitrage results in a debit or a credit. In a debit arbitrage, you will have to finance that outflow, presumably at some prevailing short-term interest rate. In a credit arbitrage, you will enjoy the opportunity to invest the inflowing funds.

In the best of circumstances, these arbitrages entail a marginal profit. Thus the necessity to finance a debit or the opportunity to reinvest a credit can make the difference between a profitable or unprofitable arbitrage.

This complication may be distressing, but it really should not be. Think of the market as a bank. If you execute a debit arbitrage, you effectively lend money to the market. You receive interest by lending a little less money than will be repaid in the end.

If you execute a credit arbitrage, you effectively borrow money from the market. You receive a discounted amount of money to be repaid at full face value when the arbitrage is unwound. The trick is to find a situation where money may be lent at above market rates or borrowed below market rates.

Early Exercise

The potential for early exercise, (exercise prior to the expiration date) affects conversions, reversals, and boxes. For example, the holder of a conversion may elect to exercise the put if futures decline well below the common strike price. The resulting short futures contract offsets the original long futures contract while the deep out-of-the-money short call may be offset at low cost.

Consider what might happen to a debit box in a declining market. If the high-struck long put is trading near its intrinsic value and is exercised prior to expiration, the high-struck call is deep out-of-the-money and can be offset at small cost. Now the position has turned into a reversal! The short futures position, acquired through exercise of the high-struck put and combined with the long low-struck call and the short low-struck put, constitutes a reversal.

The box buyer still has a risk-free arbitrage position but now can earn interest on the credit received on exercising the put. This potential advantage increases slightly the value of the debit box.

An early exercise can reduce the period of time during which a net debit is tied up and unable to earn interest. Thus the potential for early exercise generally works to the benefit of debit arbitrage traders. It may, however, work to the detriment of a credit arbitrage for just the opposite reason.

Cashflow Mismatch

A final complication revolves around the fact that futures are marked-to-market daily in cash whereas options on futures are not. Because boxes do not entail any futures positions, this complication applies only to conversions and reversals.

Gains which accrue as a result of a futures position may be reinvested. Losses may have to be financed at some cost. For example, the holder of a reversal stands to lose money in a rising market. Margin calls must be met on the short futures while unrealized gains accrue on the long call position. These margin calls must be financed by borrowing funds (collateralized by the call) or by paying money which might otherwise be earning interest.

Cashflow mismatch between futures and options can be handled by weighting the position. In other words, the number of futures contracts must be reduced slightly to reflect the financing cost of margin calls and the interest earned on positive margin flows.

Perhaps you now have the impression that option arbitrage transactions—conversions, reversals, debit boxes, and credit boxes—are not quite as simple to analyze or as riskless as they may at first appear. Imagine what it is like to execute these strategies amid the chaos of the trading pit! Yet there are individuals who do just that and manage to make a decent living to boot. They are the rascals that make it so hard for the rest of us to get off one of these trades ourselves! But they are doing their part to ensure a fair and efficient market.

While most off-floor traders will find it difficult or even impossible to execute these arbitrages, they nonetheless benefit indirectly by the fact that others are so engaged in the sense that this arbitrage activity tends to drive option prices "in-line" with their fair-market values.

QUESTIONS

1. Which statement is false? A conversion . . .
   (a) Is the opposite of a reversal.
   (b) Involves futures, puts, and calls.
   (c) Represents a form of arbitrage which can be used to take advantage of a situation where puts are underpriced relative to calls.
   (d) Is comprised of a long futures contract and a synthetic short futures.
   (e) Is comprised of two vertical spreads.
2. A reversal is a . . .
   (a) Short futures contract, long put, and short call.
   (b) Short futures, long call, and short put.
   (c) Strategy that allows you to capitalize on neutral trading markets.
   (d) Strategy that can only be put on with near-to-the-money puts and calls.
   (e) (b) and (d) above.
3. Which statement is true?
   (a) A long call and a short put constitute a synthetic short futures contract.
   (b) The return associated with a conversion equals the (market price – strike price) less (call premium less put premium).
   (c) A short call and a long put constitute a synthetic short futures contract.
   (d) A conversion executed where the market is well in excess of the strike price results in an initial net debit.
   (e) (b) and (c) above.
   (f) (a) and (d) above.
4. You put on a conversion when Swiss franc futures are at .5267, the .5300 call is at .0127, and the .5300 put is at .0160. What is the initial net _____ (debit or credit)? What is the expected return (without considering transaction costs)?
5. You put on a reversal when Swiss franc futures are at .5267, the .5200 call is at .0180, and the .5200 put is at .0109. What is the initial net _____ (debit or credit)? What is the expected return (without considering transaction costs)?
6. Which statement is false?
   (a) A box may be constructed using all puts or all calls.
   (b) A box spread consists of two vertical spreads which overlap with respect to strike prices.

    (c) A box is a form of arbitrage which is not generally practiced by off-floor or public customers.

    (d) A box may be put on by selling a low-struck call and buying a high-struck call and by buying a low-struck put and selling a high-struck put.

    (e) None of the above.

7. A debit box . . .

    (a) Consists of a bull call spread and a bear put spread.

    (b) Consists of a bear put spread and a bear call spread.

    (c) Always results in a small net profit.

    (d) Can usually be traded directly without "legging-in."

    (e) Results in a net return equal to the difference in strikes plus the net debit.

8. A box is established by buying an 86/88 call spread for $1\,^{51}/_{64ths}$ and buying a 86/88 put spread for $^{14}/_{64ths}$. What is the initial net _____ (debit or credit)? What is the expected return?

9. Which statement is false?

    (a) Cashflow mismatch between futures and options is a problem which may beset the conversion or reversal trader.

    (b) Early exercise is usually not a problem when you enter a debit box.

    (c) You do not need to know market volatility to find the price of a put given the price of a call with the same strike.

    (d) Early exercise is not a problem which may affect a conversion or reversal.

    (e) None of the above.

10. Look at option premiums in the market of your choice today. Based on quoted prices, are there any conversion or reversal opportunities? Any boxes?

9

Intermarket Option Spreads

The availability of options exercisable for a number of closely related instruments affords traders the opportunity to capitalize on anticipated *relative* price movements in a number of novel ways. In other words, intermarket spreads may be traded using options.

Futures market participants have traded such spreads using futures for many years. For example, the Notes Over Bonds (NOB) and T-bills over Eurodollar (TED) spreads have enjoyed a great deal of popularity. Options exercisable for these instruments have opened the way to trade such spreads in unique and potentially highly profitable ways.

WHAT MAKES THE SPREAD TICK?

T-bonds and T-notes, T-bills and Euros differ in many ways; some are obvious, some not so obvious. The most notable difference between the actual bonds and notes that may be delivered in satisfaction of the bond and note futures contracts traded at the Chicago Board of Trade is term remaining until *maturity.* The most notable difference between the bills and Eurodollar time deposits on which the Chicago Mercantile Exchange's futures contracts are based is one of *credit risk*.

Let us review the basic features of these instruments in order to understand how spreads using these futures contracts are traded. Building from that basis, we may extend our analysis to intermarket option spreads.

Trading the Yield Curve

The NOB spread essentially reflects movements in the yield curve between intermediate-term government securities (as represented by the

6 ½ to 10-year note futures contract) and long-term government securities (as represented by the 15-year plus bond futures contract). The yield curve can move in two basic ways, either of which may wield a positive or negative influence upon the level of the NOB spread. The yield curve may exhibit a *parallel* shift or a *nonparallel* shift, that is, the shape of the curve may fluctuate.

A parallel yield curve shift occurs when both intermediate- and long-term yields rise or fall simultaneously by a uniform or near-uniform amount. For example, both intermediate- and long-term yields may rise by 1 percent or fall by 1 percent. A nonparallel yield curve shift occurs when intermediate- and long-term yields rise or fall by different amounts.

Normally, the yield curve is upward sloping (long-term yields exceed intermediate- and short-term yields). The yield curve *steepens* if long-term yields rise faster or fall slower than intermediate- and short-term yields. The curve *flattens* when long-term yields rise slower or fall faster than intermediate- and short-term yields. Sometimes this effect becomes severe, and the curve *inverts* when short-term yields run at a premium to long-term yields.

While interest rates can move quite sharply over a short period of time, rate levels tend to change more dramatically than does the shape of the yield curve. Rates tend to move together, so parallel shifts are more common than nonparallel shifts. Furthermore, curve shape changes are usually much more gradual than parallel shifts.

In order to capitalize on anticipated parallel curve shifts, you must understand that long-term fixed income securities are more volatile than intermediate-term securities. A 1 percent change in the yield of a long-term security induces a more dramatic price movement than does a 1 percent change in the yield of an intermediate-term security. This is intuitive in that long-term investors must live with the consequences of such a change longer than do intermediate-term investors. How can you take advantage of his "directional bias" towards long-term securities?

When interest rates advance, note and bond futures prices decline. But the longer-term bond futures fall faster than do intermediate-term note futures. Thus the difference between the two prices, as reflected in the NOB spread, widens. This implies that you should go "long the NOB" by buying note and selling bond futures.

If interest rates decline, the NOB narrows. A rate decline suggests increasing prices. However, bonds rally faster than notes, so the NOB narrows. This implies that you should go "short the NOB" by selling note and buying bond futures (see Figures 9–1 and 9–2).

Yields Advance ⇒ *Buy* the NOB

Yields Decline ⇒ *Sell* the NOB

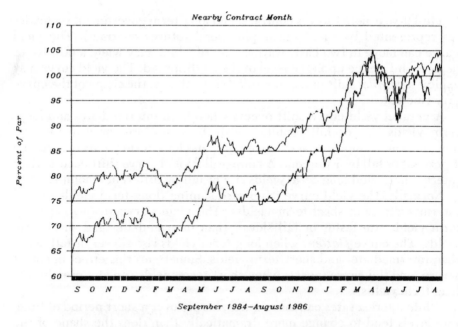

Figure 9-1 Bond (lower) vs. note (upper) futures.

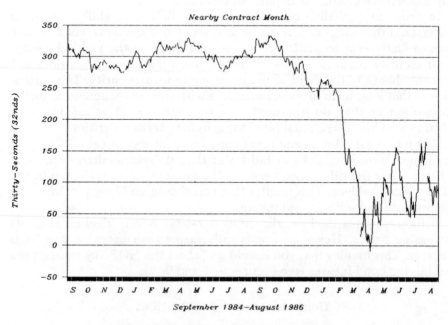

Figure 9-2 Notes over bonds (NOB) spread.

In order to capitalize on anticipated changes in the *shape* of the curve, it is necessary to balance the number of notes relative to bond futures in order to neutralize this directional bias. For example, if bond futures are expected to trend by 15 ticks for every 10 ticks that note futures move (given a *parallel* yield curve shift), then the appropriate strategy is to enter into 15 notes for every 10 bond futures contracts traded.

If the shape of the curve is expected to steepen, no matter whether yield levels are generally expected to rise or fall, the recommended strategy is to *buy the NOB* in the appropriate ratio. If the curve is expected to flatten, regardless of whether yield levels are rising or falling, the recommended strategy is to *sell the NOB* in the appropriate ratio.

Curve Steepens $\Rightarrow$ *Buy* the NOB

Curve Flattens $\Rightarrow$ *Sell* the NOB

Flight to Quality

The **TED** spread reflects the divergent credit risks between the 13-week (91-day) $1 million face value T-bill futures contract and the 90-day $1 million face value Eurodollar futures contract.

T-bills are often referred to as "riskless" investment. This is due to the fact that bills are backed by the full faith and credit of the U.S. government. Thus repayment of the face value upon maturity is assured unless the U.S. Treasury defaults. Most financial analysts regard a Treasury default as highly improbable given the catastrophic economic consequences that would result.

Eurodollars represent dollars on deposit in foreign financial institutions. In particular, the eurodollar futures price at the CME is based upon a survey of LIBOR rates. Yields on Eurodollar deposits reflect private credit risks, thus they do *not* reflect a riskless rate of return as do bills.

Because Euros reflect private credit risks, their yields are always higher than T-bill yields although this spread will change as general yield level changes (see Figures 9–3 and 9–4). In particular, if yields are rising, the TED spread tends to increase. If yields are falling, the TED spread tends to fall. This is due to a phenomenon known as *flight to quality.*

When yields are advancing, this implies that investors are demanding higher rates of return to reflect rising economic uncertainty. Many investors tend to become nervous and opt for low risk investments such as might be reflected in T-bills. Thus bill prices are bid up (yields decline) relative to Euros, and the TED widens.

When yields are declining, many investors become concerned with realizing a reasonable rate of return on their investments. Many investors are willing to accept more credit risk in order to boost their returns. They bid Euros up (yields decline) relative to bills, and the TED narrows.

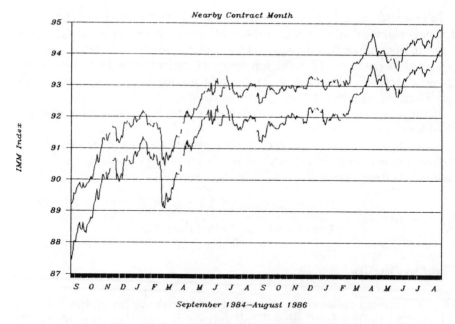

Figure 9–3   Euro (lower) vs. bill (upper) futures.

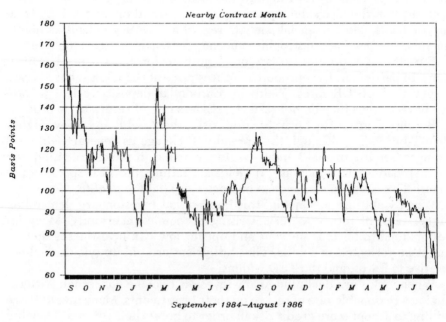

Figure 9–4   T-bills over Eurodollars (TED) spread.

The recommended strategy is to *buy the TED* when yields are advancing; *sell the TED* when yields are declining.

Yields Advance ⇒ *Buy* the TED

Yields Decline ⇒ *Sell* the TED

While the tendency for the NOB to widen or narrow as yields advance or decline is quite consistent, the TED is less reliable. Because of the lower reliability associated with the TED, our discussion below will focus on NOB option strategies. Bear in mind that the same principles generally apply with equal respect to the NOB or TED.

TRADING AN INTERMARKET OPTION SPREAD

So far, we have restricted our discussion to trading intermarket spreads with futures. Fortunately, the same basic principles which apply when trading futures spreads apply with equal force to option spreads. When yields are advancing, buy the NOB or buy the TED. When yields are declining, sell the NOB or sell the TED. The difference is that options provide more than one way to capitalize on a bullish or bearish position.

Trading the NOB Option Spread

If the NOB is expected to widen, you enter into a bullish note and bearish bond futures position. You can buy note calls and sell bond calls or sell note puts and buy bond puts. Buying calls and selling puts are both essentially bullish position; selling calls and buying puts are essentially bearish positions.

If the NOB is expected to narrow, you can enter into a bearish note and a bullish bond position. You can sell note calls and buy bond calls or buy note puts and sell bond puts.

NOB widens ⇒

(1) Buy note calls; sell bond calls.
(2) Sell note puts; buy bond puts.

NOB narrows ⇒

(3) Sell note calls; buy bond calls.
(4) Buy note puts; sell bond puts.

Unfortunately, only strategies number two and three are viable. Let us assume that one pursues strategy number four in anticipation of falling yields and a narrowing NOB. If you are right and yields fall, this implies that prices will rise, and your puts run out-of-the-money and eventually expire worthless.

If you are wrong (yields rise and prices fall) both bond and note puts fall into-the-money. But the bond falls faster than does the note, so the profit on the note put may be less than the loss on the bond put. Thus you have what amounts to a no-win situation!

If you pursue strategy number three, however, it is almost as if you cannot lose! If you are right (yields fall and prices rise) the bonds rally faster than do the notes, so the bond call is farther in-the-money than that note call. The profit on the bond call can, therefore, be expected to be greater than the loss on the note call. If you are wrong (yields rise and prices fall) both calls fall out-of-the-money and expire worthless. The question becomes: Does the initial transaction result in a net debit or a net credit?

Let us presume that you are using at-the-money (or nearest-to-the-money) bond and note options. Bond futures tend to be more volatile than note futures. This drives bond premiums up to higher levels. However, note futures trade at a higher absolute level (at least when yields are in excess of the 8 percent futures contract standard). Under certain conditions, these two factors may cancel each other out such that an at-the-money note option may trade at a premium which is quite similar to that of an at-the-money bond option.

If you can put the trade on at an initial net wash (or at a relatively modest debit), your risk is almost completely negated. If you are wrong about the market, the options fall out-of-the-money and are worthless. There is no initial investment; therefore, there is no loss. If you are right about the market, the long bond option runs deeper in-the-money than the short note option, and a profit ensues.

Example: It is May 13, 1985. September note and bond futures are at 81–25 and 71–26, respectively. The NOB is at $3^{19}/_{32}$ds. In anticipation of falling yields and a narrowing NOB, you sell a September 82 note call at $1^{15}/_{64}$ths and buy a 72 bond call at $1^{36}/_{64}$ths. The net debit is $21/_{64}$ths or $328. This represents your approximate risk in the event of falling yields.

By May 31st, note and bond futures rally to 85–22 and 76–13. The NOB is at $2^{97}/_{32}$ds. The note call rises to 3–55; the bond call rises to 4–39. Your profit equals the $48/_{64}$ths differential less the $21/_{64}$ths initial debit for a total of $422.

	Notes	*Bonds*	*NOB*
May 13:	Sell 82 call	Buy 72 call	
	@ $1^{15}/_{64}$	@ $1^{36}/_{64}$	
	[$81^{25}/_{32}$]	[$71^{26}/_{32}$]	$3^{19}/_{32}$ds

	May 31:	Buy 82 call	Sell 72 call	
May 31:		Buy 82 call @ $3^{55}/_{64}$ $[85^{22}/_{32}]$ ($2^{40}/_{64}$)	Sell 72 call @ $4^{39}/_{64}$ $[76^{13}/_{32}]$ $3^{03}/_{64}$	$297/_{32ds}$

Split-Strike NOB

So far our discussion has been restricted exclusively to the use of at- or near-the-money options. In an actual trading situation, there may not be any options which are trading near-the-money.

Since near-the-money options are more liquid than in- or out-of-the-moneys, one should normally look for near-the-money options for use in almost any option trading strategy. But it is unusual to find both note and bond options struck right at-the-money.

Example: On July 17, 1985, September 1985 notes were trading at $86^{28}/_{32ds}$ while the September bond contract was at 78–01 for a NOB equal to $^{283}/_{32ds}$. One might employ a very close-to-the-money 78 bond option. But the 86 and 88 note options are about equidistant from-the-money; hence you might consider taking a *split-strike* position in both the 86s and 88s.

If you felt that the NOB would rise as prices drop, you could have sold an 86 note put for 46/64ths, sold another 88 note put for 1–49, and bought two 78 bond puts for 1–16. This is initial investment of a single 64th or $15.625.

July 17:	Sell one 86 note put	@ $^{46}/_{64ths}$	=	$ 719
	Sell one 88 note put	@ $1^{49}/_{64ths}$	=	$1,766
	Buy two 78 bond puts	@ $1^{16}/_{64ths}$	=	$2,500
	NET DEBIT		=	$16

Earlier we indicated that the initial investment in the strategy approximates the maximum risk. This is not so with the split-strike option NOB. Paradoxically, your risk is greater when your market forecast is slightly wrong. When your prediction is way off, your risk can be limited to the initial investment.

Example: If the NOB drops as prices rise sharply, all three options fall out-of-the-money and expire worthless. Your risk is limited to the $15.625 investment. If the market remains perfectly stable, your risk equates to the in-the-money amount of the high-struck put. The 78 bond puts and the 86 note put falls out-of-the-money and worthless, but the 88 put would be exercised against you as it falls $1^{04}/_{32ds}$ in-the-money.

If the market falls and the NOB rises, you win. To illustrate: By July 31st, notes had fallen to 84–19; bonds were down to 75–06 for a 301 NOB. The two

78 bond puts could be sold for 3–00 each or 6 points; the 86 and 88 note puts could have been covered for 1–42 and 3–27, respectively, or 5–05. This is a net return of $^{59}/_{64ths}$ reduced by the initial one tick investment for a total of $^{58}/_{64ths}$ in profit.

July 31:	Buy one 86 note put	@ 1 $^{42}/_{64ths}$	=	($1,656)
	Buy one 88 note put	@ 3 $^{27}/_{64ths}$	=	($3,422)
	Sell two 78 bond puts	@ 3 $^{00}/_{64ths}$	=	$6,000
	Initial net debit		=	($16)
		NET PROFIT	=	$906

Split Bond Strikes

An obvious disadvantage of splitting the strikes on the note options is that you lose control of the short in-the-money option. If the market remains stable, the in-the-money amount of the note option must be counted as loss. If you have to split strikes, it is better to do so with the long bond options. In this way, *you* control the in-the-money option. If the market remains stable, you will accrue profit on exercise.

> **Example:** On July 12, 1985, notes were at 86–06 and bonds were at 77–14. Splitting the bond strikes in anticipation of a rising NOB and falling prices, you might have bought a 76 bond put at 53 and a 78 bond put at 1–46, selling two 86 note puts at 1–08.

July 12:	Sell two 86 note puts	@ 1 $^{08}/_{64ths}$	=	$2,250
	Buy one 76 bond put	@ $^{53}/_{64ths}$	=	($828)
	Buy one 78 bond put	@ 1 $^{46}/_{64ths}$	=	($1,719)
		NET DEBIT	=	$297

Thus your risk is restricted to the $^{19}/_{64ths}$ debit if you are very wrong about the market and prices rise sharply. If the market remains perfectly stable, however, you will recoup the $^{18}/_{32ds}$ in-the-money value of the 78 put by expiration for a $^{17}/_{64ths}$ net profit. Of course, your profit may be much more attractive if the market falls and the NOB widens.

Double Split Strikes

Strikes may be split when the market is trading closer to an odd number (73, 75, 77) than to an even number at which strikes are set (74, 76, 78). Sometimes you will find that both notes and bonds are trading closer to the odd numbers.

Example: On August 5, 1985, September 1985 notes were at 84–15; bonds were at 75–04 for a 299 NOB. In anticipation of falling prices and a rising NOB, you may buy 74 and 76 bond puts for 25 and 1–20, respectively, and sell 84 and 86 note puts for 25 and 1–51, respectively. This results in an initial net credit of $31/64$ths.

August 5:	Sell one 84 note put	@ $25/64$ths	=	$391
	Sell one 86 note put	@ $1\,51/64$ths	=	$1,797
	Buy one 74 bond put	@ $25/64$ths	=	($391)
	Buy one 76 bond put	@ $1\,20/64$ths	=	($1,312)
	NET CREDIT		=	$484

The credit generated by the double split-strike transaction illustrated in the prior example is large. Bear in mind, however, that the short 86 note put is deeper in-the-money ($1\,17/32$ds) than the long 76 bond put ($28/32$ds). If the market remained stable, you would take a bigger loss on the note option than you would profit on the bond option. This loss of $21/32$ds would offset the initial credit of $31/64$ths by $11/64$ths!

Example: By August 16th, note and bond futures rose to 86–13 and 76–24, respectively, but curiously the NOB widened to 309. At that point, you could have liquidated the position by selling the 74 and 76 puts for 2/64ths and 13/64ths and buying back the 84 and 86 puts for 2/64ths and 18/64ths for a net loss of 5/64ths. This loss is more than compensated for, however, by the initial debit of 31/64ths.

August 16:	Buy one 84 note put	@ $2/64$ths	=	($31)
	Buy one 86 note put	@ $18/64$ths	=	($281)
	Sell one 74 bond put	@ $2/64$ths	=	$31
	Sell one 76 bond put	@ $13/64$ths	=	$203
	Initial net credit		=	$484
	NET PROFIT		=	$406

This result is not surprising—the market rallied and you were left with the initial net credit. It may, however, be surprising that the NOB rallied in the face of rising prices.

This underscores an important point: A change in the shape of the yield curve may affect the NOB as readily as general shifts in yield levels. In this case, the yield curve was steepening, so the NOB widened even though prices were generally rising.

Our prior examples employed put options. You can just as readily enter an option NOB by selling note and buying bond calls in anticipation of rising prices and a falling NOB.

A final point: Try to establish an option NOB position with a net delta near zero. This insulates your position from possible adverse effects of near-term price fluctuations. Splitting strikes and adjusting the number of note to bond options allows you to maintain delta neutrality even when there are no bond and note options available with near equivalent deltas (see Figures 9–5 and 9–6).

An Initial Wash?

Under most circumstances, the worst scenario is that the return will be constrained to the initial net debit or under very favorable circumstances, a net credit. There *are*, however, other risks worth mentioning. In particular, if you sell note calls and buy bond calls, your risk is that the yield curve will steepen. If the curve steepens sharply while note yields remain relatively stable, the risk may be exacerbated. If you sell note puts and buy bond puts, your risk is that the curve will flatten. If the curve flattens while general yields fall marginally, risk is enhanced.

This source of risk is apparent but not terribly severe. Changes in the shape of the curve tend to be far less dramatic than fluctuations in

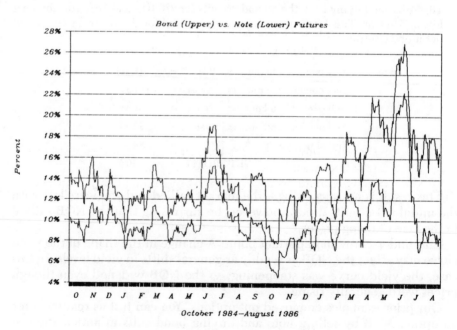

Figure 9–5   20-Day historic volatility.

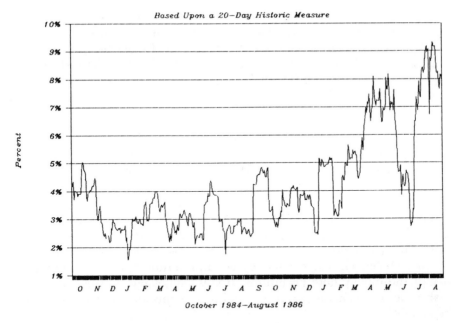

Figure 9-6   Bond less note volatility spread.

the level of interest rates. Thus a NOB trader should have plenty of time to liquidate before the shape of the curve fluctuates significantly.

Risk

Sell note puts/buy bond puts	Curve flattens
Sell note calls/buy bond calls	Curve steepens

Beyond these risks, how realistic is this expectation of establishing the spread at an initial net wash or even a modest net debit?

In May 1985 when note options were first introduced and in the imme-diately following months, yields were at a reasonably high level *over* the 8 percent futures contract standard. Consequently, the spread between the intermediate-term note futures contract and the long-term bond futures contract was quite wide. Moreover, when yields were quite high, the differential between the implied volatility of bonds and notes was rela-tively narrow. Thus it was possible to establish a NOB option spread at a relatively modest debit or even a near wash.

But when yields fall, the spread between notes and bonds tends to narrow as discussed above. Moreover, the spread between note and bond volatilities also tends to widen. This may be explained by the fact that as yields decline, the sensitivity of a bond or note to fluctuating yields becomes more pronounced. The longer-term bonds react more severely than do intermediate-term notes as yields change (see Figure 9–1).

This may be observed in the accompanying graphics which illustrate that as prices were advancing (yields falling) from October 1984 through August 1986, the volatility spread has been advancing (Figures 9–5 and 9–6).

	Price Level	Volatility
Bonds	Low	High
Notes	High	Low

It *was* possible to find near-the-money bond and note options trading at comparable premiums in May–September 1985. But by the end of the period illustrated on the graphic, (1) the volatility spread widened significantly and (2) bond and note prices became very close in terms of absolute price level. Thus at-the-money bond premiums became much higher than at-the-money note premiums. If you cannot put on the spread at a wash or at a reasonably small net debit, the spread becomes much less attractive.

INTERMARKET OPTION STRADDLE

Option spreads provide unique and attractive ways of playing changing relationships between two related yet different option instruments. Because of the limited risk feature of options, you can often take advantage of this changing relationship at nominal risk.

This section discusses yet another way to take advantage of the relationship between notes and bonds using options. Because this strategy involves *buying* both bond call (put) and note put (call) options, it is referred to as the *NOB straddle*. But, as we shall see, the NOB or *intermarket straddle* affords significant advantages over an "unmixed" straddle in either bonds or notes!

Straddle Fundamentals

A straddle is a popular option combination which entails the purchase of a put and a call (a long straddle) or the sale of a put and a call (a short straddle). These strategies may be used to capitalize on a volatile or a relatively static market environment, respectively. We will focus on the long straddle.

Example: You buy a bond call struck at 96 for 1 32/64ths and buy a 96 bond put for 1 32/64ths. Thus there is an initial net debit of 3 points or $3,000.

Buy 96 bond call	@ 1 32/64ths	=	($1,500)
Sell 96 bond put	@ 1 32/64ths	=	($1,500)

You will profit if the market rallies over the upper breakeven point of 99 (the 96 strike *plus* the initial net debit of 3 00/64ths) or declines below the lower breakeven point or 93 (the 96 strike *less* the 3 point debit) at expiration.

Why? If the market rallies to 100, for example, you will exercise the 96 call for 4 points, less the initial debit of 3 points, for $1,000 net gain. If the market falls to 92, the put may be exercised for 4 points, resulting in a net profit of $1,000.

But if the market remains relatively stable, trading between the breakeven points at expiration, you lose. For example, if the market is at the common 96 strike by expiration, both options are at-the-money and expire worthless, leaving you with the loss of the 3 point debit. Thus the long straddle may be thought of as a way to capitalize on volatile, unpredictable markets even if you cannot pick a market direction.

The NOB straddle shares the characteristics of an outright long T-bond option straddle. Generally, however, you can establish the NOB straddle for a lower initial debit. Furthermore, the NOB straddle will allow you to shade your position when you believe that there is a slightly greater chance of a bear versus a bull movement or vice versa!

Price Expectations

When yields rise and prices fall, bond futures fall faster than note futures. When the NOB widens, buy the NOB! When rates fall, prices rise but bonds rise faster than notes. When the NOB narrows, sell the NOB!

Options can also be used to take a position in the NOB. A long put is basically a bearish strategy; a long call is essentially bullish. Therefore, you can essentially *sell the NOB* in a rising market by buying note puts and buying bond calls, or you can *buy the NOB* in a falling market by buying note calls and buying bond puts. These two forms of the long NOB straddle are known as a *bull NOB straddle* and a *bear NOB straddle*, respectively.

Remember: A long straddle essentially indicates no directional market bias. The assumption is that the market will fluctuate in one direction or the other rather dramatically.

	Volatility	
	High	*Low*
NOB Rising (Prices Falling)	Buy note call/ Buy bond put	Sell note put/ Sell bond call
NOB Falling (Prices Rising)	Buy note put/ Buy bond call	Sell note call/ Sell bond put

What if you believe that the market will be volatile, but you are leaning in one direction or the other? This is the time to execute a long NOB straddle. For example, assume that you believe there is a 70 percent probability of a large bull move and a 30 percent probability of a large bear move. Under these circumstances, buy a bullish NOB straddle by buying both note puts and bond calls.

If your market bias is correct—interest rates drop and prices rise significantly—the long bond call will move into-the-money and appreciate faster than the note put declines. In the process, the bond call delta will approach 1.0; the note put delta will fall towards 0. Thus you will be making money at an accelerating pace.

The note put acts as a safety net in the event that rates change in the direction opposite your market sentiment. The advantage of using a long T-note option as one of the straddle legs is the reduced cost of trading the NOB straddle vis-a-vis a T-bond straddle.

Example: Near the close on March 5, 1986, June 1986 note futures were trading at 99–19; June bond futures were trading at 95–19 for a NOB of 4 points or $128/32$ds. At that time, the note put struck at 100–00 was trading at 1–57 ($1,890.63), while the bond call option struck at 96–00 was trading at 2–15 ($2,234.38). The bull NOB straddle could have been established at a total net debit of $4,125.

Buy 100 note put	@ $1\,^{57}/_{64}$ths	= ($1,891)
Buy 96 bond call	@ $2\,^{15}/_{64}$ths	= ($2,234)
	NET DEBIT =	$4,125

If the NOB straddle is held until expiration, profits may accrue if interest rates increase or decrease significantly. If note and bond futures rally to 105–00 and 101–00, respectively, the 96 bond call would be worth $5,000; the 100 note put expires worthless. Profit equals $5,000 from the long bond call less the $4,125 required to establish the position or $875 (see Figure 9–7).

The value of the position at expiration is positive if the settlement price of T-note futures is greater than the T-bond option strike price plus the settlement value of the NOB spread.

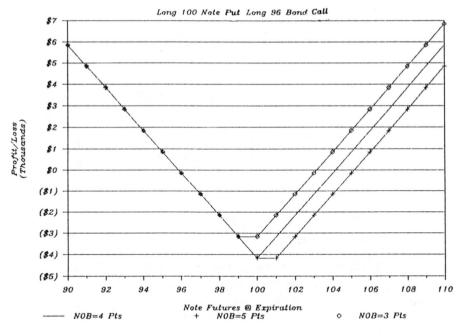

Figure 9–7   Long bull NOB straddle.

For example, if T-bonds close at 96–00 and the NOB trades to 3 points, the note put expires one point in-the-money. Hence a declining NOB spread may give rise to an increase in the value of the NOB straddle at expiration. Conversely, an increase in the NOB spread may lead to a lower value of the NOB straddle at expiration.

This profit may be compared with an "unmixed" or "straight" bond straddle. On March 4, 1986, the bond put at 96 was trading at 2–41 ($2,640.63). Compare this to the 100 note put struck at 100 for 1–57 ($1,890.63). Thus the bull NOB reduces the initial debit (and increases potential profitability) by about $750.

Putting It All Together

If your market sentiment leans more toward the bearish side, greater profits may be attainable with a long bear NOB straddle.

Example: The *bear* NOB strategy would consist of a 96 bond put purchased for 2–41 ($2,640.63) and a 100 note call purchased for 1–33 ($1,516.33).

Buy 100 note call	@ $1\,^{33}/_{64ths}$	= ($1,516)
Buy 96 bond put	@ $2\,^{41}/_{64ths}$	= ($2,641)
	NET DEBIT =	$4,157

In a rising rate environment, bond futures generally decline much faster than note futures decline. If rates rise and the NOB widens, a bond put would be expected to increase in value faster than a note call declines in value. If bond futures close at 90–00 and note futures close at 95–00, the NOB straddle has a value of 6–00 or $6,000. Profits equal the $6,000 expiration value less the initial net debit of $4,156.25 or $1,843.75 (see Figure 9–8).

Of course, if you believe that rates will remain relatively stable while the NOB fluctuates, this implies that you may wish to *sell* NOB straddles. For example, sell a note put and sell a bond call when the NOB is expected to advance, or sell a note call and sell a bond put when the NOB is expected to fall.

The probability that the NOB will fluctuate significantly while rates remain stable is minimal. Perhaps the only scenario where that may be possible is if the shape of the curve is changing while yields remain

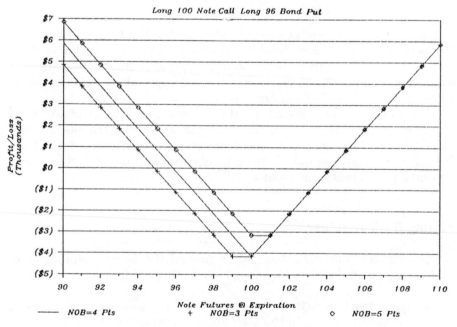

Figure 9–8   Long bear NOB straddle.

relatively stable. For example, if the curve steepens slightly while rates remain otherwise stable, you may sell note puts/sell bond calls. If the curve flattens, sell note calls/sell bond puts. Under must circumstances, however, these strategies cannot be recommended.

QUESTIONS

1. Which statement is false?
   (a) The NOB stands for Notes Over Bonds.
   (b) The NOB generally rallies when prices fall.
   (c) The NOB is insensitive to the changing shape of the yield curve.
   (d) The NOB rallies when rates rise.
   (e) The NOB declines when prices rise.
2. The implied volatility for the near-the-money note call is 8.1 percent; the implied volatility for the near-the-money bond call equals 11.5 percent. What is the expected movement in the notes given a 1 point move in the bonds?
3. A steepening yield curve . . .
   (a) Means that intermediate-term rates are falling relative to short-term rates.
   (b) Suggests that you should buy bonds and sell notes.
   (c) May be capitalized on by buying the NOB in the ratio of approximately 13 notes to 10 bonds.
   (d) Suggests that you should sell bond puts and buy note puts.
   (e) May cut into a profit associated with going long bond calls and short note puts in a falling rate environment.
4. You believe that the yield curve will decline in a parallel fashion. What do you do?
   (a) Sell note calls/buy bond calls.
   (b) Sell note puts/buy bond puts.
   (c) Buy note puts/sell bond puts.
   (d) Buy note calls/sell bond calls.
   (e) None of the above.
5. Do you believe that rates will advance or decline over the next week? If you believe they will advance, look at the bond and note puts; if you believe they will decline, look at the calls. Compare the near-the-money bond options with the note option. Are there any low-risk option NOB strategies? If not, why not (where are the implied volatilities of the note and bond options)?

Answers to Questions

INTRODUCTION TO OPTIONS

1. d
2. a
3. d
4. c
5. e
6. 91.79
7. (a) 0.45, 0.09
   (b) 0.4236
8. d
9. b
10. 0.35
11. b
12. e
13. c

OPTION PRICING CONCEPTS

1. c
2. a
3. (a) Premium = Sum(n = 1 to t)[Prob(t) (Max(Market(t) − Strike,0))]
   $$= .5(\$25) + .5(0)$$
   $$= \$12.50$$
   (b) Delta = Change in premium/Change in Underlying
   $$= (25 - 0)/(375 - 325) = 25/50 = 0.50$$
   (c) Premium = $1/(1 + .1)^{.5}[\$12.50]$
   $$= .9535 \, [\$12.50]$$
   $$= \$11.92$$

4. (a)

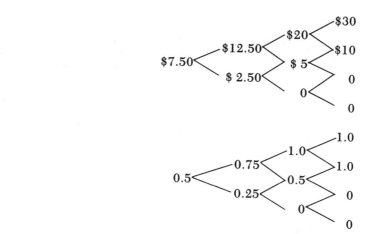

(b)

5. d

6. (a) $C = e^{-(.3287)(.075)}[.4280(.6293) - .4200(.6064)]$
    $= .9756[0.2693 - 0.2546] = 0.0143$ or *1.43 cents per mark*
  $d_1 = [\ln(.4280/.4200) + 0.5(.11)^2(.3287)]/(.11)\sqrt{(.3287)}$
    $= [0.0188685 + 0.0019886]/0.0630656 = 0.3307$
  $N(.3307) = .6293$
  $d_2 = .3307 - (.11)\sqrt{(.3287)} = 0.2676$
  $N(.2676) = .6064$

 (b) delta $= e^{-rt}N(d_1)$
     $= .9756(.6293) = 0.61$

 (c) $P = 0.0143 - .9644(.4280 - .4200)$
    $= 0.0065$ or *0.65 cents per mark*

RISK, REWARD, AND PROBABILITY

1. N $= \ln(.4236/.4173) / 0.15(30/365)$
   $= \ln(1.0151)/0.0123$
   $= 0.01498/0.0123$
   $= 1.2154$ corresponding to .8888 on normal distribution table indicating that there is a $1 - 0.89$ or 11% probability that you will rally over the B/E.

2. N $= \ln(84/83.75)/0.12(60/365)$
   $= 0.15$ or .5596—this indicates a 44% probability that the market will wind up over 84 by expiration.

 The B/E equals $82\,^{48}/_{64ths}$.

 N $= \ln(82.75/83.75)/0.12(60/365)$
   $= -.6089$ or .2709 or a 27% probability that the market will wind up under the B/E

 Thus, there is a 29% probability $100 - (44 + 27)$ that the market will wind up between the $82\,^{48}/_{64ths}$ B/E and the 84 strike price.

3.		Prem.	Vol.	B/E	Prob.
In-Mny	84 Calls	4^{01}/64ths	12.6%	88^{01}/64ths	38.21%
In-Mny	86 Calls	2^{41}/64ths	12.1%	88^{41}/64ths	29.46%
Out-Mny	88 Calls	1^{42}/64ths	12.1%	89^{42}/64ths	17.88%
Out-Mny	90 Calls	1^{01}/64ths	12.5%	91^{01}/64ths	8.53%
In-Mny	90 Calls	3^{48}/64ths	12.2%	86^{16}/64ths	36.32%
In-Mny	88 Calls	2^{33}/64ths	12.5%	85^{31}/64ths	26.44%
Out-Mny	86 Calls	1^{37}/64ths	12.7%	84^{27}/64ths	15.63%
Out-Mny	84 Calls	^{60}/64ths	13.2%	83^{04}/64ths	7.21%

4. aggressive
5. c
6. (a) in-the-money, short put
   (b) 95^{24}/32ds

OPTION SPREADS

1. c
2. e
3. (a) 2 – 48 less 1 – 32 equals 1 – 16 or $1,250 debit.
   (b) $1,250 or the initial net debit.
   (c) The difference in strikes ($2,000) less the initial net debit ($1,250) or $750.
   (d) 84 plus the debit of 1^{8}/32ds or 85^{08}/32ds.
   (e) N = ln(85.25/86) / 0.12(60/365)
       = ln(.9912791)/0.019726
       = – 0.0087592/0.019726
       = – 0.4440424 corresponding to .3300 on normal distribution table indicating that there is a 1 – 0.33 or 67% probability that the market will remain over the B/E.
4. a
5. c
6. b
7. b
8. (a) 3^{20}/64ths (3.3125) less 1^{40}/64ths (1.625) equals *$1,687.50* or the initial net debit.
   (b) Difference in strikes ($2,000) less the initial debit ($1,687.50) or *312.50*—this is a profit!
9. (a) 1.72 less 2(0.74) equals 0.24 cents per DM or *$300.00* given a 125,000 DM contract.
   (b) The difference in strikes (.02) less the initial debit (0.0024) or *1.76* cents/Mark; At the upper strike price of *0.4400*.

THREE-DIMENSIONAL OPTION TRADING

1. c
2. 93.43, 92.57

3. a
4. (a) put, call
   (b) debit, 0.44, 91.56, 92.94
5. b
6. d
7. (a) long
   (b) debit

   $-0.04 + 2(.14) - .39 = -0.15$ or $375
   (@ $25 per basis point).

   (c) Max profit $= (50 \times \$25) - \$375 = \$875$

   B/Es = 92.00 plus or minus 35 basis points
      = 91.65 to 92.35
8. c
9. c
10. Expected change in the premium given a change in volatility.
11. Expected change in the premium given a change in term.
12. Expected change in the delta given a change in the market price.

HEDGING WITH OPTIONS

1. b
2. d
3. e
4. d
5. (a) The in-the-money amount of the call (2 pts.) less the $2\,^{32}/_{64ths}$ premium for a gain of $^{32}/_{64ths}$ or $500.
   (b) A loss of 2 pts ($2,000) on the long bond insulated by the $2\,^{32}/_{64ths}$ premium for a gain of $^{32}/_{64ths}$ or $500.
   (c) A loss of 5 pts ($5,000) on the bond insulated by the $2\,^{32}/_{64ths}$ premium for a loss of $2\,^{32}/_{64ths}$ or $2,500.
6. (a) to 0.4000: loss on DMs   = (0.0350)
                gain on option = 0.0260
                      TOTAL = (0.0090) or $-\$1,125$/contract
         to 0.4400: gain on DMs   = 0.0050
                loss on option = (0.0140)
                      TOTAL = (0.0090) or $-\$1,125$/contract
         to 0.4600: gain on DMs   = 0.0250
                loss on option = (0.0140)
                      TOTAL = 0.0110 or $\$1,375$/contract
   (b) to 0.4000: loss on DMs   = (0.0350)
                gain on option = 0.0210
                      TOTAL = (0.0140) or $-\$1,750$/contract
         to 0.4300: loss on DMs   = (0.0050)
                loss on option = (0.0090)
                      TOTAL = (0.0140) or $-\$1,750$/contract
         to 0.4600: gain on DMs   = 0.0250
                loss on option = (0.0090)
                      TOTAL = 0.0160 or $\$2,000$/contract

7. a
8. e
9. d
10. b
11. Buy puts on bonds; buy puts on DMs.
13. c
14. e
15. d
16. (a) $1/0.45 = 2.22$ per million or one hundred eleven (111) $1 million face value options.
    (b) You need $1/0.38 = 2.63$ per million or one hundred thirty-two (132) $1 million face value options.

    Therefore, you sell an additional 21 calls.
17. (a) $1.2300(1/0.56) = 2.20$ puts per $100,000 face value or four hundred thirty-nine (439) options.
    (b) $1.2300(1/0.64) = 1.92$ puts per $100,000 face value or three hundred eighty-four (384) options.

    Therefore, you sell 55 puts.
18. c
19. d

FLOATING RATE RISK MANAGEMENT

1. d
2. a
3. (a) Buy a series of successively deferred put options.
    (b) A stack means that you buy options exclusively in the nearby month, periodically "rolling forward."

    A strip/stack means that you strip out as far as liquidity permits, stacking additional contracts in the farthest deferred month which still enjoys liquidity.

OPTION ARBITRAGE

1. e
2. b
3. c
4. debit

    Debit = .0160 less .0127 or 0.0033 or $412.50 per 125,000 Swiss franc contract.

    Return = (Market − Strike) less (Call − Put)
    $$= (.5267 - .5300) \text{ less } (.0127 - .0160)$$
    $$= (-.0033) \text{ less } (-.0033)$$
    $$= \text{zero}$$

5. debit

Debit = .0109 less .0180 or 0.0071 or $887.50 per 125,000 Swiss franc contract.

Return = (Strike – Market) less (Put – Call)

= (.5200 – .5267) less (.0109 – .0180)

= (– .0067) less (– .0071)

= 0.0004 or $50 per 125,000 SF contract.

6. a
7. a
8. debit

Debit = $1^{51}/_{64ths}$ plus $^{14}/_{64ths}$ or $2^{01}/_{64ths.}$

Return = $2,000 (difference in strikes) less $2^{01}/_{64ths}$ or $– ^1/_{64th}$ = a loss of $15,625.

9. d

INTERMARKET OPTION SPREADS

1. c
2. Ratio = 11.5%/8.6% = 1.3372

You expect a 0.7478 or $^{24}/_{32ds}$ move in notes.

3. e
4. a

Index